THE KINGDOM
AND
THE POWER

THE KINGDOM
AND
THE POWER

◆

Rediscovering the Centrality of the Church

PETER J. LEITHART

PUBLISHING
P.O. BOX 817 • PHILLIPSBURG • NEW JERSEY 08865

© 1993 by Peter J. Leithart

Unless otherwise indicated Scripture quotations are from the New American Standard Bible. Copyright by The Lockman Foundation 1960, 1962, 1963, 1968, 1971, 1972, 1973, 1975, 1977.

Manufactured in the United States of America.

Library of Congress Cataloging-in-Publication Data

Leithart, Peter J.
    The kingdom and the power : rediscovering the centrality of the church / Peter J. Leithart.
        p.   cm.
    Includes bibliographical references and index.
    ISBN 0-87552-300-5
    1. Kingdom of God. 2. Church. 3. Sociology, Christian. 4. Church and state—United States. I. Title.
BT94.L394 1993
231.7'2—dc20   93-17941

Contents

Acknowledgments

Origen said in his commentary on the Lord's Prayer that to live is to be indebted, a maxim that is doubly true for writers. It would be literally impossible even to recall all my intellectual and material debts, but several cannot pass without mention.

Special thanks to James B. Jordan, who generously published some of the articles on which this book is based, who read through the bulk of the manuscript before publication, and whose gifts and insights never fail to astonish, as he constantly and (to all appearances) effortlessly throws fresh light on well-known and obscure Scriptures.

Professors John M. Frame, Vern S. Poythress, Richard B. Gaffin, Jr., and William Edgar read and commented on the paper that contained the seed ideas from which this book grew.

Thanks to George Grant, now of Legacy Communications, whose regular writing assignments from Coral Ridge Ministries kept food on the table as I wrote the book, and whose infectious enthusiasm has sustained me.

Thanks to the people of Reformed Heritage Presbyterian Church, and especially to those who regularly attended the evening worship service, for listening patiently as I stammered toward my conclusions.

Bryce Craig and Thom Notaro of Presbyterian and Reformed Publishing Company have been careful midwives during the delicate final stages of the book's too-lengthy labor and delivery.

My wife, Noel, has supported me in innumerable ways through the most trying of times and deserves most of the credit for anything I have accomplished. Our five children turned into six while the book awaited publication, and all have contributed to making our home a small kingdom, our table a source of continual joy.

I am, by necessity though not by choice, a hearty adherent of what Michael Kinsley has called "Strout's Law" of journalism ("sell every piece three times"). Accordingly, certain sections of this book have appeared previously in *The Biblical Worldview, The Chalcedon Report, Biblical Horizons,* and the now-defunct *Geneva Papers.* Thanks to the editors of those publications, Gary DeMar, Garry Moes, James Jordan, and Michael Gilstrap, for their interest in those earlier essays.

Finally, my parents, Dr. Paul and Mildred Leithart, were instruments of the Spirit in teaching me early to love both Jesus and His church. This book is dedicated to them.

Introduction

In the fall of 1991 I began a series of sermons on the first several chapters of Leviticus. My decision to preach on an obscure and difficult book (in the morning service, no less!) runs against the grain of contemporary pastoral theory. And I must admit that, despite my fascination with the details of the sacrificial system, I did not arrive easily at the decision to preach on it. Early on in my series, in fact, I spent most of one sermon explaining why a study of Leviticus is valuable for Christians. I am convinced that Leviticus is not only valuable but essential to a proper understanding of the New Testament. But anyone who preaches on Leviticus to an American congregation at the end of the twentieth century owes somebody an explanation.

I feel a similar compulsion to defend my decision to write this book. After all, over the past century hundreds of scholarly articles and books on the kingdom have been published, to which scores of recent popular works on various aspects of the kingdom of God have been added. What can possibly justify my presumption to add another boulder to this avalanche?

A brief survey of popular approaches to the kingdom should help to answer that question. Most of the works I have studied in the research and writing of this book tend to be dominated by one of the following theological models:[1]

- The *millennial* model dominates dispensationalist treatments of the kingdom of God, both popular and academic. According to this model, the kingdom, though (perhaps) already present in some sense, will become a concrete reality only in the future, after Christ's bodily return and while He reigns from a throne in Jerusalem for a thousand years. That thousand-year era will be marked by unparalleled peace and prosperity. This model could be called, more generally, a "futurist" model, because of its almost exclusive emphasis on the future coming of the kingdom.
- The *eschatological* model is dominant among New Testament scholars of various stripes. Though there are many fine shades of difference in formulation, nearly all scholars agree that the New Testament era is one of eschatological "tension." The kingdom, normally defined abstractly as "God's rule," has already come, but is not yet consummated; the future kingdom of God has broken into this present world with the coming of the Christ, but God's absolute sovereignty is still contested. The church thus lives between the "already" of the First Advent and the "not yet" of the Final Advent. This model tends to portray the kingdom mainly in temporal terms, as the "new age" inaugurated with the coming of the Messiah. In contrast to the "futurist" model, the eschatological model, while not denying a future consummation, places emphasis on the present reality of God's reign.
- An increasing number of evangelical Christians, particularly those influenced by the Christian Reconstructionist Movement, operate with what might be called an *ethical* or *social activist* model of the kingdom. According to this model, the kingdom is realized on earth as people submit themselves in every area of life to the law of the exalted Christ. "Building the kingdom" is closely joined with constructing a Christian world civilization and taking political and cultural dominion, primarily

through evangelism and discipleship, but in part at least through political means.

- In more traditional Protestant churches, what might be called a *mystical* model of the kingdom of God remains prevalent, though largely undeveloped theologically. Taking Jesus' statement that "the kingdom of God is within you" (Luke 17:21, KJV) as their slogan, adherents of this viewpoint understand the kingdom as God's presence and rule in the hearts of His people. If the kingdom is believed to have any outward manifestation, it is in evangelism and Christian service.
- Among many Roman Catholic and Eastern Orthodox theologians and some "mainline" Protestants, a *sacramental* or *liturgical* model of the kingdom is predominant. According to this model, the power and blessing of the heavenly kingdom are made present by the Spirit to the church primarily in her worship and through her sacraments. Sacramental worship is the present form of the kingdom, though the kingdom's power exerts itself beyond the hour and place of worship. This model might be seen as a particular variation on the *ecclesiastical* model of the kingdom, which has been dominant throughout much of the history of the church. Without identifying the present imperfect church with the future kingdom, the ecclesiastical model brings kingdom and church into close proximity to one another.

Each of these models has, I believe, captured a genuinely biblical insight. But the various aspects of the kingdom highlighted by these models must not be separated from one another. In my study, I have found that most evangelical treatments of the kingdom are dominated by one of the first four models, or by a synthesis of them.

There is much good in these evangelical discussions of the kingdom.[2] What is lacking in evangelical scholarship and evangelicalism in general is an adequate appreciation of and emphasis on the validity—in my judgment, the centrality—of the ecclesiastical or sacramental model of the kingdom. When evangelicals teach or write about the kingdom, they typically include little or nothing about the relationship of the kingdom and the sacraments or of the kingdom and worship, and only a very inadequate statement on the relationship of the kingdom to the church. And yet, as Christians have seen throughout the centuries, all of these relationships are indispensable to a full understanding of the kingdom of God.

The evangelical aversion to the church, I came to recognize, was a source of both political and ecclesiastical disarray. The ecclesiastical problems are obvious. Even among evangelicals who place more emphasis on the church, there is very little stress on the centrality of worship, the sacraments, and discipline in the life of the church. The failure of evangelical Christians to act like the church has not been lost on that increasing number of evangelicals who have chosen to embark on pilgrimages to Canterbury, Rome, or Constantinople. Faced with a choice between a high Catholic ecclesiology and no ecclesiology, they have understandably chosen the former.

The political problems are more subtle. Though I do not think the Bible teaches that kingdom and church are identical, it is clear that the social dimension of the kingdom—its chief visible, earthly, communal manifestation—is the church. Though other institutions may indeed serve the purposes of God and advance His righteousness, no other institution can lay claim to being the community of the "sons of the kingdom" (Matt. 8:11–12).

When the church is set aside as the primary institution of the kingdom, Christians find a substitute to serve as the communal form and chief instrument of the kingdom of God. In American history, this substitute has generally been found in the "Redeemer Nation." What is called "American civil religion" is the product of a failure of ecclesiology.[3]

National political issues have, as a result, displaced theological and ecclesiastical concerns in the "agenda" and priorities of many churches.[4] As a result, churches, especially those dominated by an activist model of the kingdom, fail to address the world in a distinctively Christian manner—that is, as the church. They tend to fall captive to conservative political ideologies and run the risk of being reduced to yet another interest group. Whatever the political merits of such a strategy, it is theologically offensive to treat the church as an interest group.

Activist Christians tend to assume that, if the church is to be politically influential, her first task is to become more political. They need to feel the full force of Richard John Neuhaus's superb formula: "The first *political* task of the Church is to be the Church."[5] If in the course of this book I seem to verge into an exclusively "ecclesiological" model of the kingdom, it is not because I denigrate the Christian's political and social role; it is because I wish to stress that the church's task—even her political task—is not directly political.

Though I began this project with academic questions in mind, I believe that this book holds practical consequences for the church's life in the coming decades. The Supreme Court's *Casey* decision sent shock waves through the evangelical activist community. These waves turned into a full-scale earthquake when newly inaugurated President Bill Clinton celebrated the twentieth anniversary of *Roe v. Wade* by summarily overturning the anti-abortion policies of his two predecessors. After nearly two decades of struggle, the pro-life movement is back precisely where it began, if not worse.

Such political setbacks are likely to produce despair and cynicism among some Christians and reevaluation of priorities among others. It is my hope that this book will challenge such Christians with what I believe is a more comprehensively biblical model of Christian action in the world.

I am well aware of the limitations of my effort. I have not dealt with any of the issues I have raised in a comprehensive way. I have not, for example, provided an exposition of every New Testament passage that mentions or alludes to the kingdom of God. Nor have I provided a detailed, full-length portrait of the church's contemporary condition. Instead, I have attempted to sketch, in more or less broad strokes, what I believe is a more adequate, a more *biblical,* paradigm for understanding the kingdom of God. I hope, by God's grace, that this book helps the church in some small way to face the challenges that lie before her.

In the writing and research for this book, however, I have often felt the force of Calvin's comment on Christ's presence in the Supper. In the fourth book of the *Institutes,* he wrote of his inadequacy to the task he had set for himself.

> . . . whenever this matter [of the presence of Christ] is discussed, when I have tried to say all, I feel that I have as yet said little in proportion to its worth. And although my mind can think beyond what my tongue can utter, yet even my mind is conquered and overwhelmed by the greatness of the thing. Therefore, nothing remains but to break forth in wonder at this mystery, which plainly neither the mind is able to conceive nor the tongue to express.[6]

The kingdom, like the presence of Christ in the Supper, is something more felt than explained.

Origen, in his ninth homily on Genesis, echoed this same sense of wonder as he considered the depths of the revelation of God in Scripture.

> The further we progress in reading, the greater grows the accumulation of mysteries for us. And just as if someone should embark on the sea bourne by a small boat, as long as he is near land he has little to fear. But, when he has advanced little by little into the deep and has begun to be lifted on high by the swelling waves or brought down to the depths by the same gaping waves then truly great fear and terror permeate his mind because he has entrusted a small craft to such immense waves. So also we seem to have suffered, who, small in merits and slight in ability, dare to enter so vast a sea of mysteries.

ONE

✦

What Is the Kingdom of God?

It is early morning, June 19, 1988. I am standing in the middle of Spring Street in midtown Atlanta as sunlight begins to filter through the long narrow spaces between buildings into the chilly street below. A few miles away at the Omni, final preparations for the 1988 Democratic National Convention are being made. For an entire week the bleary eyes of the nation's political junkies will be fixed on Atlanta as the Democratic Party meets to perform its quadrennial rite of initiation for its latest political messiah.

On Spring Street, however, another drama is about to unfold before me, one that will electrify the Christian community, propel a hitherto obscure activist into the national spotlight, and reveal the deep fissures that divide the American people. It is a drama that will confirm that America is in the midst of a second civil war, one that is already far bloodier than the first.

Around eight o'clock some 135 men and women quietly walk or trot up Spring Street toward the Atlanta Surgi-Center, Atlanta's largest abortion "clinic." It is a varied group: Young and old, men and women. Some—a very few—clerical collars are visible. A mountainous bearded man wearing a flowery Hawaiian shirt takes what appears to be the "linchpin" position directly in front of the door. The rest gather three or four rows deep on the steps at the entrance of the clinic, sit down, and wait—quietly, soberly, resolutely. Some pray. Some sing hymns. A friend of mine, who will later become the Atlanta coordinator for Operation Rescue, paces up and down the sidewalk, talking into and listening to a black walkie-talkie.

Minutes later the abortionist arrives. Standing, the rescuers form a human wall. There is a tense moment as the abortionist, a policeman on each arm, tries to push his way to the door. After several attempts, he backs off. Through a megaphone, the police captain orders the rescuers to disperse. There is another tense moment, a long silence. I have the feeling that one of the rescuers will stand to say that it's all been a very bad mistake or a big joke, we didn't mean to upset the police, have a nice day. No one budges.

After huddling for a few moments with his officers, the police captain orders his men to begin making arrests. When one of the policemen spots my friend with the walkie-talkie, my friend falls to the ground and is carried to a waiting van.

Then I get that sinking feeling you get when you have crossed a bridge and there is no turning back. For those 135 rescuers, there is no turning back. What some pro-life activists would later call the "Battle of Atlanta" has begun.

✦   ✦   ✦

The night before, I attended a pre-rescue rally at Perimeter Presbyterian Church on the outskirts of Atlanta. Randall Terry, now well known as the founder and leader of Operation Rescue, spoke with warmth and fervor. He reminded us of the babies being slaughtered. He warned us of impending judgment. He encouraged us by saying that those who fight for the unborn would be considered heroes by future generations. It was not so much a sermon as a summons to battle. Terry sounded less like Spurgeon than like Henry V before the battle of St. Crispin's Day.[1] Despite Terry's moving and passionate appeals, I remained unconvinced. I decided not to participate in the rescue. I would wait and see.

As I stood up the street from the Surgi-Center the next morning, handing out pamphlets and talking with passers-by and policemen, I saw my pastor and several other close friends being arrested. Observing their implacable resolution, their orderliness, their prayerfulness, I began to doubt my decision not to participate in the rescue. I felt an urge to cross the sidewalk to take my place among the rescuers. Deep down, in spite of all my doubts about the wisdom of the rescue, I felt instinctively that I was on the wrong side of that sidewalk.

I did not follow my urge that morning, but as I walked back to my car, I knew that I had witnessed a memorable event. What has stayed with me from that late spring morning in Atlanta is not so much my sense of guilt for failing to fight abortion more boldly. It is not so much my desire to stand with my friends in a good cause, or the unsettling memory of seeing my pastor and close friends roughly packed into a police van. Instead, what has stayed with me is the conviction that America is a battleground. More than ever, I have sensed that the boundary lines are being drawn more sharply, that the middle ground is rapidly falling away, and that we face the necessity of taking sides. I realized that I had witnessed a major battle in a very real war.

A Nation at War

The conclusions I drew from observing the 1988 rescue were not at all unique. Over the past decade, many commentators have argued that contemporary America is the scene of a *Kulturkampf*, a "cultural war."[2] Competing visions of the past, present, and future are struggling for dominance of America.[3]

Kulturkampf is a historical and sociological term. In biblical language, we can describe our time as a time of *judgment*. In Scripture, judgment means more than "punishment." When God judges nations, He punishes His enemies, but that is not all He does. Judgment also means that God comes near to discriminate, to make distinctions. In Scripture, judgment is pictured not only by the image of the wine press, but also by the image of the winnowing fan (Lam. 1:15; Matt. 3:12, 17). When God judges, He separates sheep and goats, wheat and tares. The apostle Peter wrote that in one particular period of judgment, "the earth and its works will be discovered" (2 Peter 3:10).[4] Times of judgment reveal the hearts of men and force them to a crisis of choice. And when people are forced to make choices, they are drawn into conflict with those who make different choices. To live in a time of judgment is to live in a time of conflict.

No one has described the intellectual front of the cultural war more vigorously than Notre Dame's moral philosopher, Alasdair MacIntyre. MacIntyre has argued in several books that modern Western moral debate is in chaos. We argue about what "ought" to be; we act as if we had some authoritative foundation for ethical absolutes; we discuss what is "good"—we do all this as if we all knew and agreed on what these words mean.

But this assumed agreement is an illusion. Though we use the same words, the words carry very different and sometimes opposite meanings. For some, economic justice means that everyone should have close to an equal share of a nation's aggregate wealth; for others, it means that everyone's paycheck should reflect the free market value of his work. For some, being compassionate means helping a poor, unmarried woman to obtain an abortion, or rescuing a baby seal from a ruthless Eskimo; for others, compassion requires that we block abortion clinics to prevent that same woman from murdering her child and let the Eskimo provide for his children. For some, freedom means liberty to display graphic photographs of homosexual acts in prominent museums at taxpayers' expense; for others, freedom means the liberty to do what is right.

We have, MacIntyre contends, no common moral principles, no common conceptions of justice, no common ideas of rationality. We do not even agree on how we go about deciding what we should agree on. Americans are deeply divided on the most fundamental principles of morality. Moral discussion has thus become little more than interminable verbal warfare.[5]

The war, however, is not confined to the lofty towers of the nation's prestigious universities. It has political as well as intellectual dimensions. Nor is the political war confined to the issue of abortion. As the late Francis Schaeffer often pointed out, one of the great weaknesses of modern evangelicalism[6] is its tendency to see things in pieces, rather than in wholes. The cultural warfare touches every sector of American public life. Consider a few recent publicly debated issues:

- *There is a war over education.* The nation's public schools are in disarray. Test scores continue to decline, illiteracy is on the rise, and students graduate from high school without the slightest appreciation of their culture and its past. Multiculturalism would institutionalize ignorance of the Western achievement. Discipline is almost nonexistent in many schools; violent crime has replaced speaking out of turn as the chief discipline problem. Some suggest that the solution is to raise salaries to attract more qualified teachers; other suggest that tighter discipline will solve many of our educational problems; others want to give parents a choice of schools. Unwilling to wait for the slow wheels of reform to turn, many parents are putting their children into private schools or teaching them at home. In many universities, moreover, Western civilization as a whole is under attack from what Roger Kimball has called "tenured radicals."[7]
- *There is a war over the family.* Radical feminists see the family as an inherently oppressive institution and have made significant gains in "feminizing" law, education, and American culture in general. Gay rights activists have pushed for legal redefinitions of the family that would legitimize homosexual families. Partly because of changes in law that made divorce easier to obtain, di-

vorce rates have risen dramatically. The traditional two-parent family with children is rapidly becoming obsolete.[8]

- *There is a war over popular culture.* Movies, television, and, more recently, music videos have become increasingly violent and pornographic over the past two decades. And these forms of "entertainment" permeate our lives. Producers defend their products by appealing to a Constitutional "right to free expression." In response, some groups have used boycotts to pressure sponsors of sexually explicit and violent productions to clean up the airwaves.

- *There is a war over the proper care of the environment.* The '90s are emerging as the Green decade. Radical environmentalists implicitly claim that the greatest threat to the environment is capitalistic exploitation and press for more comprehensive international political institutions to protect the environment. Others claim that genuine environmental concerns are best addressed by the free market.[9]

All these issues have been contested for some time, but the warfare has taken on a new intensity in recent years especially, owing to efforts of Operation Rescue, the warfare over abortion. Operation Rescue took the war to the streets. The original rescue of June 19, 1988 drew pro-life activists from across the nation, sparking a major pro-life effort. Rescues in Atlanta continued into the first two weeks of August as three hundred people were arrested and, by August 14, over two hundred were in jail. Because many refused to give their names, identifying themselves only as "Baby Jane Doe" or "Baby John Doe," they were not able to post bond.

National Christian news media reported the story widely. The "700 Club" devoted an hour to the rescue, and hundreds of people called to ask how they could get involved. Jerry Falwell visited Atlanta and dropped hints that he might be arrested in a future rescue. Even the major secular media picked up the story. The TV news magazine "48 Hours" spent an entire show exploring the rescue movement. Since 1988, Operation Rescue has conducted similar campaigns in Wichita, Kansas, Buffalo, New York, and Baton Rouge, Louisiana.

Operation Rescue has drawn this kind of attention because its activities make visible the warfare that has been raging since the 1970s. Operation Rescue has vividly revealed the divisions within our society and, by forcing abortion into public awareness, widened those divisions. Before Operation Rescue made its national debut, the abortion fight was mainly a war of words: debates, proposed legislation, court judgments. Abortion was caught up in the ritualized and comparatively peaceful conflict of the legal and political processes. For most Americans it was easy to forget that it was a war at all. With Operation Rescue the confrontation became palpably physical. Rescuers provided the empirical evidence that America has become a battleground over the abortion issue, and that the cold war over abortion has turned hot.

Operation Rescue also unveiled the limits of America's vaunted "pluralism." At the rescues, policemen physically dragged pro-life activists, sometimes kicking and throwing them, while gently carrying women into the clinic so that they could kill their babies. Operation Rescue showed that the uniformed representatives of the "system" were decidedly on the side of the abortionists.

Kingdoms in Conflict?

Truly we face a vicious attack from powerful enemies in high places. And yet in the midst of the battle, we are very blessed. Despite the war, we can give thanks. We constitute the greatest nation on the face of the earth. She is in fact the greatest empire that has ever existed, truly the "last great hope of mankind." We enjoy a degree of justice and liberty, prosperity and peace beyond the imagination of any other people. We have an unsurpassed heritage, boasting many of the greatest thinkers, artists, and leaders in all of human history.

Indeed, despite the present conflict and turmoil, we will overcome our adversaries and endure forever. No matter how powerful our enemies, no matter how vicious their attacks, we will rise up to advance across the globe, and other nations will, like birds seeking refuge in a spreading tree, find security in the shade of our branches. We will defeat any and all enemies, within and without, in our cosmic warfare.

Do these last statements surprise you? Have I lapsed into the overheated rhetoric of an extremist patriot? I assure you that I am completely serious, and I believe every word that I have written.

But perhaps that little pronoun "we" has confused you. You may have assumed that "we" meant "we Americans" or "we conservative Americans" or "we right-thinking Americans." What I have been describing is in fact not the United States of America, but the church, the priestly kingdom and holy nation of God (1 Peter 2:9). Men and women find true liberty, peace, and joy only in the church. She is the original melting pot. Only citizens of heaven have access to true riches and enjoy true security. The kingdom of God is the cosmic tree in which the nations find shelter. It is the church against which even the gates of hell shall not prevail.

I confess, of course, that my use of "we" was deliberately ambiguous. I wanted to challenge you to think more carefully—more biblically—about two closely related issues: the past and current condition of America, and the nature of the conflict that American Christians face today. We need to think carefully about who "we" are and who "they" are, where the dividing line is to be drawn, and what kind of war we are fighting.

Surely God has used the people and power of the United States in remarkable ways. Missionaries from the United States have criss-crossed the globe preaching the gospel. Charitable donations from the United States have fed and clothed thousands of hungry and naked children in other lands. American armies have fought to protect the liberty of other nations against tyrants, and so on. It would be unfair to ignore those contributions. Even today, as Richard John Neuhaus has said, "On balance and considering the alternatives, the influence of the United States is a force for good in the world."[10]

But it is precisely this history that makes the "we" ambiguous. For some American Christians, Neuhaus's *qualified* appreciation of American influence verges on treason. Christianity's profound influence on American life has made it easy for American Christians to think that this nation is something *more* than a relative force for good. Throughout history some have seen America as peculiarly a "Redeemer Nation," with a global and even apocalyptic mission. As historian Sidney Mead put it, some have viewed America as "the primary agent of God's meaningful activity in history."[11] Such a view contradicts the biblical teaching that the church is God's primary agent in history.

Extreme nationalism of the nineteenth-century sort may be a thing of the past. But it is difficult for many Americans, especially in the aftermath of such triumphs as Operation Desert Storm, to shake off the sense that "we Americans" are somehow God's chosen people, that somehow God is (or, at least, should be) on "our" side. The cultural war is thus depicted as a conflict between those who would preserve the traditional American way of life ("us") and those who wish to change things ("them"), between traditionalists and progressives, conservatives and liberals. Many Christians view conservatives as the children of light and liberals as the children of darkness.[12] Liberals, it is further argued, hold the positions of prestige in politics, the academy, and the media. The cultural war is thus portrayed as a contrast between a conservative "moral majority" and an oppressive and devilish liberal elite.

This view of America's cultural war, understandable as it is in the light of American history, tends to ignore a basic fact of contemporary American life: America's Christian consensus has disappeared. As Armenian Orthodox writer Vigen Guroian has written, "While three quarters of Americans might describe themselves as religious, there is little other evidence to indicate that such religiosity always includes the content or conviction of biblical faith."[13] And, despite the rhetoric of a "moral majority," Americans no more share a moral consensus than a religious one. The battle over abortion alone should be sufficient proof of that. It is simply no longer possible to say "we Americans" want a restoration of "traditional morality." By all indications, many of "us" do not.

Some Christians seem to recognize that the Christian consensus in America has evaporated. When they talk of "we," they mean "we Christians," not "we Americans." That use of "we" embodies a more accurate assessment of American's condition. It recognizes that no appeal can be made to a general American moral or religious consensus. Yet these same Christians continue to portray "them" as an oppressive elite. Randall Terry's call for Christians to become "'valiant warriors' to take back the levers of power in our nation's power bases,"[14] for example, assumes that America's cultural crisis is mainly a problem of having the wrong hands on the levers.

Statements such as Terry's indicate that many Christians have not yet adjusted to the collapse of Christendom. Christians fail to recognize that, though their numbers are great in America, the United States is in no sense guided by Christian norms and cannot be understood as a Christian nation. Christian America and Christian Europe are things of the past. They were in many ways wonderful while they lasted, and we can hope that future generations will see a rebirth of Christian civilization in a more mature form. In the West, that prospect is, to all appearances, a distant one.

For the present, Western Christians find themselves in some important respects in the same situation as the Christians of the early centuries A.D. We face not merely a hostile elite, but a hostile culture. Orthodox Christians must stop thinking of ourselves as the temporarily exiled rulers of America who can be restored to power if only an election or two would go our way. We must start accepting the truth that, sociologically speaking, we are a minority subculture. If this accurately describes the current state of American Christianity, the task before the church is not to "take back the levers of power," but rather to convert a pagan world.[15]

Our cultural crisis, in short, goes much deeper than moral majoritarians suspect. It is not as if the top floors of the edifice of Christendom need some remodeling. The entire building has collapsed, and now, if it is to be rebuilt at all, it must be rebuilt from the ground floor. The problem is not that America has been the site of a coup that can be corrected by a counter-coup. America is the site of a death, and the only known antidote for death is resurrection.

Holy War

The "moral majority" analysis offers, in my judgment, a too-optimistic diagnosis of the affliction that plagues American life. More seriously, it tends to divert attention, theologically and practically, from more significant conflicts. My reflections on the "we" and "they" of the cultural war would be mere sociological observations but for the fact that our understanding of the times influences our priorities and actions. As Nobel economist James Buchanan has observed, the "status quo" has a unique authority; we start here, not somewhere else. If we have misread the status quo, we are in danger of missing the real war and of putting too much of our energies and time into minor skirmishes. A misreading of the character of our situation will lead us to misjudge priorities and to wield the wrong weapons.

In this connection, theologian James B. Jordan has helpfully drawn attention to the biblical distinction between "holy war" and "normal war." "Normal war" includes political and legal activities, as well as military operations. In the terms we have been using, America's cultural war is one particular instance of normal war. While acknowledging the obligation of Christians to engage in normal war, Jordan emphasizes the *"primacy of the Holy War."*

When Jordan stresses the primacy of holy war, he does not mean that Christians should arm themselves for an evangelical *jihad*. In the New Testament, holy war is carried out by the *church*, and the church's primary weapon is the *gospel*, which comes to expression in the world through the Word, the sacraments, and the church's community life. Thus, "the first order of Holy War is always the continual re-creation of the Church, as the Holy Spirit proceeds from eternity into time continually bringing new life and energy to God's people."[16]

Recognition of the primacy of holy war forces us to re-assess our priorities. We will have to ask again, What are the most important issues confronting American Christians? How are we to combat the evils that we see around us? In some cases, the battlegrounds in the holy war overlap considerably to the battlegrounds of the cultural war. Abortion, for example, is an evil that Christians should vigorously fight with every political and spiritual weapon that comes to hand. Frequently, however, a skirmish in the holy war will seem irrelevant to those engaged in the cultural war. If holy war is primary, however, the activities of holy war—sacramental worship, Bible teaching, evangelism, prayer—take on a new prominence as the chief priorities and weapons of American Christians.

A historical example may help make the point. Sixteenth-century Europe witnessed a cultural war of sorts. The rebirth of classical learning, the widely acknowledged corruption of the church, and the rising power of centralized states had already upset the medieval system. Yet, certainly the most dramatic and significant event of the period was the result of a guilt-ridden monk's struggle to understand the righteousness of God. It was Luther's recovery of the gospel that radically and permanently changed European civilization.

In another example, the Reformation spilt apart at the Colloquy of Marburg in 1529.[17] There Luther dramatically refused to compromise on the doctrine of the real presence of Christ in the Lord's Supper. Despite efforts at reconciliation, the Zwinglians and Lutherans went their separate ways. According to Indian scholar J. P. Singh Uberoi, Marburg not only splintered the Reformation, but began the splintering of the modern mind. In particular, Zwingli's belief that the Eucharist was merely symbolic is the source of the "dualism or double monism" that Uberoi says is characteristic of the modern world view. "Spirit, word and sign had finally parted company at Marburg in 1529; and myth or ritual . . . was no longer literally *and* symbolically real and true. . . . Zwingli was the chief architect of the new schism and . . . Europe and the world followed Zwingli in the event. Zwingli, the reformer of Zurich, was in his system of thought the first philosopher . . . of the modern world."[18] While the debate over the real presence may have seemed tangential to the "great issues" of the day, Uberoi suggests that its influence was crucial.

Please note several things that I am *not* saying. I am not saying that Christian political and social activism is wrong or unimportant. The legal, political, and social questions that face America are exceedingly important, and Christians should address them and take action. But there are other, more important questions to ask and answer, more powerful weapons than law and politics, and more important battles to wage.

Nor am I saying merely that religious questions are more important than "political" questions, though that is true enough. I am saying that religious questions are more important *to politics* than any of the political questions. Religious commitments are expressed in one's positions on political issues. The most important *political* question that Christians can put to America's leaders is, "Who do you say that I am?" (Matt. 16:15).

Finally, I am not saying that the "liberal elite" equals the "spiritual forces of wickedness in heavenly places," or that the cultural war" is identical to the "holy war." Instead, I am saying that there is a warfare "behind" the warfare, a *Religionskrieg* behind the *Kulturkampf*, a holy war behind the cultural war. The holy war cuts across the various divisions of the cultural war; it is waged on a different "plane." Yet, though the holy war is not identical to the cultural war, neither is it irrelevant to the cultural war; they intersect in ways that we cannot fully fathom. The two are different but related, distinct but not separate.

Thus, my ambiguous use of "we" was intended to push toward a deeper consideration of the nature of the war Christians face today. It is not primarily the cultural war, important as that is. The "we" means "we Christians," and the "they" can be nothing less than "spiritual forces of wickedness in the heavenly places" (Eph. 6:12). "We" means the church, while "they" are what the Bible calls the "world." The conflict "behind" the cultural war is the conflict of the kingdom of God against the kingdom of Satan. That is the really big conflict of history, and that is the conflict whose outcome will determine the outcome of the cultural war.

What Is the Kingdom of God?

These thoughts lead us to ask how the kingdom of God is related to the cultural war. For some today, "building the kingdom" is closely and directly related to "restoring America." The kingdom is thought to be mainly concerned with social and political transformation and reform. The kingdom of God is mainly a matter of "normal war."

In Scripture, however, the kingdom of God is most directly related to the holy war. The kingdom is a matter of holy war primarily and relates only indirectly to the "normal" war of political and legal action. The relationship between serving the kingdom and "restoring America" is thus not a simple and direct one. Indeed, as Herbert Schlossberg has astutely observed, genuine Christian faith—truly seeking the kingdom—may actually be subversive of the contemporary American order.

If we are rightly to understand the relationship between the holy war and America's cultural war, we must, obviously, seek to understand what the kingdom of God is. If we are to be soldiers fighting a holy war for the kingdom of God, we need to know how God expects us to fight, the weapons, tactics and strategies He wishes us to employ, the goals of our battle, and the prospects of victory.

Different understandings of the kingdom of God have led Christians to a wide variety of practices in the past.

- When John Cassian, the founder of Western monasticism, asked the hermits of Egypt why they had retreated to the desert, their answer was that they were there "to seek the kingdom of God."[19]
- During the mid-fourteenth century, bands of several hundred flagellants each spread across Europe, wandering from town to town. Stripped to the waist, they walked down the main streets of the towns, beating themselves with leather whips until the blood flowed. Why this outpouring of self-flagellation and penance? Because the flagellants were convinced that the kingdom of heaven was near.
- In late 1533 a group of radical Anabaptists gained control of the city of Munster in Westphalia. By March of the following year they had banished all who refused baptism. A Dutch "prophet" known as John of Leyden was proclaimed king, and laws were passed to permit polygamy and to establish a system of common property. A proclamation was issued calling the saints to exterminate the ungodly. Why did the Anabaptists seize Munster and establish their strange "theocracy" there? Because they were convinced that in doing this they were establishing the kingdom of God on earth.

These dangers may seem remote from our hyper-sophisticated "postmodern" world. Few Christians retreat to the desert to contemplate God. No Christian today, we think, is forcibly erecting theocracies. If Christians were walking through the streets of New York or Chicago beating themselves with whips, surely Dan Rather would have told us. But the "kingdom of God" is still used as a justification for a wide range of activities.

- Liberation theologians from Africa to Latin America to Asia see the kingdom manifested largely in political and social change. The Roman Catholic journal *Crisis* reprinted a letter from Cardinal Paulo Evaristo Arns of Sao Paulo, Brazil, to Fidel Castro. Cardinal Arns congratulated Castro on the thirtieth anniversary of the Cuban Revolution, adding that "Christian faith discovers in the achievements of the Revolution signs of the kingdom of God."[20] The phrase "sign of the kingdom," historically used in connection with the sacraments, is applied by liberation theologians to Marxist revolutions and regimes of the most brutal and oppressive kind. Why do they support such regimes? Because liberation theologians believe that revolutionary political activity is a sign of the kingdom of God on earth.
- Since the late 1970s, thousands of evangelical Christians have entered the political arena for the first time. In some states they have made efforts to take control of existing political parties. Christian lobbying and advocacy groups have formed. In 1988, a leading charismatic, Pat Robertson, ran for president. Why are so many evangelicals entering the political process? Many do so because they believe that political action is a way to build the kingdom of God.

Some Christians have retreated into monasteries to "seek the kingdom," while others enter the political arena in a crusade to "build the kingdom." Some see the kingdom manifested in revolutionary violence, while for others the kingdom is manifested in pacifist nonresistance. Eastern Orthodox Christians find the kingdom manifest in the sacraments and liturgy of the church, while others believe that nearly every Christian activity except worship is a way of building the kingdom. This wide variety shows that Christians have very different understandings of what the kingdom of God is.

Defining the kingdom of God is no easy task. In the Bible, this phrase and its equivalents ("kingdom of heaven," "the kingdom," etc.) are used in a staggering variety of ways.

The phrase can refer to the place where God's people joyfully feast in His presence (Luke 22:29–30). It can refer to the rule of the triune God, and particularly to the rule of Jesus Christ (Ps. 145:13; Col. 1:13). It can refer to those people who submit to the rule of the Lord (1 Peter 2:9). It can refer to the transfigured new heavens and new earth (Matt. 25:34).

How can we put all these different elements together? Considered in all its facets, the kingdom of God can be defined as *the new world order that Christ established in His life, death, resurrection, and ascension, a new order of things that will be fully revealed and established only at Christ's return.*[21] Several aspects of this definition should be noted.

First, I do not mean to deny that the triune God has always ruled or His kingdom is from everlasting to everlasting. But Jesus taught that the coming of the kingdom of God was near (Matt. 4:17). Though God has always ruled and always will, Jesus achieved something of such novelty that He could preach as if the kingdom of God had never before existed.

Second, by this definition, the kingdom of God is an existing reality. Christ established His kingdom in His First Advent. At the same time, the kingdom of God is not fully manifested and revealed. The main features of the new world order are already in place, but the "new heavens and new earth" have not yet been consummated. The future of the world has come into the middle of the world's history. This "eschatological tension" is what some biblical scholars call the "already and not yet" character of the kingdom.

Everywhere in the New Testament, we find this emphasis. We have *already* tasted the powers of the *age to come* (Heb. 6:4–6); we *already* feast with and on Christ, as a *foretaste* of the Marriage Supper of the Lamb (1 Cor. 10:16; Rev. 19:7); we are *already* citizens of heaven, our lives *already* hidden with Christ in God, *already* ascended to the heavenly Jerusalem, though the creation still groans for our adoption as sons (Eph. 2:6; Col. 3:1–4; Heb. 12:18–24; Rom. 8:22); we are *already* new creations in Christ, though we have *not yet* put on immortality (2 Cor. 5:17; 1 Cor. 15:50–57); the Spirit is the earnest of our future inheritance (2 Cor. 1:22; 5:5; Eph. 1:14); and so on.

It is clear from the first three (Synoptic) Gospels that the kingdom of God was the major theme of Jesus' preaching and teaching. Each author summarized Jesus' teaching and ministry under the heading of "the kingdom of heaven" or "the kingdom of God" (Matt. 4:17; Mark 1:14–15; Luke 4:42–43). But the Gospels show that Jesus preached a specific message about the kingdom: the kingdom of God is *near* (Matt. 4:17). The imminent coming of the kingdom was the main theme of Jesus' preaching and teaching.

Once we recognize Jesus' emphasis on the nearness of the kingdom, we are faced with two options. Either Jesus was right, and the kingdom did come; or Jesus was wrong. Orthodox Christians cannot accept the latter conclusion. The only alternative is to accept at face value the New Testament's claim that the kingdom of God has *already* come, though it has *not yet* been fully revealed, established, and manifested.[22]

The remaining imperfections of this world order result from the continuing power of sin. Though Christ rules now, His enemies are not yet put under His feet (1 Cor. 15:25). Only when the last enemy, death, is defeated, will the kingdom of God be perfected and the transfiguration of the creation be completed with the resurrection of the dead (1 Cor. 15). Until God's war against the wicked is won, the kingdom will not come in its fullest reality.

Features of the Kingdom

The new world order is a result of the revolutionary work of Jesus Christ. I call it "revolutionary" because it brings about a reversal of fortune, a radical transformation of an existing situation. The New Testament frequently uses the language of revolution to describe the effects of Christ's First Advent. Mary, like Hannah before her, sang the praises of the God who scatters the proud, who brings down rulers and exalts the humble, who fills the hungry and sends the rich empty away (Luke 1:46–55). Jesus Himself drew on the imagery of the Jubilee in His first sermon in Nazareth: His coming marked the beginning of the favorable year of the Lord, the time of release for prisoners, for the restoration of sight to the blind, for the preaching of good news to the poor (Luke 4:18–19). The Beatitudes in both Matthew and Luke imply a radical reversal of human expectations (Matt. 5:3–12; Luke 6:20–26).

It must be stressed, however, that, though the coming of the kingdom marks a revolution in the world order, it is a lawful and righteous revolution. The coming of Christ was not only a revolutionary event, but also the revelation of the righteousness of God (Rom. 1:17). My use of the words "revolution" and "revolutionary," therefore, should not be taken to imply a modern, anarchistic revolution.

Jesus revolutionized the world in three ways. First, He has achieved a *revolution in the heavens*. Under the old covenant system, Satan was in a position of power over men. He was in heaven (Job 1–2). By His life, death, resurrection, and ascension, Jesus cast Satan from heaven and took His place at the right hand of the Majesty on high. The coming of the kingdom of God means that Christ has been exalted to the right hand of the Father, is now reigning (Eph. 1:19–23), and will reign until He has made a footstool of His enemies (1 Cor. 15:25). The nations have been given to Him as His inheritance (Ps. 2), and He is ruling to bring the nations to worship and obedience to His Father. In Christ, the saints have also been exalted to heavenly thrones (Eph. 2:6).

Second, Christ achieved a *revolution at the sanctuary* by opening the true, heavenly sanctuary. From the time of Adam and Eve, and throughout the old covenant, men were permitted to draw near to God only in very rare circumstances. They were excluded from the sanctuary, God's house (Lev. 16:1–2). When Christ died, the veil that separated the inner sanctuary was torn in two, a sign of the desecration of the earthly temple and an earthly symbol of the opening of the heavenly tabernacle (Matt. 27:51). By faith, we are now permitted to enter into the true, heavenly sanctuary (Heb. 9–10). The coming of the kingdom of God means that Christ has

19

opened up a way into heaven *for us* and that we can enjoy all the blessings of God's glorious presence. We can feast in the Holy Place and, invigorated by heavenly food and drink, undertake to transform the world into an image of heaven.

Third, Christ achieved a *revolution on earth*. Throughout the Old Testament, God's works in history centered on a single nation, Israel. But in the New Testament, Israel has been fulfilled in the new Israel, the Christian church. In the church, the dividing wall has been broken down, and Jew and Gentile are united in one new Man, Jesus Christ (Eph. 2:14–15). The new Israel is a race of rulers, fulfilling the original mandate to Adam. In Christ, she is heir and possessor of all things (Eph. 2:6; 1 Cor. 3:21–23). Empowered by her union with the risen Christ through the Spirit, the church has been given the mission of making disciples of the nations and furthering God's will on earth as it is in heaven (Matt. 6:10; 28:18–20).

These three features are closely interconnected. Christ has ascended to His throne and now gives gifts to His people. One of these gifts is the right to sit in heavenly places with Him, sharing in His rule over all things. Another of the royal gifts of King Jesus is the right to sit at His Table to feast on heavenly bread. Those who partake of the one loaf are formed into a priestly nation. Renewed by these heavenly, Spiritual blessings, Christ's people go into the world, under the blessing of God, to fulfill God's purposes for the human race.

It should also be noted that this definition of the kingdom of God is thoroughly Christ-centered. Theologians since the time of Origen (early third century) have recognized that Jesus is revealed in the Gospels to be the incarnation and personification of the kingdom. Where Christ is present, there is the kingdom. So also, each "feature" of the kingdom as I have described it focuses on Christ. The kingdom is in heaven because Christ is seated there at His Father's right hand; the kingdom is in the sanctuary because there Christ makes Himself present in Word and sacrament; the kingdom is in the church because Christ has promised to be present wherever two or three are gathered in His name. The kingdom is where the body of Christ is found, whether we speak of His body incarnate, sacramental, or ecclesiastical.

Conclusion

It strikes many modern Christians as surpassingly odd that, with the Roman Empire collapsing about their ears and the barbarians invading from the north and east, Christian leaders of the first centuries were preoccupied with debates about whether the Son's eternal relation to the Father should be described as *homoousion* ("same substance"), *homoiousion* ("like substance"), or *homoion* ("like"). Unless we are Lutherans, we might think Luther a fanatic for his ferocious defense of his formulation of the real presence of Christ in the sacrament at the Marburg Colloquy. (In Luther's Small Catechism, the body and blood are said to be "in, with, and under" the bread and wine.)

While the church fathers and Reformers are hardly above criticism, the contention of this book is that *we* are the oddities, not they; *we* are the ones obsessed with trivialities. The church fathers and Reformers had a more biblical sense of priorities than we have. We have permitted the idolaters of power and mammon to set our priorities for us; we have let them convince us that the really big issues confronting the world are political, and that they can be solved through political means. We have inverted the biblical stress on the priority of holy war over normal war.

Our forefathers knew better. They would tell us that the debates over *homoousion* are of vastly greater significance—ultimately, of vastly greater political significance—than the debates over Saddam Hussein. They would warn us that Arius remains a greater threat to our social well-being than acid rain. Reforming the welfare state is important, but our forefathers would have insisted that reforming worship is a more pressing need. Liturgy is closer to the heart of the church's concern than a hundred pieces of legislation. The next assembly for communion will have a more profound effect on the world than the next assembly of Congress. Baptism is a more crucial reality than the size of the federal budget.

The view of the kingdom sketched in this chapter, and filled out in this book, may appear to be a call for a reversal of the recent move of evangelical Christians into the public arena. But I am not advocating a renewed "pietism," a withdrawal from engagement with the world. What I am calling for, on the contrary, is a return to the early church's belief that, as historian Jaroslav Pelikan has commented, the "notes" of the church (one, holy, catholic, apostolic) are central to Christian mission and to the Christian social and political mission particularly. This book is not a summons to retreat from the world, but a rally cry to conservative Christians to engage the world—not as isolated Christians or as an interest group, but *as the church*. It is the burden of this book to stress the primacy of holy war, which, being translated, means the primacy of the church.

TWO

◆

I Saw Satan Fall

Thirteen mutilated corpses. Some were missing hearts, brains, and other organs. The missing organs were later found nearby in stinking, steaming pots—cooked, along with assorted animal parts, in blood.

This was the ghastly spectacle that greeted Mexican police in Matamoros near the Texas border in mid-April 1989, while they were investigating the disappearance of a Texas college student, Mark Kilroy. Officials later concluded that the ritual killings had been performed by a satanist, drug-dealing cult known as Palo Nayombe, and members of the cult were arrested. The group, police surmised, had hoped to protect itself from capture by offering human sacrifices.

The Matamoros murders received widespread media coverage and shocked the nation, but the incident was hardly unique. Geraldo Rivera's program on satanism, telecast the previous autumn, had been jeered by sophisticated elites. Yet all over the nation police departments are reporting an increase in the incidence of crimes by satanist cults. Only a month before the discoveries at Matamoros, a symposium on satanism and the occult had been conducted for police in Austin, Texas.[1]

Interest in the occult and satanism is increasing at an alarming rate. More alarming still, it has entered the mainstream of American life. Nearly every secular bookstore in the nation displays shelf after shelf of New Age and occult books, which are, not insignificantly, usually housed near the religion section. In Pelham, Alabama, near where my family and I live, two palm readers had at one time hung out their shingles. (One of them, apparently hoping to "cover her bases," also has a statue of the Virgin Mary in front of her house.) That's right, Pelham, *Alabama*. And it seems that every town between Birmingham and Auburn has its local psychic. The heart of the Bible Belt is going New Age!

If we focus our attention on sensational incidents like the grizzly slaughter at Matamoros or the pop-occultism of New Age humanism, however, we may miss the larger point. Most of the iceberg remains submerged. Satanic influence does not always appear so blatantly evil. Often, as Hannah Arendt has noted, evil can seem perfectly banal. Satan can appear disguised as an angel of light. He can also wear the disguise of a state legislator who fights to keep abortion "safe and legal," a yuppie whose dominating passion is his own net worth, a preacher bewitched by another gospel.

We must be careful not to shift blame. We dare not say, as did Eve, "The Devil made me do it." We are sinful enough ourselves, and we do not need direct satanic influence to commit even the most unspeakable evil. But the man who practices sin is a slave to sin (John 8:34), and the man who acts satanically is a slave to Satan. Racial slavery may (or may not) be a thing of the past, but the world remains heavily populated with slaves.

Surely, as someone once said, "Satan is alive and well on planet earth."

The Prince of This World

Or is he? It may seem insufferably naive even to raise this question. Of course Satan is alive and well. It is obvious to anyone who reads the *National Enquirer* or the *New York Daily News* and to anyone who watches television talk shows. Like the desert hermits, it seems we can hardly open our eyes without discovering Satan busily at work.

Christians must always be careful, however, to live by faith in God's Word and promise, not by a very limited and erring understanding of the world. The real question is, What does the Bible teach about Satan?[2]

The Kingdom of Creation

Answering that question leads us back to the first chapters of the Bible, where Moses recorded the account of creation. There we learn that God did not create man as a slave, but quite the opposite. God's first instructions to Adam and Eve were, "Be fruitful and multiply, and fill the earth, and subdue it, and rule" (Gen. 1:28). We have heard these words so often that we no longer feel their breathtaking force. God commanded two people, a man and a woman, to be king and queen of the whole creation and to produce a worldwide race of kings and queens to rule the creation. They and their children were to learn more and more about God's good creation, to discover ever new uses of the things God had made, to bring the world more and more completely into service to God and man. Over time, they were to build from the raw materials of creation a glorious temple-city on earth as a replica and image of the heavenly city of God.[3]

When God said, "Let them rule," however, He was not only telling Adam and Eve what to do. He was also *defining* what men and women would be. Adam and Eve were commanded to rule, and they were created as ruling creatures. God commanded them to learn about the creation, and He made them learning creatures. He told Adam and Eve to construct a culture that would glorify Him, and He made them culture-building creatures. The royal task of "ruling and subduing" is, as much as the procreative task of "filling the earth," a "natural" activity for men and women made in the image of God.

Many popular novels and movies bring out this fact of humanity's created nature. Robinson Crusoe was shipwrecked

25

on an almost deserted island, but he did not live as an animal, nor was he transformed into Rousseau's untainted noble savage. Instead he built, he invented, he innovated—he formed a small-scale civilization. The Swiss Family Robinson did the same. Wherever people go, they strive to improve, exploit, "glorify" their environment because that is the way God made them.[4]

Adam was created not only to be a ruling king, but also to be a worshiping and guarding priest (Gen. 2:15). Priesthood involves several activities,[5] but certainly one of a priest's chief duties is worship. In Scripture, worship is closely bound up with God's kingship. As we shall see later in more detail, the temple, where Israel gathered for worship, was the palace of the Great King (Pss. 80:1; 99:1). To worship God is to acknowledge His kingship, to lift Him up and honor Him as King. He is *enthroned* on the praises of His people (Ps. 22:3). In their priestly worship, Adam and Eve were to exalt and celebrate God's kingship.

Like kingship, priesthood was both a command to and a definition of man. God commanded Adam and Eve to worship Him, having designed them to be worshiping creatures. Paul made this point in Romans 1. Those who refuse to worship the Lord do not cease worshiping altogether. Instead, "they exchanged the truth of God for a lie, and worshiped and served the creature rather than the Creator" (Rom. 1:25). Worship, like ruling, is "built into" men. It is "natural" for people to bow before something. If they do not bow before the living God, they will bow before idols.[6]

Since Adam was a priest as well as a king, it is clear that God did not give up His kingship when He created humanity. God is the original King, and His Word carries absolute authority and omnipotent power. He ruled over Adam and Eve through what the Bible calls the "covenant." The late South African theologian Cornelis van der Waal identified three key elements of all biblical covenants: promise, demand, and threat.[7] God *promised* life to Adam and Eve, *commanded* them not to eat from the tree of the knowledge of good and evil, and *threatened* them with death if they disobeyed His command. God ruled Adam and Eve as their covenant King.

Though God remained sovereign, He planned to *share* His rule with Adam and Eve. This was one of the promises implicit in the covenantal arrangements in Eden: Adam and Eve were one day to inherit the privileges of eating from the tree of knowledge and ruling with God. Older theologians called Adam God's "vice-gerent," or, in more familiar language, God's prince. He was the son of the King (Luke 3:38). Adam was to rule, but only according to the commands of God's covenant and for His glory. Adam was to be a king, but only as he continually acknowledged the superiority of the divine King. For Adam and Eve, ruling was not to be the ultimate business of life. Their chief goal was to honor their Creator. Worship, not dominion, was to be primary. They were to be priests, honoring the Lord, before they were kings, ruling with Him.

To empower them for their calling, God allowed Adam and Eve to meet with Him in the Garden of Eden. The Garden was a sanctuary, a place of God's special, glorious presence. Located on a mountain, the Garden was symbolically the center of the world and of human life.[8] As they appeared before the Glorious Presence in the Garden each Sabbath, Adam and Eve were to be transformed into His image, advancing from glory to glory. God would have spoken to them from above the trees, instructing them how they were to fulfill their calling. The Tree of Life at the center of the Garden bore fruit to refresh, strengthen, gladden, and transform Adam and Eve. As they ate the fruit, God would have communicated His life-giving Spirit to them. Eating from the tree of the Garden, they would have received God's blessing—power to fulfill His purposes for them.[9] God's blessing and His gift of life were to be communicated to Adam and Eve through the feast at the Garden-sanctuary.

The life of Adam and Eve was therefore to be completely circumscribed by worship. On the first day, they were to appear before the Lord in the Garden to worship and commune with Him, to enter into His sabbath rest. Empowered by God's blessing, they were to go about their royal tasks for six days, only to return at the end of the week to offer themselves and their works to the Lord for His evaluation and judgment and to be refreshed for another week of royal labor. The life of Adam and Eve displays human history in miniature. Human history began in the Garden with Adam and Eve worshiping God, and will end with the church gathered in a glorious temple-city. Worship is the alpha and the omega of human life and history.

These, then, are the features of God's original kingdom, the world order of creation:

- *God is the King,* but He intends to *share His rule* over the creation with men and women.
- Adam and Eve were to produce a *race of rulers* that would use the raw materials of creation to form a *replica of the heavenly temple-city* of God.
- They were to build the earthly temple-city in *obedience* to God's covenant law and *for His glory.*
- To empower them for their task, God *blessed* them with life by giving them *access to His Garden* and by letting them eat the fruit of the *Tree of Life.*
- Priestly *worship* in God's sanctuary is the *beginning and goal* of the life of the kingdom.

Throughout redemptive history, though the forms have changed in significant ways, God's kingdom has had these same basic structures and this same basic program.[10]

Training Grounds

Child training experts often suggest that parents use what are called "training grounds." A training ground gives a child an opportunity to learn responsibility at low risk. Parents give their child a little responsibility in a controlled environment, to see how he will handle it. If he handles it well, he will be rewarded with a bit more. For example, parents might give their young boy a quarter a week in allowance. By the time he is a teenager, they might increase his allowance to five or ten dollars a week. By gradually increasing his allowance, parents help him grow up into responsible stewardship.

God placed Adam and Eve in just such a "training ground." He wanted them to share in His rule, but He knew that they would not be ready immediately. To test and train them, God placed a second tree, the Tree of Knowledge, in the center of the Garden beside the Tree of Life, but He forbade Adam and Eve to eat from it (Gen. 2:16–17). Some scholars call this second tree the "judgment tree."[11] It symbolized the capacity to distinguish or judge between good and evil. Knowledge of good and evil is mature wisdom, the chief virtue of judges and kings (2 Sam. 14:17; 1 Kings 3:9). God would eventually have permitted Adam and Eve to eat of this tree. He wanted them to become mature kings and to participate in His royal judgments, but first they needed to grow up. They needed to show their faith in God. Before they were given greater responsibility, they needed to learn how to obey their covenant Lord. Before receiving true riches, they had to learn how to handle their allowance.

Adam and Eve, as we all know, were unfaithful in their training ground. Dissatisfied with their allowance, they demanded their entire inheritance. Impatient with waiting for God's permission, they wanted to exercise their right to rule. Ignoring God's command, they tried to attain wisdom apart from the fear of the Lord (Prov. 1:7). They wanted to rule without acknowledging God's rule, to be kings without first being priests. They put dominion ahead of worship.[12]

Because of the sin of Adam and Eve, God punished them by disrupting the original structures of His kingdom. God carried out the threat of the covenant He had made with Adam and Eve.

First, *the sanctuary, the center of human life, was closed off.* God had originally permitted Adam and Eve to meet Him in the Garden, to drink of the waters of Paradise, and to eat from the Tree of Life. After Adam and Eve defiled themselves, however, God cast them out of the Garden and stationed guardian cherubim at the entrance to prevent their return (Gen. 3:24). Unclean Adam and Eve were cut off from the presence and glory of God; naked and ashamed, they dared not approach Him. God in His anger said, "Truly they shall not enter into My rest." They were no longer allowed to eat the fruit of the Tree of Life. To be in God's presence is life, and to be denied access to God's presence is death. God's threat was literally true: "In the day that you eat from it you shall surely die" (Gen. 2:17).

Second, *man's kingship and priesthood were perverted.* Adam and Eve's descendants continued to rule over the earth and to develop technologically and culturally. Cain built a city. Jabal became the first to engage in animal husbandry; his brother Jubal invented musical instruments; and Tubal-cain made implements of bronze and iron (Gen. 4:20–22). But these technical and cultural achievements were marred by the ungodly uses to which they were put. Lamech "ruled and subdued" the earth, but he did so for his own name, not to magnify the name of the Lord (Gen. 4:23–24; 11:4). The descendants of Cain were created to build a replica of the temple-city of God; they did indeed build, but what they built was the defiled city of fallen man.

Man's dominion became perverted because he had perverted his priesthood. Before Cain killed his brother or built an ungodly city, he offered unacceptable sacrifices to the Lord (Gen. 4:1–5). Cain's original sin, like his father's, was a sin against priesthood. Similarly, civilization is perverted not because of a lack of technical ability; civilization is perverted because sinners do not joyfully submit themselves to the commands of the covenant King and do not offer their works to Him in worship. It is because the sons of Adam have abandoned the worship of the Creator for the worship of the creature that God delivers them over to shameful lusts and to all manner of sin and disorder (Rom. 1:18–32). The problem of human culture is not that men fail to rule the earth; the problem is that men rule in rebellion against their overlord and for their own pleasure and glory.

30

Third, *the human race was divided*. Through Seth, Adam and Eve did have godly descendants (Gen. 5). They remained obedient to the Lord and walked with Him as prophets (Jude 14). Curiously, Scripture records virtually nothing about the cultural achievements of the descendants of Seth.[13] Cult and culture, worship and dominion, kingship and priesthood, were separated. The human race was divided between the line of Cain and the line of Seth, between the seed of the woman and the seed of the Serpent.

Enslaved to Satan

Worst of all, Adam and Eve, created to be rulers, became slaves of sin and of Satan. Peter wrote, "By what a man is overcome, by this he is enslaved" (2 Peter 2:19b). Adam was conquered in his contest with Satan, and, as the victor, Satan claimed Adam and his children as plunder. Rousseau notwithstanding, people are not born free. Since Adam's sin, they come from the womb dragging chains.

Satan's enslavement of the human race was not, of course, outside of God's control. Satan did not have an inherent "right" to rule the world, as if the physical world is evil. The creation was very good when it was made, and it remains good (1 Tim. 4:4–5). As St. Augustine emphasized again and again, Adam's enslavement to Satan was "penal." The disruption of the order of God's kingdom was God's way of punishing Adam and Eve and their children. He punished their rebellion by delivering them into bondage to Satan. As always, the punishment fit the crime; Adam and Eve obeyed the word of the Serpent, and so God made them bow their necks under Satan's heavy yoke. Sinners are cursed not primarily because they are slaves of Satan, but because they are objects of the just anger of God. If Satan is the "prince of this world," it is only because the Holy God permits him to be so.

To understand how human slavery to Satan is a result of God's anger with covenant breakers, we need to remind ourselves that the name "Satan" means "accuser." The Bible pictures Satan as the creation's most unscrupulous prosecuting

31

attorney. He makes use of every opportunity to secure a conviction. When Adam and Eve disobeyed God, they gave Satan more legal ammunition than he could have hoped for. Satan could successfully prosecute Adam and Eve because they really were guilty. He "had the goods" on them. His case was "airtight." He knew that Adam and Eve and their children were "guilty as sin." And he pressed charges at every opportunity. The power that Satan has is primarily *legal* power over sinners.

This is why, throughout the Old Testament, Satan was permitted into God's courtroom, to accuse the righteous before the heavenly throne of judgment (Job 1–2; Zech. 3:1–5). Satan called on God to carry out His covenant vengeance against Adam and the whole human race. We can imagine Satan trying to "take the moral high ground," demanding that God execute His justice against sinners. "You're supposed to be a Holy God," Satan might say. "These people are such vile sinners. Why don't you just destroy them, and show them who's boss? Vindicate yourself, if you are God!" Satan is in a position of authority not because of his own inherent power, but because men are sinners.

Satan also had power because of the fear of death. Again, the basic problem is sin. The "sting of death is sin," Paul wrote (1 Cor. 15:56). Because of sin, Satan could hold over humanity the threat of death, like the sword that dangled over the head of Damocles.

If man was to achieve the plan that God had set for him from the beginning, he had to be delivered from his oppressive overlord. But, even more importantly, he had to be delivered from sin and from the wrath of God, because it was sin that gave Satan a foothold, and it was the holy God who had delivered the human race into slavery in the first place.

Happily, God had promised that the Seed of the woman would crush Satan's head, delivering the slaves from prison and bringing to fruition the original order and purposes of the kingdom (Gen. 3:15). For millennia, enslaved men suffered in darkness, waiting for that promised deliverance.

Jesus' Conquest of Satan

Throughout much of the world, political leaders gain power by plots, assassinations, and conquests. Journalist David Lamb reports, "Fifteen countries in [sub-Saharan] Africa have had one coup since independence, thirteen others have had two or more. By 1983, no fewer than fifty governments had been overthrown in independent Africa, and twenty-eight of Africa's countries had experienced coups d'etat."[14] Even in some nations that hold elections, voters must brave gunfire to get to the polls. We in the United States have always elected our leaders peacefully, in secret ballots, without coercion. We can hardly imagine living under a political system in which revolutionary violence plays such a large role.

The peacefulness of our political system makes it difficult for us to imagine certain events in Old Testament history. The Old Testament is as full of stories of conquest, assassination, and conspiracy as any Third World newspaper. One of the main threads of Old Testament history is the story of the fulfillment of God's promise to give the land of Canaan to the children of Abraham. Once delivered from Egypt, Israel was instructed to wage holy war against selected Canaanite peoples, wiping the land clean (Ex. 23:23). This story is so familiar, and it has been so sentimentalized by picture books and popular movies, that we sometimes forget it is the story of a long and bloody conquest.

Types of the Redeemer

Why did God include so many stories of battle, bloodshed, and warfare in the Old Testament? This question has been asked by Christians throughout the centuries. Marcion's conclusion that the God of the Old Testament was a different God from the God of the New was early rejected by the Christian church. Orthodox Christianity has taught, by contrast, that the Old Testament is a picture book filled with "types" of the coming Messiah and His work of deliverance.

"Types" are like sonograms, the pictures taken of babies *in utero*. When you look at a sonogram, you can just barely make out the fuzzy shape of a baby. On the right is something that looks a bit like a hand, and on the left something that resembles a foot. Only someone with more expertise can determine the baby's sex.

The Old Testament is filled with shadowy, fuzzy, embryonic pictures of the Messiah.[15]

- Joseph, who was delivered by his own brothers into slavery, suffered in prison, and was then exalted to be ruler over Egypt and to feed the world, is a type of Jesus, who died, was buried, rose again, and ascended to take His throne and give gifts to men.
- Nehemiah, who led the reborn people of Israel in the building of a new temple, is a type of Jesus who as Head of a new Israel is building the church.
- Jonah, who spent three days in the belly of the fish at the bottom of the sea and was then restored to life, is a type of Jesus, who was buried in the belly of the earth and who rose again on the third day.
- The sacrifices and priesthood described in such detail in the book of Leviticus were, the book of Hebrews tells us, one grand preview of the drama of Jesus' death, resurrection, and ascension.

In the same way, the conquering work of Joshua and David is a type of the work of Jesus. If that is the case, Jesus' life and ministry can be seen as a military campaign. He spent His life on earth waging holy war.

That description may seem a bit odd. We tend to picture Jesus as a bearded man wearing a long white robe, looking to heaven, holding a lamb on His shoulders. There is nothing wrong with that picture: Jesus *is* the Good Shepherd (John 10:11). But Jesus is not *only* the Good Shepherd. He is also the One who comes from Edom with His garments stained red with the blood of His enemies (Isa. 63:1–6). Jesus is the conquering Warrior, the Captain of the hosts of the Lord, who rides a white horse at the head of a vast army (Rev. 19:11–16). Like Samson and Saul, Jesus was endowed with the Spirit of power to wage war against the oppressors of His people (Judg. 14:6, 19; 15:14; 1 Sam. 11:6–11; Matt. 3:13–4:11).[16] Jesus was the "Nazirite," consecrated for holy war (Matt. 2:23).[17] He Himself characterized His inauguaration of the kingdom as a violent campaign opposed by violent men (Matt. 11:12).[18]

David is one of the leading "types" of Christ in the Old Testament. In coming to establish the kingdom of God, Jesus brought into reality what David had accomplished "typologically." David gained mastery of the land by defeating the Philistines. Jesus, the Son of David, also gained His throne by defeating the enemy of His kingdom. Of course, Jesus did not defeat the human enemies of Israel. He did not form a conspiracy to throw off the oppression of Rome. His fulfillment vastly exceeds the type. Jesus waged holy war against Satan himself. He crushed the head of the Serpent by satisfying the justice of His Father (Gen. 3:15). This was the first phase in Jesus' revolution: defeating His greatest enemy and the greatest enemy of His people.

G. K. Chesterton was fond of pointing out that there is often more good theology and ethics in fairy tales than in some thick books of systematic theology. In "Sleeping Beauty," we have a wonderful picture of the work of Christ on behalf of His church. In Walt Disney's animated version of that tale, Prince Philip climbs a jagged black mountain, cuts through deadly thorns with his sword, and grapples with the dragon-witch to rescue his beloved. A more fitting picture of Jesus' work can hardly be imagined. Jesus appears in the Gospels not as an Oriental guru—a proto-Gandhian proclaiming love and nonviolence—but as a princely Lover, passionately willing to suffer all things to rescue His Bride from her captor.

Christus Victor

In past ages, it was common for battles to be fought by the commanders of two armies in hand-to-hand combat. David's defeat of Goliath catalyzed a great Israelite victory over the Philistines (1 Sam. 17). As late as the sixteenth century, the frustrated Holy Roman Emperor Charles V offered to finish his long war with France once and for all by challenging the French king, Francis I, to a duel. In our day, this kind of behavior would be frowned upon, to put it mildly. Imagine Clinton and Hussein mixing it up in Madison Square Garden!

Here again, our political and military traditions make it difficult for us to grasp the full import of such biblical events as the temptation of Jesus (Matt. 4:1–11; Luke 4:1–12). For some, the main point of the temptation is to provide believers with an example of how to parry Satan's temptations. Some have psychologized the story of the temptation by interpreting it as a dramatic portrayal of Jesus' inner struggles, His doubts and fears. There is certainly great practical value in studying how Jesus overcame the temptations of Satan. But the main point of the event is to show Jesus not as our example, but as our hero. The temptation does not tell us first of all what *we* should do, but what Christ *has* done, once and for all. Our hero, Jesus Christ, went to the wilderness to engage in "hand-to-hand" combat with Satan. The commanders of two opposing armies met to decide the war, and the fate of their armies hung in the balance.

Satan had gained mastery of the human race by defeating a man in holy war. Only a New Man could deliver humanity from its slavery. Jesus thus battled with Satan in His capacity as the Last Adam, as the "Son of God."[19] The similarities between Satan's temptation of Adam and Eve and his temptation of Jesus are remarkable. Like Adam, Jesus was tempted to eat forbidden food, to put God to the test, and to fall down in homage to Satan. Like Adam, Jesus was tempted about food, faith, and worship.

But the differences between Adam's temptation and Jesus' are equally striking. Adam was tempted in a Garden-sanctuary; Jesus in the wilderness. When Adam was tempted, he still had access to the Tree of Life; Jesus had been fasting for forty days and nights. In other words, Jesus defeated Satan on his own "turf." Jesus defeated Satan not in the Garden, but in the howling waste. God does not deliver His people by flicking a switch from a distant throne. He delivers them by entering into their weakness and struggle, by giving over His own Son to pain and suffering and finally to the shameful death of a cross. Like Prince Philip, Jesus stormed the dragon's fortress and emerged triumphant. By resisting Satan's temptation and fulfilling the perfect righteousness demanded by His Father, Jesus satisfied His Father's offended justice and began to deliver His people from their "penal servitude" to Satan.

It is significant that Jesus defeated Satan by the Word. The First Adam failed to defeat Satan because he doubted the covenant Word of God; Adam did not even pick up his most effective weapon of war. But the chief weapon of the Last Adam's arsenal of holy war was the sword of the Spirit (Heb. 4:12–13).

The same was true of all of Jesus' battles against Satan and his demons. The temptation in the wilderness, after all, was not Jesus' only battle with Satan. Like all good military campaigns, Jesus' assault on Satan involved several offensives. He constantly encountered demons in His travels through Judea and Galilee. Wherever He went, His main activities included not only preaching, teaching, and healing, but also exorcising demons (Matt. 4:23–24). Even the demons recognized why Jesus had come. "What do we have to do with You, Jesus of Nazareth? Have you come to destroy us? I know who You are—the Holy One of God" (Mark 1:24). Being the Stronger Man, Jesus bound the strong man and plundered His house, freeing those who had been enslaved to him (Mark 3:27). Before Jesus could begin to restore the world and begin to build a new temple-city, He had to exorcise the old. As the true Holy Warrior, He exorcised demons with the two-edged sword that proceeded from His mouth.

Jesus' battles against Satan were directly connected with the coming of the kingdom of God. Jesus said that when He drove out demons by the Spirit of God, it was a sign that "the kingdom of God has come upon you" (Matt. 12:28–29; Luke

11:20). The coming of the kingdom means that God in Christ has acted powerfully in history to conquer Satan, to break the yoke of Satan's oppression, just as He had formerly delivered Israel from Pharaoh by stretching forth His "finger" (Luke 11:20; cf. Ex. 8:19).

It should be noted that Jesus' defeat of Satan had not only spiritual but physical consequences. Many of His miracles of healing were also exorcisms of demons (Matt. 9:32; 12:22; Mark 9:25; Luke 13:11, 16). Though the relationships between the spiritual and physical are mysterious, it is clear that the kingdom of God is not a purely spiritual reality, nor is Satan's dominion over sinners a purely spiritual dominion. Human beings in body and soul were enslaved to sin and Satan. And everything that Satan held in bondage was freed by the power of the Spirit-filled Holy Warrior. Jesus' goal was the restoration of the total fabric of human life, both physical and spiritual. All was to be redeemed from the curse of slavery to Satan.

Victory Disguised as Defeat

Jesus' encounters with Satan and with demons during His life were minor skirmishes compared with Jesus' decisive battle in His death and resurrection. In His death, He triumphed over rulers and authorities, making a public display of them (Col. 2:15). "Through death" He rendered "powerless him who had the power of death, that is, the devil" (Heb. 2:14). By His resurrection, Jesus swallowed up death in victory and removed the sting of death (1 Cor. 15:54–55).

Jesus' death was a victory over Satan. Let that sink in a bit. At this point, all similarity between Jesus and Prince Philip ceases. The drama of the gospel far surpasses any merely human drama. Jesus did not enter His final contest armed with a sword and shield, but laid down all His weapons at the entrance of the Coliseum. Like a lamb before its shearers, Jesus became defenseless and put Himself at the mercy of His enemies. Jesus defeated His enemy not by killing him but by letting Himself be killed. He slaughtered His enemy by offering

Himself for slaughter. He crushed the Serpent's head by letting His heel be bruised. He trampled down death by death.

The cross, a symbol of victory! We might as well say that the hammer and sickle were a symbol of freedom! At the cross all human wisdom becomes foolishness. At the cross we learn that the foolishness of God is wiser than men, that the weakness of God is stronger even than Satan. The new cosmic mountain is not a garden, but Golgotha, the place of the skull. No longer do four rivers of water flow to the ends of the earth, but a river of blood. To this mountain Jesus, lifted up, will draw all men (John 12:32).

How could Jesus triumph over Satan in His death? We can understand this only if we recall that Satan is a parasite. He depends for his power and authority entirely upon the sinfulness of men and women. So long as we are still accounted guilty before the heavenly Judge, Satan has solid legal grounds to accuse us. Once the debt is paid, once the penalty has been administered, Satan's head is crushed, and he falls from heaven like lightening. He no longer has an airtight case against God's people; he has no case at all. When the Judge pronounces a "not guilty," the accuser must fall silent.

By paying the debt that Adam's children owed to the Father, Jesus, the Last Adam, has delivered them from slavery to Satan. Because He is the propitiation for sin, Jesus delivers His people from the covenant curse. For similar reasons, Christ's resurrection removed the "sting of death," sin. By raising His Son from the dead, the Father vindicated, justified Him.[20] Because Jesus has offered the perfect and final sacrifice for sin, and because He has been raised, He has triumphed over Satan.

By His life, death, and resurrection, Jesus has thrown Satan from his position of authority and power in heaven. The prince of this world is cast out (John 12:31). The accuser of the brethren has been thrown down (Rev. 12:10). The Son of God has destroyed the works of the Devil. There has been a righteous and just revolution in the highest heavens. The kingdom has come.

Conclusion

Before church on Easter morning several years ago, a group of boys was gathered on the front porch of the small church where I preach near Birmingham, Alabama, gazing intently into a white plastic bucket. As I came closer, I could see that they were looking at a copperhead, about eight or ten inches long, that had been found in the swampy field behind the church. (My first thought was that snake handling might attract visitors!) The snake's head had been partly crushed (honestly!), and some of the "innards" were oozing out. Despite its injury, when one of the boys bumped the bucket, the snake twisted around violently, ready to strike. Though wounded beyond recovery, the snake was still dangerous to pick it up (though one of our elders tried, apparently claiming the promise of Mark 16:18!).

That snake is a picture of the power of Satan in the world after Jesus' death and resurrection. By His death and resurrection Jesus has dealt a mortal blow to Satan—the Serpent's head has been crushed. His most powerful weapons have been taken from him. He has been decisively defeated at Calvary and has fallen from his position of authority in heaven.

But he is still a threat. Though in a losing battle, Satan fights on. Peter still had to warn his readers that Satan was like a roaring lion seeking to devour them (1 Peter 5:8). So long as we remain sinners, we will have to battle to resist Satan's temptations and accusations. Though the "prince of this world" has been cast out, it is still as foolish to "flirt with the devil" as it would be to toy with a wounded copperhead.

THREE

✦

One Like the Son of Man

People say they read for relaxation. The truth is, attentive reading is a complex process that taxes even the best minds. If you read a detective novel, for example, you cannot afford to miss anything. Apparently trivial details often turn out to be clues of great significance. The deep footprint found under the victim's window in chapter 10 reminds you that Colonel Killwell was wearing muddy riding boots when he greeted you in the foyer in chapter 3—and you murmur a knowing "Aha!" under your breath.

As you read a detective novel, your mind travels in a circle, or, better, a spiral. To understand the end, you need to remember the beginning. Start at the last chapter, and you miss most of the point. Curiously, the reverse is just as true. To understand the beginning fully, you need to know the end. That is why you "see" so much more when you read a book a second time. During the second reading, you shiver the first time the speckled band is mentioned. During the second reading, the howl across the moors seems doubly eerie.

Reading and studying the Bible is in many ways like reading a detective story. Fundamentally, the many stories of the Bible are different episodes of a single story. To understand the significance of one part of the Bible, you need to under-

41

stand what went before and what comes after. The attentive reader of the Bible finds himself delightedly muttering the very same "Aha!" when he discovers themes from Joshua resurfacing in John or realizes that Luke is alluding to the laws of Leviticus.

Like reading a detective novel, reading Scripture means reading in a spiral. To understand the New Testament, you must know the Old, but to understand the Old, you must know the New. To make things even more complicated, like the epicycles on planetary orbits in Ptolemaic astronomy, there are many small spirals along the perimeter of the big spiral. Every part of the Old Testament refers both forward and backward—forward to the sufferings and glory of Christ, backward, ultimately, to Eden. David is as much an antitype of Adam (and Moses and Joshua) as he is a prototype of Christ.

These thoughts are especially important to keep in mind when we try to piece together a large biblical theme like the kingdom of God. To capture the full meaning of Jesus' preaching and teaching on the kingdom of God, it is essential not to forget anything that went before. When we find footprints, we need to remember who's been wearing boots.

A Man on David's Throne

When the Old Testament prophets looked forward to the coming messianic kingdom, they didn't spin visions out of air. The prophets were not only looking forward but looking back as well. Guided by the Holy Spirit, they drew much of their prophetic imagery from the golden age of the kingdom of Israel, when David and Solomon ruled a unified nation from the holy city of Jerusalem. Their reigns were to the prophets what the 1960s are to now-middle-aged hippies and young would-be radicals—a time when giants stalked the land.

The Davidic period was undoubtedly a high point of Israel's history. It was then that the promises of God to Abraham reached their clearest and most complete fulfillment (Gen. 12:1–3). David the warrior-king defeated the enemies of Israel and brought rest to the land, completing the conquest begun under Joshua (2 Sam. 7:1, 11; 1 Kings 5:4). The fame of David and Solomon spread throughout the ancient Near East. Rulers from distant lands brought tribute to the Israelite kings and came to learn wisdom (1 Kings 10:1–10). Under Solomon, the Lord fulfilled His promise to dwell among His people by taking up residence in the temple (1 Kings 6–8).

After the reigns of David and Solomon, however, Israel was divided between the northern and southern kingdoms (1 Kings 12). Divided from each other, both kingdoms eventually turned from the Lord and His covenant. Because of their idolatry and unfaithfulness, the Lord uprooted His people from the Land of Promise and scattered them among the nations. As Hosea predicted, Israel remained "for many days without king or prince" (Hos. 3:4).

Despite the Lord's discipline of Israel, the prophets emphasized, His promise would not return void. The Lord, after all, had confirmed His promise with an oath (Ps. 89). The prophets therefore predicted that the golden age would return in even greater splendor, and there would arise a king to take David's throne. While chronicling the decline and fall of the Davidic dynasty, 2 Kings and 2 Chronicles at the same time held out the promise of its restoration. Second Kings ends with the story of the exiled Davidic king Jehoiachin. In the thirty-seventh year of his exile, as a token of the coming restoration of the Davidic kingdom, Jehoiachin was released from prison, set upon a throne above other kings, given a new set of clothes, and allowed to eat at the table of the Babylonian king Evil-Merodach (2 Kings 25:27–30). Second Chronicles ends on a similarly hopeful note, with the decree of Cyrus the Persian that a house should be built for the Lord in Jerusalem (2 Chron. 36:22–23).

Along similar lines, Ezekiel envisioned a reunited kingdom ruled by David himself (Ezek. 34:23; 37:24). A new and more glorious temple would be erected, a temple from which the Lord would not depart. Water flowing from the temple would cleanse and refresh the land (Ezek. 40–48). Through Jeremiah, the Lord promised the coming of a "righteous Branch" for David, who would rule in justice over Israel (Jer. 23:5–6). Isaiah set his sights more widely, prophesying of a Davidic king who would rule not only Israel, but the nations as well (Isa. 9:1–7; 11:1–10; cf. Ps. 72). The temple mountain of Zion would become the new world-center, a glorified Garden of Eden, and the nations would, following the footsteps of the Queen of Sheba, stream to Jerusalem to worship the Lord and learn from His Word (Isa. 2:2–4).

Great David's Greater Son

Jesus clearly had these prophecies and hopes in mind when He appeared to proclaim that the kingdom of God was near. His hearers understood that He was heralding the restoration of the Davidic kingdom. They understood that the Day of the Lord was imminent, that God would shortly visit Israel in power and glory, and in mercy and judgment. Jesus was claiming to be the David of Ezekiel's prophecy, coming to conquer His enemies and to bind together His divided people. When the crowds heard His announcement, all the pieces of the Old Testament prophetic puzzle came flooding back into their minds, and, at least for some, suddenly they all fit together.

For those closest to Jesus, His status as the promised Son of David, the fulfillment of the prophetic hopes, was clearly explained. Gabriel told Mary that the Lord would give Jesus the throne of His father David, to reign over Jacob eternally (Luke 1:32). Peter confessed that Jesus was the anointed Son of God, the Greater Solomon come to build a new temple (Matt. 16:13–20).[1] These understood that Jesus was the Heir of David's throne.

Though the Old Testament prophecies were fulfilled in Jesus, they were fulfilled in an unexpected way. That is not to say that the prophecies were misleading. Jesus constantly rebuked His disciples and the Jewish leaders for not seeing the sufferings and glories of Christ displayed in the Old Testament Scriptures (Luke 24:25–27). Yet, though the living Child was the same One pictured in the prophetic "sonogram," He looked very different. Jesus was the One pictured in the fragments of the prophetic puzzle, but when the finished portrait emerged, the total effect was so breathtaking as to be a stone of stumbling and a rock of offense.

The Kingdom Is at Hand

Today many earnest, Bible-believing Christians are still waiting for the prophecies of a restored Davidic kingdom to be fulfilled. They believe, of course, that Jesus is the promised Messiah, but not that He has yet restored the Davidic kingdom. They accept that He is Heir to the throne of David, but not that He is now sitting on the throne of David or reigning over the nations. Instead, they expect that David's throne will someday be set up in Jerusalem, and that Jesus will rule on earth for a thousand years.

But the New Testament teaches something very different. The central message of Jesus' teaching was, "The time is *fulfilled,* and the kingdom of God is *at hand"* (Mark 1:15, emphasis added). With these words, Jesus announced that the restored Davidic kingdom prophesied by Isaiah, Jeremiah, and Ezekiel would be established *soon.* The Jews listening to Jesus could not have understood His words in any other way. Either Jesus was right, or He was wrong. The New Testament teaches that He was right.

This is proved by a careful reading of the New Testament's interpretation of two messianic psalms. Psalm 2 is clearly a messianic psalm. The king is called the Lord's Anointed and is installed to His throne by the Lord Himself (vv. 2, 6; see 2 Sam. 2:4, 7; 12:7). He is enthroned on Zion (v. 6) and called the "son of God" (v. 7; see 2 Sam. 7:14); it is said that He would reign over the nations and kings of the earth (vv. 8–12). But when was this prophecy (or when will it be) fulfilled? When would this messianic King be enthroned on Zion?

Happily, the New Testament does not leave us in any doubt about the answer to those questions. Preaching in the synagogue of Pisidian Antioch, Paul quoted this very psalm. "And we preach to you the good news of the promise made to the fathers, that God has fulfilled this promise to our children in that He raised up Jesus, as it is also written in the second Psalm, 'Thou art My Son; Today I have begotten Thee'" (Acts 13:32–33). The promised coming of a universal Davidic king was fulfilled in the resurrection of Jesus. Simply put, Paul taught that the messianic King prophesied in Psalm 2 has already ascended to His throne.

Psalm 110 is another clearly messianic psalm. Both Jesus and the Jews understood that this psalm spoke of the "Christ," the Messiah (Matt. 22:41–46). Like Psalm 2, Psalm 110 prophesies of a divinely installed King (v. 1) who rules over His enemies (v. 2), shattering and judging those who rebel (vv. 5–6) until all His enemies are made a footstool for His feet (v. 1). Again, the question is, When did (or will) the Messiah depicted in this psalm take His place at the right hand of the Lord?

Again, the New Testament gives an unequivocal answer. Peter taught in his Pentecost sermon that this prophetic psalm was fulfilled in the ascension of Jesus into heaven:

> This Jesus God raised up again, to which we are all witnesses. Therefore having been exalted to the right hand of God, and having received from the Father the promise of the Holy Spirit, He has poured forth this which you see and hear. For it was not David who ascended into heaven, but he himself says: "The Lord said to My Lord, Sit at My right hand, Until I make Thine enemies a footstool for Thy feet." Therefore let all the house of Israel know for certain that God has made Him both Lord and Christ—this Jesus whom you crucified. (Acts 2:32–36)

There can be only one conclusion from these clear New Testament statements: the prophecies of Psalms 2 and 110 were fulfilled by the resurrection and ascension of Jesus Christ.

We don't have to wait around for Him to ascend to David's throne on Zion. Jesus Christ has been ruling with a rod of iron, dashing His enemies in pieces like pottery. All the while He has been seated at the right hand of the Father, ruling in the midst of His enemies and making them a footstool for His feet. For two millennia Jesus has occupied the throne of David, and He is seated there today.

Those who deny that Jesus has already restored the Davidic kingdom fundamentally misconstrue the character of Old Testament history and prophecy and of New Testament fulfillment. The Old Testament, the writer to the Hebrews tells us, reveals Christ in types and shadows (Heb. 8:5; 10:1). The old covenant system, in other words, had built-in limitations. It was designed precisely to point forward to something better. The earthly and historical structures of David's kingdom were pledges of the future coming of the heavenly and eschatological kingdom of the Messiah. The stress on "shadows" in the book of Hebrews should not be understood in a gnostic or Neoplatonic sense, as if the earthly things of the old covenant were evil or unreal or as if the new covenant has nothing to do with earthly history. The new covenant, as we shall see, has the restoration of the creation as its ultimate aim, and the old covenant types and shadows were good and glorious in themselves. But the new covenant fulfillment is better and more glorious. Even Abraham, sojourning in the land that his seed would inherit, was looking for the heavenly country that we have inherited (Heb. 11:16).

Jesus' fulfillment of the Old Testament types and shadows thus involves a glorification, a transfiguration and glorification of the type into the reality. Jesus' kingship does not replace David's kingship. God did not change His mind, and start over with a new dynasty. He did not back down on the oath He swore to David, but showed His righteousness by keeping it even to His own hurt (Ps. 89:35–37; cf. Ps. 15:7).

Yet, though Jesus' kingship does not replace the Davidic dynasty, neither does Jesus' kingship merely mimic David's. The New Testament Davidic King *is* the rightful Heir to the

Old Testament dynasty, but the Davidic kingship itself has been transfigured by the death, resurrection, and ascension of Jesus. In Jesus' heavenly enthronement at His Father's right hand, the Davidic kingship is not replaced, but fulfilled—brought to its complete fullness, its maturity, its intended goal.

A careful student of the Old Testament Scriptures would have concluded that David's kingship pointed to something and Someone incomparably greater. When David ascended to his throne, for the first time in history a man sat upon the "throne of the Lord" (1 Chron. 28:5; 29:23). But it was clear to any Israelite who knew his Bible that David was not sitting on *the* throne of the Lord. Everyone knew that the Lord's throne is in heaven (Pss. 11:4; 103:19; Isa. 66:1), and David, great as he was, had not ascended to heaven. Thus, just as the earthly tabernacle was a copy of the true, heavenly sanctuary, so also the earthly throne of David and Solomon, glorious as it was, was a mere shadow of the heavenly throne at the right hand of the Father (Rev. 4–5). Having achieved our redemption, Jesus Christ ascended to a glorious white throne in comparison to which Solomon's splendid ivory throne is nothing more than a pale shadow (2 Chron. 9:17–21; Matt. 25:31; Rev. 20:11).[2]

The Last Adam

Jesus' fulfillment of the Davidic dynasty comes into sharper focus when we examine the Davidic kingdom in the light of Adam's original commission to rule the earth. God never changed His original intentions for humanity. Even after Adam and Eve sinned, God still planned to share His rule over creation with men. But He knew that sinners were not ready to assume that responsibility. They were children, too immature to handle the duties and privileges of full-grown sons. The entire old covenant era was a "training ground" for minors (Gal. 3:23–4:7).

Under the Old Testament, however, there was some progress. With the kingdom of David and Solomon, God's people entered what Augustine called their "advanced youth,"[3] their adolescence. By God's grace, they had progressed to a point where He permitted them to share more fully in His rule over the earth. The kingship of David and Solomon, in other words, was a fulfillment not only of the promises made to Abraham, but of God's commission to Adam as well. Adam, the "son of God," was to be God's prince; Solomon, the wise king, was called "God's son" (2 Sam. 7:14). In David and Solomon we see in miniature what God had intended all sons of Adam to achieve.

Indeed, the entire kingdom of Israel was a glorified form of the original creation-kingdom of God.

- Adam and Eve were to multiply and fill the earth; under the rule of their kings, the people of Israel multiplied to become like sand on the seashore (1 Kings 4:20; Gen. 22:17).
- Adam and Eve, along with their children, were to rule the earth; under David and Solomon, the Israelites secured and ruled a land flowing with milk and honey (Ps. 47:3).
- Adam and Eve were to be refreshed by God's Spirit in the Garden; Solomon built a temple in which God lived and was worshiped by the Israelites.

At the same time, Israel's fulfillment of the Adamic commission was only partial and provisional.

- God told Adam to subdue and rule the earth; David and Solomon and their subjects ruled a small nation on the Eastern Mediterranean.
- God told Adam and Eve to fill the earth; the Israelites, though numerous, filled only a small corner of the world's surface.
- God gave Adam access to His Garden and His table; though the temple was in their midst, the Israelites were not permitted to draw near into the Most Holy Place.

The kingdom of Israel was, as Augustine put it, both historical and prophetic. It marked a genuine advance in the history of fallen mankind. But it also pointed beyond to something better, a complete fulfillment of the Adamic order, one that would come through a Greater David, a New Adam.

The Son of Man

One of the delights of reading detective stories is the anticipation of not knowing "whodunit" until the final chapter. The author drops clues throughout the story: a fingerprint, a small facial tick, a missing sheaf of documents, an open window. Yet, in a skillfully written detective story the reader is uncertain until the revelations of the climactic scene who is the hero and who the villain. There is a fine line here. If the solution to the mystery is too surprising, the reader will feel cheated. Still, the best mystery stories leave the reader in a state of bemused surprise. Having suspected every character in turn, he learns to his astonishment that the butler did it after all.

From reading the early chapters of the biblical story, one might conclude that man is the villain of God's book. But the final chapter of the mystery of redemption contains a surprise ending. Man, whose sin brought God's curse, returns to bring blessing. Of course, the Bible does not teach that man climbed back up to God through his own efforts. The Man that brings redemption is the heavenly Man, and He is also God incarnate. It is God who saves us. Yet, we must not forget that Jesus is also true Man, and that just as by one man sin and death entered the world, so also it is by one *Man* that forgiveness and life abound to many (Rom. 5:12–21). Adam reappears in the final chapter, this time not as the villain but as the hero.

Matthew begins his Gospel with a subtle hint that Jesus is the New Adam, the surprise hero of redemption. The first verse of the New Testament says that the Gospel is the "book of the genealogy of Jesus Christ, the Son of David, the Son of Abraham." The phrase "book of the genealogy" or a similar phrase is used to structure the entire book of Genesis

(Gen. 2:4; 5:1; etc.). Matthew is hinting that his Gospel is a new Genesis, and that Jesus is the New Adam in his story of the new creation.

Jesus made this same point by constantly describing Himself as the "Son of Man." In order to understand the meaning of this phrase, we need to look at its Old Testament background. The phrase is found in Daniel 7:13–14, where Daniel sees in a vision one "like a Son of Man" coming up to the "Ancient of Days." The "Son of Man" is given "dominion, glory and a kingdom, that all the peoples, nations, and men of every language might serve Him." "Son of Man," then, is the title of the One who receives absolute authority from God to rule over all men and nations.

Another key occurrence of this phrase is found in Psalm 8:4. Considering the glory of the heavens, David asked, "What is man, that Thou dost take thought of him? And the son of man, that Thou dost care for him?" The psalm continues with a description of man's dominion over the works of God's hands, a reference to the original creation of Adam in Genesis 1. The "son of man" in Psalm 8 is clearly Adam, or a New Adam, the one commissioned to subdue and rule the earth for the glory of God.

Finally, the Lord frequently addressed Ezekiel, the priest, as "son of man" (Ezek. 1:3; 2:1, 3, 6, 8; etc.). In Ezekiel, the "son of man" is the prophet-priest.

Jesus thus identified Himself as the "Son of Man" because He was the Greater Adam, the One who had come to fulfill completely the commission that Adam failed to fulfill, the Man who would share fully in God's rule over creation. Jesus is also the true and final Prophet, and the High Priest after the order of Melchizedek. As the Son of Man, Jesus fulfills Adam's royal and priestly callings. Throughout the Gospels, when Jesus calls Himself "Son of Man," He is referring to His authority as Last Adam, the true human Priest-King.[4]

Other New Testament passages reinforce this point. Jesus appeared to John at the beginning of the book of Revelation as the glorified Last Adam (Rev. 1:12–16). Paul's reference to Christ as the "image of the invisible God" recalls the description of the first Adam as the "image of God" (Col. 1:15).5 The writer of Hebrews applies Psalm 8 to Jesus (Heb. 2:5–9): God has subjected all things to Jesus and "left nothing that is not subject to Him." As Last Adam, Jesus has already fulfilled the "dominion mandate."

Jesus thus ascended to His throne as both the Son of David and the Last Adam. He fulfilled not only the prophetic promises about a Davidic king, but also God's plan for Adam. He fulfills the purposes not only of Israel, but of mankind. When He ascended to the right hand of the Father in heaven, a man began to share in God's rule in the most direct way imaginable. From the moment of the Ascension, a man began to sit on *the* throne of the Lord, the heavenly throne. In one holy person, Jesus Christ is both the divine King and the Last Adam.

Jesus attained to this fulfilled kingship by remaining faithful to the terms of God's covenant. Because He obeyed the covenant law, Jesus inherited the covenant promise. Unlike the First Adam, the Last Adam did not grasp for equality with God, but humbled Himself and became obedient unto death (Phil. 2:5–11). Unlike Adam, Jesus did not put dominion ahead of worship. He was a self-sacrificing Priest before He was a reigning King. And because of His faithful obedience Jesus was highly exalted above all rule and authority and power and dominion and every name that is named.

Greater Than Angels

Just as Jesus' reign from His heavenly throne transforms and transcends David's earthly reign, so also Jesus' dominion as the Last Adam far exceeds the dominion of the First Adam. Adam was commissioned to rule over the animals, birds, and fish (Gen. 1:28). Later, God invested Noah, another Adam, with authority over other men (Gen. 9:5–6). Saul, David, Solomon, and other Israelite kings were given authority to rule over God's own people.

But the scope of Jesus' dominion is even greater. It includes all animals and all men, but extends far beyond to embrace the whole creation. Many of the church fathers interpreted the "rule and authority and power and dominion" over which Jesus is said to reign in Ephesians 1:21 as various ranks of angelic beings subjected to Christ. Whether or not that is an accurate interpretation of the passage, it is clear from other passages that the angels are subjected to Jesus. The writer to the Hebrews tells us that Jesus has "become as much better than the angels, as He has inherited a more excellent name than they" (Heb. 1:4), and applies Psalm 97:7 to Jesus: "Let all the angels of God worship Him" (Heb. 1:6).

These testimonies to Jesus' superiority to the angels do not surprise us because we know that Jesus is God. But the writer to the Hebrews is talking about Jesus, the God-man, the Last Adam. The eternal Son did not "become" superior to the angels; He always was superior. These statements can be said only of the *incarnate* Son. The man Jesus has all authority, not only over earthly things but over heavenly things as well (Matt. 28:18–20). The angels are now subject to a man!

Adam's dominion over the animals was thus a *type*, a mere shadow of the Last Adam's dominion over bestial men, principalities and powers, life and death, angels, Satan and demons, things present and things to come, and every other creature. This is not to say that earthly dominion is in any way cancelled out by the coming of Christ. The Bible assumes throughout that human beings are royal creatures, created to rule on earth over the lower creation. Jesus' heavenly dominion does not cancel or replace the earthly dominion of the First Adam, but rather fulfills it, completes it, brings it to maturity. Adam's earthly dominion was the alpha point of human dominion. Jesus reveals the omega point: we shall judge angels (1 Cor. 6:3).[6]

First the natural, then the spiritual, Paul said. Adam was of the earth, earthy, and so his dominion is of the earth, earthy. But the Last Adam is the heavenly Man, who comes from above and returns from whence He came, and who by His resurrection has become life-giving Spirit. Likewise, the unique dominion of the Last Adam is Spiritual and heavenly.

All Authority in Heaven and on Earth

One of the cornerstones of the American Constitutional system is the division of power between the legislative, executive, and judicial branches of the federal government. Those headlines can help us to understand the implications of Jesus' reign as Last Adam and Son of David.

Lawgiver

Christ claimed all authority in heaven and earth (Matt. 28:18–20). Authority means the right to be obeyed. To say that Jesus has authority means that when He speaks He has an absolute right to be heard. His Word is law. Jesus is exalted as the covenant King, and along with His promises, He makes demands. All people everywhere are commanded to repent and turn to Him in trust and obedience and swear covenant loyalty to Him (Acts 6:7; 17:30). This was Jesus' central message while on earth: *"Repent,* for the kingdom of heaven is at hand" (Matt. 4:17, emphasis added). The coming of the kingdom created a momentous crisis; it is the coming of the Lawgiver, the Greater Moses (Matt. 5–7). Repentance—turning from sin to God—is the only reasonable response.

Human rulers have limited authority over a limited number of people. Not so the heavenly King. There is no person that King Jesus does not claim as His own possession, and there is no area of life in which King Jesus does not issue His commands. The King requires total surrender, "radical obedience." He demands a righteousness that surpasses that of the scribes and Pharisees, a righteousness that takes seriously the jots and tittles of the law, as well as fulfilling the weightier matters (Matt. 5:17–20). Jesus requires not merely righteous *acts,* but also righteous *motives* (1 Cor. 10:31) and righteous *desires* (Matt. 5:21–48). Jesus has authority over the outward man and the inner man, the public man and the private man, the act and the thought. Every facet and every moment of the life of every person are lived out under the dominion of the Last Adam. Our duty is to acknowledge His dominion, submit humbly to it, bring our lives into conformity with His demands, and call others to do the same. As John M. Frame has put it, "All the issues of life hinge on the human response to God's word."[7]

Throughout the ancient Near East, the ascension of a king to his throne was a time for celebration and giving tribute. Similarly, the Lord is pictured in certain psalms as a conquering King ascending to His throne on Mount Zion amidst throngs of angelic chariots, receiving the tribute of His vanquished enemies (Ps. 68). So also, Jesus has been given a name above all other names, so that every knee will bow and every tongue confess that He is Lord (Phil. 2:5–11). The first obligation that all men owe to the Lord's Anointed is to render tribute. Our first act of repentance toward the enthroned Son of David is to kiss Him, lest He be angry (Ps. 2:12, KJV).

Jesus' legislative authority encompasses political leaders and nations as well as individuals. Psalm 2 draws an explicitly political conclusion from the fact that the Son of God reigns from Zion: "Now therefore, O kings, show discernment; take warning, O judges of the earth. Worship the Lord with reverence, and rejoice with trembling; do homage to the Son, lest He become angry, and you perish in the way, for His wrath may soon be kindled" (Ps. 2:10–12). All nations are to worship and serve Him (Ps. 72:10–11, 17). As the Son of Man, Jesus has taken the imperial throne of Nebuchadnezzar, the "king of kings," and "has been given dominion, glory and a kingdom, that all the peoples, nations, and men of every language might serve Him" (Dan. 7:13–14; see Jer. 27:6–7; Ezek. 26:7; Dan. 2:37). The kingdoms of the world have already become the kingdoms of the Lord and of His Christ, and He will reign forever (Rev. 11:15).[8] In every facet of national and social life, all the peoples of the earth are obligated to submit to the laws of Christ.

Judge and Executioner of Justice

According to Leon Morris, judgment in Scripture does not refer to abstract and impassive intellectual discrimination, or to a "neutral" weighing of evidence. Rather, "judgment is the process whereby one discerns between the right and the wrong *and takes action as a result.*" Judgment includes discrimination, but it leads to vindication of the right.[9] Biblically, it is impossible to distinguish sharply between judicial and executive acts. A righteous judge not only declares a just sentence, but also acts to enforce justice.

It is clear that Jesus Christ acts as royal Judge and sovereign Executioner as well as supreme Legislator. His words are not only authoritative, but powerful. When He speaks, things happen; when He passes judgment, the sentence is executed.[10]

Jesus said His earthly mission was one of judgment. "For judgment I came into this world" (John 9:39). The crisis of the coming of the kingdom created divisions. Mountains were levelled and valleys were raised. Those who believed were delivered from the wrath to come, and those who rejected Christ condemned themselves. Families were split wide open (Matt. 10:34–39; Luke 12:51–53). Jesus not only caused divisions, but like the judges of old, vindicated the oppressed (Luke 4:17–21).

In His exaltation, Jesus continues to act as Judge. All judgment has been delivered into the hands of the Son of Man (John 5:22, 27). He will someday return bodily to judge the living and the dead (Matt. 25:31–46). Christ's office as Judge was frequently invoked in the preaching of the apostles as the motive for repentance. Peter explained to Cornelius that Jesus had commanded the disciples "to preach to the people, and solemnly to testify that this is the One who has been appointed by God as Judge of the living and the dead" (Acts 10:42). Paul told the skeptical philosophers on Mars Hill that God "has fixed a day in which He will judge the world in righteousness through a Man whom He has appointed, having furnished proof to all men by raising Him from the dead" (Acts 17:31).

To say that Jesus Himself carries out His judicial decisions is to say that He controls all things. As Judge He not only determines what He shall do, but also does what He has determined. He steps forth from His heavenly chambers as the divine Warrior conquering and to conquer. He turns the heart of the King whatever way He pleases (Prov. 21:1), having mercy on whom He will have mercy and hardening whom He will (Rom. 9:18). His Word not only is authoritative and powerful, but is His personal presence for mercy and judgment.[11]

Christ's control is as comprehensive as His authority. He is Head over *all* things (Eph. 1:21–23). It is unbiblical to limit Christ's reign to "ruling in the hearts of His people." He does indeed rule in the hearts of His people, but He also rules the heart of Pharaoh (Prov. 21:1; Rom. 9:17–18). The temporal and eternal destiny of every man and every thing is at His sovereign disposal. As God-man, He governs the angels, sending them out to do His bidding. He feeds the animals and causes the grass to grow. He governs the courses of the planets and the orbits of electrons. He rules the clouds that bring hurricanes to the Gulf Coast and the butterfly flapping its wings in Peking.[12]

Through a Glass Darkly

Jesus not only controls all creation by His Word, but also intervenes in the lives of individual men and women to bless or to curse. It might seem extraordinarily bad taste, for example, to suggest that Jesus Christ struck Herod Agrippa and killed him because of his pride, but that is precisely what the Bible says. "An angel of the Lord struck him because he did not give glory to God, and he was eaten by worms and died" (Acts 12:23). Because Herod did not glorify God, Jesus Christ crushed him with His rod of iron.

It must be admitted, however, that the reasons for Christ's judgments and interventions in individual lives are not always so clear as in the case of Herod Agrippa. We must always remember that His ways are not our ways, nor His thoughts our thoughts.

Theodore was bishop of Tarsus, the hometown of the apostle Paul. During his tenure, Tarsus was overrun by invaders, and Theodore was forced to flee to Rome. No longer a young man, he doubtless expected to spend the remaining years of his life in exile.

The more you read of the lives of past and present heroes of the faith, the more you realize that their lives often seem to be little more than a tissue woven of frustration and failure. We know by faith in God's promise that this is not the case. In the Bible, knowing something by faith is the opposite of knowing it empirically. To say that we know by faith that our struggles are not in vain means that we do not always see the fruit. We are frequently left quite in the dark about what God is doing in our lives.

In Theodore's case, Christ's providential guidance eventually became clear. After some time at Rome, he learned that the post of archbishop of Canterbury was vacant. Despite the pope's fear that Theodore might introduce Eastern customs into Britain, he sent the aging bishop to Canterbury in 668. With the energy of a man half his age, Theodore organized the English church, establishing new congregations and holding regional church councils. The Venerable Bede said that Theodore was the first archbishop to have oversight of the whole English church. In his spare time, Theodore helped to organize schools that taught the Anglo-Saxons Greek, Latin, and arithmetic.

The pains and frustrations of Christians do not, of course, always give way to the spectacular achievements of a Theodore. The comfort of the Christian is that God redeems our failures and by His power turns them into triumphs. He weaves the hay and stubble of our lives into golden crowns. We are certain that Christ is ruling all things for the good of His people (Rom. 8:28), even when we cannot see what that good might be. We are more than conquerors *in the midst of* persecution and famine and nakedness and peril and sword

(Rom. 8:35–37). Our comfort is that we worship a God who triumphs through a cross.

Jesus controls the rise and fall of nations as well as the lives of individuals. The nations that seek to throw off the fetters of the Anointed are dashed by His rod of iron (Ps. 2). The ten kings that gave their power and authority to the beast were overcome by the Lamb, the King of Kings and Lord of Lords (Rev. 17:12–14).

Yet, Christ's rod is often no easier to discern in the history of nations than in individual stories. We know that the Berlin wall crumbled because Jesus Christ determined that it had fulfilled His purposes. But it is much more difficult for us to see how the mess in Yugoslavia and the former Soviet republics is working together for God's glory. This caution is what C. S. Lewis had in mind when in his *Christian Reflections* he warned against Christian historicism, the effort to read God's will out of history. Insofar as Lewis had a simplistic historicism in mind, we must agree. It is not always a simple thing to see the rod of Christ at work in history of nations. Blessings can look like curses, and curses like blessings.

But we do have another vantage point. Through the lenses provided by Scripture, we can look at history not only from the bottom up, but also from the top down. We have not only an earthly perspective, but also a heavenly perspective. We see things not only from the valley of the shadow of death, but also from the mountaintop sanctuary of God (Pss. 37; 73).

This is the perspective of the book of Hebrews and the Revelation of John. From this viewpoint, the viewpoint of faith—which is the certainty of *things not seen* (Heb. 11:1)—we can "see" the purposes of God being fulfilled in the tumultuous rise and fall of nations, and in the struggles and pains of our individual lives. By faith we know that Christ shakes the world so that those things which cannot be shaken will remain. We do not see all things subjected to Him, but by faith we *do* "see" Jesus (Heb. 2:8–9). His enthronement is a guarantee and pledge that God's purposes for man and for the world will not be frustrated.

We can "see" all this, however, only if we walk as did General William Booth who, in the words of Vachel Lindsey's stirring poem, "died blind/ Yet by faith he trod/ Eyes still dazzled by the ways of God." Only in the "blindness" of faith can we see in the apparent mess of human history the dazzling spectacle of the triumph of the Lamb (Matt. 13:31–33; Mark 4:26–29).[13]

Head of the All Things for the Church

Sinners are often given to extremes, and this is no less true of redeemed sinners than of unredeemed. Throughout the history of the church, Christians have tended to fall into extremes of emphasizing one or the other side of Christ's heavenly rule.

Some have emphasized that Jesus is the King of Kings and Lord of Lords, and that His rule is absolutely universal. Christ's kingdom is not restricted to the church. All areas of life are under His rule. Christ rules the state, the family, and the private association, as well as the church. The church as an institution is only one among many objects and instruments of Christ's rule over all things, they conclude.[14]

Others have emphasized that Christ rules His church by the Word and Spirit. Indeed, it seems that the predominant view of the kingdom throughout the history of the church has been that the church *is* the kingdom of God. Christ's rule is a rule of grace and mercy, and He rules His people in order to save them and bring them into the heavenly kingdom. The King gives gifts to His people, and His people respond in joyful worship and obedience. The kingdom is Christ's rule over the church.[15]

We are faced with the question, then, Does Christ rule over all things or over the church? As in so many theological disputes, the answer to this dilemma is a firm and unequivocal, yes!

I have emphasized in this chapter that Jesus rules as the Son of David and the Last Adam over all things in heaven, on earth, and under the earth. At the same time, however, I will insist equally strongly that His rule has a particular focus and center. Paul wrote to the Ephesians that Christ has been exalted far above all rule and authority and power and dominion, and has been made head of all things *for the church* (Eph. 1:20–23). Paul did not deny that Christ rules all things. On the contrary, he stretched the limits of language to express the absolutely comprehensive dimensions of Christ's rule. But Paul also recognized that the central concern of Christ's rule is the church, the assembly of God's people.

I cannot emphasize this point too strongly. Some Christians today use the phrase, "kingdom of God," to refer mainly to activities other than church activities. For some, "kingdom" is not only broader than, but opposed to "church"; "kingdom work" almost by definition refers to Christian activities that take place outside the "four walls of the church." In this view, worship, the sacraments, and Christian fellowship are *not* "kingdom activities," while picketing, lobbying, and Christian activism *are* "kingdom activities." There are genuine insights in this viewpoint: Christ's rule is universal, all we do is done for His glory, and He reigns over every facet of individual and social life. But these insights can become grossly distorted. In fact, the Bible teaches that the church is central to the kingdom of God. Worship is not peripheral but *central* to the kingdom. It seems that when it is said that the church is no *more* important than other institutions, what is often meant is that she is really *less* important.

When we think carefully about it, however, we can see that Christ's universal rule and His rule of the church are inseparable. Each requires and assumes the other.[16] Jesus, to be sure, rules for the sake of His chosen people, to bring them into the life of the kingdom, to restore in them the fullness of the image of God, to make them His instruments for the fulfillment of His purposes for creation, and finally to bring them into the final kingdom of the perfected heavens and earth.

To achieve these ends, however, it is not enough for Christ to rule over His people through His Spirit. To save His elect to the uttermost, He must also open doors for the preaching of the gospel of the kingdom, deliver His people from their enemies, bestow blessings on them, and discipline them in love. And to do these things, He must rule more than His own people. As the Westminster Shorter Catechism puts it, Jesus rules not only by "subduing us to Himself" and "ruling and defending us," but also by "restraining and conquering all His and our enemies" (Q. 26).

If Christ is finally to bring His people to the heavenly kingdom and to accomplish His historical purposes for and in them, He must not only rule over the church, but also defeat the enemies that are arrayed against the church. If His rule over the church is to be effective, He must also rule all things. If Christ is to save the young man in rural China, He must control the bureaucrat who grants the missionary his visa. If Christ is to take the gospel to the Ethiopian eunuch, He must govern the persecutors who force Philip to flee Jerusalem (Acts 8:4–8, 26–40). If He is to bring Theodore of Tarsus to Canterbury, He must rule the Arab armies in Syria.

Scripture explicitly teaches that Jesus Christ rules all things as well as the church. He is "Head" over all things (v. 22), as well as over the church (Eph. 5:23). Headship implies authority and rule. Christ is also said to "fill all things in every way" (1:23); in fulfillment of God's command to Adam, He "fills" the whole creation with His presence.[17] At the same time, the church is called the "fullness" of Christ (1:23). Christ is present among His people in a way that He is not present in the whole creation, and His headship over the church is different from His headship over all things. There is a headship over the church, and there is a headship over the world; there is a filling appropriate to the church, and a filling appropriate to the creation as a whole. We distort the Scriptures if either of these truths is denied, or if either is subordinated to the other.

Jesus, moreover, does not rule the church merely to perfect and build the church. The church exists for the life of the world. Thus the two dimensions of Christ's rule circle back on each other: Christ rules the world for the sake of the church, and He rules the church for the sake of the world. And He rules both to bring honor and glory to His heavenly Father.

Conclusion

Many of the church fathers interpreted Psalm 24 as a prophecy of the ascension of Christ. The repetition of the question, "Who is this King of glory?" was understood as the question posed by the angels as they watched Christ ascend through the angelic throngs toward His heavenly throne. Psalm 24 was an expression of the angels' astonishment at the ascension.

Chrysostom described the source of this astonishment.

Today we are raised up into heaven, we who seemed unworthy even of earth. We are exalted above the heavens, we arrive at the kingly throne. The nature which caused the Cherubim to keep guard over Paradise is seated today above the Cherubim. Was it not enough to be elevated above the heavens? Was it not enough to have place among the angels? Was not such a glory beyond all expression? But He rose above the angels, He passed the Cherubim, He went higher than the Seraphim, He bypassed the Thrones, He did not stop until He arrived at the very Throne of God.[18]

The angels stand amazed. They have come to the final chapter of the story of redemption, the final act of the drama of salvation, with its marvelous surprise ending. The Last Adam—a Man!—has ascended to the heavenly throne, and the angels bow in adoration. Though made for a little while lower than the angels, with the coming of the kingdom humanity has, in Christ, come into its own.

FOUR

✦

In the Heavenlies

In one of the sermons in his collection *The Weight of Glory*, C. S. Lewis made some insightful observations about people's obsession with access to the amorphous reality he called the "Inner Ring."[1] Inner Rings, Lewis explained, are attractive in part because they provide power, but the desire for the Inner Ring is not so much a desire for power as a desire simply to be "inside," a desire for that "delicious sense of secret intimacy."

Inner Rings, Lewis recognized, are unavoidable, and are in some contexts useful. But the obsessive desire to gain access to an Inner Ring is insidious, tempting a good man to do very bad things. Indeed, the quest for access to the Inner Ring is illusory, like peeling an onion. "If you succeed there will be nothing left." This is because "the circle cannot have from within the charm it had from outside. By the very act of admitting you it has lost its magic." Other groups exist for the sake of an end: a music club for the sake of music, the mob for the sake of mobbery, the president's Cabinet for the sake of governing. The Inner Ring, by contrast, "exists for exclusion. . . . Exclusion is no accident: it is the essence."

This desire for access to the Inner Ring, twisted and dangerous as it can be, is at base a distortion of a legitimate and even godly desire. God, we have seen, has always intended to permit His people to draw near into the true Inner Ring of intimate companionship with Him. As the images of God, men and women have a "built-in" desire to fulfill their Creator's intentions. Sinners, however, corrupt this God-given desire for intimacy into what Lewis calls a "lust for the esoteric"—a lust described with marvelous extravagance in Umberto Eco's novel, *Foucault's Pendulum*.

The issue, then, is, To which Inner Ring shall we seek access and on what terms? The consistent teaching of Scripture is that the true "Inner Ring" is the kingdom of God; to be in the true Inner Ring is to be in communion with the Father, Son, and Spirit (John 17:21). The Bible also insists that we are given access to this Inner Ring only in Jesus Christ. We cannot take heaven by storm; we must accept it as a gift and on the Giver's terms.

Part of the coming of the kingdom in the work of Christ is God's gift of Himself and of heavenly rule to His people. In this chapter, we will focus on the heavenly "Inner Ring" as a place of authority and power, and in chapter 5 we will focus on the intimacy of the "Inner Ring" of the sanctuary. We shall see that the coming of the kingdom means that the true Inner Ring is, at long last, opened to us.

The Reign of the Saints

During the Puritan Revolution, a host of sects with colorful names were disgorged from the Pandora's box of English religious culture. Prominent among these were the Fifth Monarchy Men. Convinced that the fourth monarchy of Daniel's visions was coming to an end, they believed the reign of the saints was about to begin and prepared themselves to seize control of the levers of power by force of arms.

Few American Christians would agree that God's people should violently seize political power. Even the few groups that speak about a Christian "take-over" of the United States plan a peaceful coup, not a violent one. The scars of the religious wars of Europe's early modern period have yet to heal, and some Christians are hesitant even to utter "politics" and "religion" in the same sentence.

Though it is indeed quite sensible to keep one's distance from violent religious movements, too many Christians go to the opposite extreme of denying that Christians should or do rule in any sense at all. Against this, the Bible unequivocally teaches that the reign of the Messiah includes the rule and dominion of His people. It is entirely biblical to say that those who are united to Christ share with Him in His reign over heaven and earth. He is supremely crowned with kingly glory and honor (Heb. 2:9), but through His suffering He has also brought many sons to glory (Heb. 2:10).

We find this truth emphasized throughout the book of Revelation. When John is first caught up into heaven, he sees the Lamb sitting upon the throne—but he also sees twenty-four elders wearing crowns and sitting on heavenly thrones (Rev. 4:4). The Son has been given a rod with which He rules the nations—and He promises a rod to those who persevere in faith to the end (Rev. 2:26–27). The Faithful and True Witness promises to grant His faithful people the right to sit on His own throne, just as He sits on His Father's throne (Rev. 3:14, 21). The Lamb has purchased a people, making them kings and priests who will reign on the earth (Rev. 5:10). United to the Son, the sons of God are admitted to the Inner Ring, and the King whispers His secrets in their ears. He no longer treats us as slaves, but as friends (John 15:15), and a King's friends are given important posts in His government.

In the Old Testament, the inseparability of the rule of the Messiah and the rule of the saints is most clearly set out in Daniel 7:22, 27 (cf. Isa. 54:3; 60:1–3, 10–14; Mic. 4:11ff.). Daniel prophesied that after the dominion of the one horn is destroyed, "the sovereignty, the dominion, and the greatness of all the kingdoms under the whole heaven will be given to the people of the saints of the Highest One." This situation of saints reigning with the Son of Man is called "His kingdom" (Dan. 7:27). The reign of God's people is bound up with the reign of God's Anointed. One cannot exist without the other.

It appears from some passages of Scripture that the saints must die before they ascend to their heavenly thrones. But the passage in Daniel forces us to a different conclusion. If the reign of the Messiah and the reign of the saints are two sides of the same reality, then the beginning of the reign of the Messiah is also the beginning of the reign of His saints. Since, as we saw in chapter 3, the Messiah's reign has already begun, then the saints are reigning now.

The New Testament confirms this conclusion. To the Ephesians Paul wrote that the saints have ascended into the heavenlies in union with Jesus Christ. Though we were dead in sins, we have been brought to life through baptism into Christ's resurrection (Eph. 2:1–5; Rom. 6:1–11). More than that, we have been baptized into Christ's ascension: God has "raised us up with Him, and seated us with Him in the heavenly places, in Christ Jesus" (Eph. 2:6).

What does it mean to be seated in heavenly places in Christ? Earlier in the same letter Paul told the Ephesians that Jesus Himself is seated at the right hand of the Father "in the heavenly places" (Eph. 1:20) above all powers and authorities in heaven and earth. A seat in the heavenlies is a seat of authority (Eph. 1:21–23). A seat in the heavenlies is a *throne!* Christians are enthroned in the heavenlies because they are "in Christ," united to the Son of Man who has been exalted high above all rule and authority and dominion and power.

Death Dethroned

In Romans 5:12–21, Paul made some of these same points. The passage contrasts two "reigns," two kingdoms: the reign of sin and death on the one hand, and the reign of grace on the other (vv. 17, 21). The transition from the reign of sin and death to the reign of grace occurred with the coming of the Last Adam, through whom the grace of God abounds to many (v. 15). The death and resurrection of Jesus were the decisive events in the change from one kingdom to the other.

Through the obedience unto death of the New Man, many were made righteous and given life. By His obedience, the reign of sin and death was swallowed up in the reign of grace (v. 19). Since the reign of grace is a result of Christ's death and resurrection, it is clear that it has already begun.

Paul's contrast of these two kingdoms in Romans 5:17 is not precisely parallel, however. He did not contrast the reign of death with the reign of life; instead, the reign of death has been succeeded by the reign "in life" of *those who receive* the abundance of grace and of the gift of righteousness" (emphasis added). Charles Cranfield comments, "The effectiveness and unspeakable generosity of the divine grace are such that it will not merely bring about the replacement of the reign of death by the reign of life, but it will actually make those who receive its riches to become kings themselves, that is, to live 'the true kingly life,' purposed by God for man."[2] In other words, the reign of death was replaced by the reign of the church, and this occurred when the Last Adam was sent to give grace and mercy.

Paul makes is abundantly clear that the reign of the church is not merited or seized, but accepted by faith. The reign of the church is the reign of those who have *received* grace and righteousness. We inherit the kingdom, the right to sit enthroned in the heavenlies, not by the works of the law, but through faith. Only those who humbly accept God's mercy and patiently wait upon the Lord are admitted to the true Inner Ring.

The coming of the kingdom of grace means, then, that the saints rule in life. United to the Last Adam, Christians are restored Adamic kings, fulfilling the creation mandate. United to the Son of David and Greater Solomon, Christians are Davids and Solomons, fulfilling the types and shadows of the Law. United to the true Israel, Jesus Christ, the church is a renewed Israel, given the task of conquering and occupying the Land of Promise. Christ has accomplished a revolution in the heavens: Satan is cast down, and Christ and His people enthroned. The proud are scattered and kings cast down from their thrones, and, by grace, the poor and humble are exalted (Luke 1:46–55).

Heavenly Dominion

A psychotherapist subjecting the apostle Paul to analysis would likely conclude that he was delusional. Here is Paul, by his own admission imprisoned and beaten time without number, stoned and near death, shipwrecked three times, frequently suffering in hunger, thirst, cold and exposure (2 Cor. 11:23–27). And yet this same Paul speaks of being seated upon a heavenly throne, sharing in the rule of Christ over the cosmos. Surely here, if anywhere, we have a prime candidate for a padded cell deep in the heart of the National Institute of Mental Health, a psychotic sufficiently deranged to merit a PBS documentary, perhaps even a CBS mini-series, and at least an appearance or two on "Donahue."

Empirically, the church, throughout history and equally today, is undeniably afflicted, perplexed, persecuted, struck down (2 Cor. 4:8–10). Yet the Scriptures unequivocally teach that Christians are already seated on thrones in the heavenlies, that we reign *now*, "in life." We are tempted to avoid one or the other horn of this apparent dilemma. We are inclined either to deny that the church rules, or to suppose fondly that someday, in some millennial paradise, the affliction, perplexity, and persecution of the church will come to an end.

But we must take the bull by both of its paradoxical horns. The church rules and conquers *in the midst* of and through her suffering (Rom. 8:31–37) so that the surpassing greatness of the power may be of God and not of herself (2 Cor. 4:7); for when she is weak, then is she strong. Despite appearances to the contrary, the church rules now on earth. James B. Jordan has well summarized the biblical teaching: paradoxical as it may seem, the church, like Jacob, *limps to victory*.[3]

But what exactly does this mean? Is it anything more than a striking paradox, a rhetorical trick, to say that the church

rules in the midst of suffering? Aren't we just playing seman-
tic games? To understand the meaning of the rule of the
church, and how it is compatible with the church's suffering,
we need to examine the biblical doctrine of "dominion" a bit
more.

John Wyclif defined dominion as comprising ownership
and authority.[4] In chapter 3, we noted that the dominion of
the Last Adam is comprehensive in both respects. He is both
Head and Heir of all things. Though the implications remain
to be worked out in history and at the Second Coming, Jesus
has already fulfilled the "dominion mandate" by His obedience in life and death, by His resurrection and ascension.[5] He
has all authority, and all things are His possession. But what
does this fact have to do with the rule of the saints? To answer this question, let us consider each element of Wyclif's
definition in turn.

Ye Shall Judge Angels

Like Christ's own authority, the authority of the saints extends
beyond that of the first Adam and far exceeds the authority
of Old Testament kings of Israel. The dominion of Adam and
of Israel was a shadowy type of the dominion of the saints,
and the reality far exceeds the types. In the Old Testament,
the people of God conquered and ruled over the abominable
nations that surrounded them. In their wars with the Canaan-
ites and Philistines, however, Joshua and David were attack-
ing the symptoms and not the disease, as the subsequent history of Israel abundantly proved. Israel's mastery over the idolatrous nations that surrounded her did not prevent her from
falling into idolatry.

In Christ, the church already has authority over all things,
visible and invisible. We battle (and conquer!) not flesh-and-
blood Philistines, but principalities and powers, spiritual
forces of wickedness in heavenly places (Eph. 6:12). In
Christ's name, the church resists the Devil, and he flees (Matt.
10:8; James 4:7). In Christ, the church mounts a head-on assault on the Dragon. Christian dominion is dominion *fulfilled*

in Christ, brought to its maturity, its completion, its destined goal.

The primary imperative of Christian dominion is not, then, to rule over the animals, fish, and birds. Christians are not given shadowy earthly thrones as David and Solomon were. We are seated on thrones in heaven itself (Eph. 2:6). We will judge angels (1 Cor. 6:3), and already Satan is being crushed under our feet (Rom. 16:20). Like the apostles, the church has been given power in the gospel to drive out unclean spirits (Matt. 10:1, 8), and the heavenly authority to bind and to loose (Matt. 18:18–19). Like Christ's own dominion, the unique dominion of the church is heavenly and spiritual in the sense that it originates in the Spirit poured out by the ascended Christ.

Cultural dominion is good. It is good for the righteous to sit on earthly thrones. Christians can serve God by building bigger bridges, better mousetraps, and just republics. One of the fruits of Christianity, indeed, is genuine technological and cultural development. The Bible assumes throughout that human beings are cultural creatures, and our lives as citizens of heaven are inevitably intertwined with earthly concerns and pursuits. Christ does not save *from* culture but saves *within* culture, and Christ is, in Niebuhr's phrase, the transformer of culture.

True as all this is, the dominion that Christ gives His people is not first of all cultural, technological, or political. The saints' unique dominion is not of an earthly character. To echo James, even demons can have a form of dominion (James 2:19). But the Scriptures teach that all who are "in Christ" have an authority denied to all those who are outside Christ; only those who are "in Christ" are seated on *heavenly* thrones. Only those in Christ have access to the *real* Inner Ring of power and privilege.

Instruments of Righteousness

Practically, the heavenly and spiritual character of Christian dominion holds two main implications. First, though Christian dominion is heavenly and spiritual in character, it is exercised on earth over earthly powers and kingdoms. Despite the apparent weakness of the church, she is fulfilling the creation mandate to fill the earth with worshipers of God and rule the earth in obedience. The church in the book of Acts, for example, appears oppressed and downtrodden, but a closer look will show that the church in fact rules in the midst of suffering and persecution. Who's really in charge in the book of Acts? Certainly not the Roman authorities, whose prisons became sieves the minute a Christian was chained up (Acts 12:1–19; 16:19–34). Certainly not the Jews who persecuted Christians, for despite their efforts the word spread, and converts multiplied. Indeed, far from harming the church, Paul's imprisonment actually emboldened the saints to preach the gospel (Phil. 1:12–14). The New Testament shows us that the church conquers the world in the midst of her enemies.

Long before Constantine painted crosses on the shields of the soldiers of the Roman army, the church militant was busily conquering her enemies. Long before cathedrals began to dominate the landscape, the church was ruling the world from the catacombs.

Second, because Christian dominion is essentially dominion over principalities and powers, over spiritual wickedness in high places, over sin and Satan, it is manifested primarily in sanctification, in conformity to the image of Christ, in increasing maturity. The growth of the kingdom in history is visible primarily as growth in righteousness, holiness, love, and the other fruits of the kingdom. The fruits of the kingdom are certainly related to cultural advancement, but they are not identical to them. The church has frequently acquired power with no apparent increase of righteousness. Even after his celebrated conversion, the Frankish king Clovis did not stop splitting his rivals' heads with his battle axe.

Paul's continuing discussion of the reign of sin and the reign of grace in Romans 6 shows that the reign of the saints is primarily a reign over sin. All people are inescapably slaves either of sin or of grace. Sin reigns with such tenacity that its hold can be broken in only one way: death. Only the dead are free from sin. How, then, can a person be freed from sin and still live on to serve God? Only by dying and rising again with Christ in baptism (Rom. 6:1–4). Sin is no longer master of those who have died and risen with Christ. Being dead in Christ, we have the power to say an emphatic no! to sin (vv. 12, 14). Not only has the dominion of sin been broken, but we have been given dominion *over* sin. Not only are we delivered from being conquered by sin, but we can actually conquer sin.[6]

Upon reflection we realize that authority over sin and Satan is the kind of dominion that Adamic men most need. Sin does not deprive people of dominion in its cultural and political forms. The wicked Cainites took dominion; they ruled the earth, but in an ungodly way. When He acts to fulfill His purposes for humanity and for the creation, God does not have to restore the ability to subdue and rule; sinners never lost that ability, just as they never ceased to worship. What sinners lack is the ability to subdue and rule righteously and for His glory and to worship the Creator rather than the creature. Therefore what God must restore is the proper relationship between man's priestly and his kingly calling, the priority of worship over dominion. If humanity is to fulfill God's purposes, God must first restore man to Himself.

And in Christ, that is what God has done. The heart of the new covenant promise is that we are reconciled to God, justified by grace through faith, adopted into His family, made members of the body of Christ. Having received the Spirit of Christ, we can put sin to death and rise in newness of life (Col. 3:5–11). Christ fulfills the promise of the new covenant by giving rebels new hearts and a superabundance of His Spirit so that we can obey His laws and commandments (Ezek. 36:26–27). He transforms the selfish into living sacrifices (Rom. 12:1–2). He molds chasers after vain idols into worshipers of the Father (John 4:23). He delivers sinners from slavery and enables them to acknowledge the King in obedience and worship.

Theologians have for centuries defined the image of God as righteousness, holiness, and knowledge (Eph. 4:24; Col. 3:10). This is not an exhaustive definition. Being images of God also means that men and women rule, judge, speak, and reveal God's character in all they are and do. But the theologians who have used Ephesians 4:24 and Colossians 3:10 as a definition of the image of God are correct in a crucial sense. For when Adam sinned, he was corrupted in precisely these respects; he became unrighteous, unholy, an enemy of God. And the Last Adam has restored believers in these respects: Christ has justified the ungodly; He is our sanctification; in Him there is reconciliation. Jesus has restored the image of God in these respects because these are what Adamic men needed to fulfill God's purposes to rule and worship *rightly*.

Only in Christ do humans have a right to rule the creation. Empirically, however, the exercise of earthly dominion does not belong solely to Christians. What is unique about the Christian is his death and resurrection with Christ, which enables him to be godly in the earthly dominion he presently shares with all. Christians are unique not in living earthly lives, but in being called to live heavenly lives in the midst of their earthly lives. Christians are not called to put on the old man, whose corruption they inherited from Adam. They are called instead to put on the New Man.

All Things Are Yours

In principle, because she is united to Christ, the Heir of all things, the church also has comprehensive rights of ownership; the church is the queen at the King's right hand. We are co-heirs with Him. Paul wrote to the Corinthians that "all things belong to you, whether Paul or Apollos or Cephas or the world or life or death or things present or things to come; all things belong to you, and you belong to Christ; and Christ belongs to God" (1 Cor. 3:21–23). As the true seed of Abraham, Christians are heirs of the world (Rom. 4:13).

What does it mean practically to say that all things belong to the saints? It means, first, that legal title to the earth belongs to the saints. Ultimately, it means that the saints will inherit the earth (Matt. 5:5) and the kingdom of God (Matt. 25:34). I believe, too, that it means that God will progressively deliver the world into the hands of His faithful people.

But this is clearly *not* what Paul had in mind when he wrote 1 Corinthians 3. He said that "all things *are* yours," not "all things *will be* yours." He was talking about ownership rights that the saints already enjoy by virtue of their union with Christ. Paul did not say that we must wait for the Millennium to own all things, but that Christians own all things now. Though this right of ownership encompasses the whole creation, visible and invisible, it is evidently not a visible, empirical kind of ownership. By all appearances 1 Corinthians 3 seems to apply better to assorted Japanese investors than to the church. Is it, then, simply another striking paradox to say that we who own all things are frequently hungry, thirsty, homeless, and in want?

It would be difficult to find a better description of the heart of Christian ownership than that given by Martin Luther.

> . . . every Christian is by faith so exalted above all things that, by virtue of a spiritual power, he is lord of all things without exception, so that nothing can do him any harm. . . . Our ordinary experience in life shows us that we are subjected to all, suffer many things, and even die. . . . The power of which we speak is spiritual. It rules in the midst of enemies and is powerful in the midst of oppression. This means nothing else than that "power is made perfect in weakness" [2 Cor. 12:9] and that in all things I can find profit toward salvation [Rom. 8:28], so that the cross and death itself are compelled to serve me and to work together for my salvation. This is a splendid privilege and hard to attain, a truly omnipotent power, a spiritual dominion in which there is nothing so good and nothing so evil but that it shall work together for good to me, if only I believe.[7]

St. Augustine made a similar point in the first book of the *City of God.* The bishop of Hippo had set out to answer the charge that Christianity was responsible for the fall of Rome. Part of his reply was that Rome was judged because of its sin, but he realized that Christians as much as any had suffered during the barbarian invasions. How was this to be explained?

To put it simply, Augustine's answer to that question was that no Christian was truly harmed by the barbarian invasions. True, some were deprived of their possessions, but this simply reinforced Jesus' warning against laying up treasures on earth. Christians who had heeded that warning were not deprived of their true, heavenly treasures. Likewise, some Christians were killed, but "death is not to be judged an evil which is the end of a good life." And although some Christians were enslaved, so were Daniel, his three friends, and other prophets. God would no more abandon Roman Christians enslaved to barbarians than He abandoned Joseph to his Egyptian masters.[8]

Far from harming the Christians of Rome, then, the barbarian invasions were a great benefit to them.

> For even in the likeness of the sufferings [of righteous and wicked], there remains an unlikeness in the sufferers; and though exposed to the same anguish, virtue and vice are not the same thing. For as the same fire causes gold to glow brightly, and chaff to smoke; and under the same flail the straw is beaten small, while the grain is cleansed; and as the lees are not mixed with oil, though squeezed out of the vat by the same pressure, so the same violence of affliction proves, purges, clarifies the good, but damns, ruins, exterminates the wicked.[9]

The New Testament makes this point again and again. Christians have dominion over death. Death can do us no harm, because we have already died, and our lives are hid with Christ in God (Col. 3:1–4). Death indeed is the Christian's servant: to live is Christ, but to die is gain (Phil. 1:21). Sufferings cannot harm us, but rather perfect us and prove us to be sons (Heb. 12:4–13). Nothing can separate us from the favor of God (Rom. 8:31–37). Indeed, nakedness, peril, sword, and all other afflictions simply draw us closer to the Father. The Japanese may presently own half of the world, but outside of Christ they do not own life and death, things present and things to come. A man may be catered to by a horde of obsequious servants, but only those who are in Christ are served by death, suffering, and everything else. Because we are in Christ, all our experiences—even those which are evil in themselves—become so many pathways to God, so many tokens of His love and favor, so many signposts along our pilgrimage toward His eternal kingdom.[10]

Clearly, Christians do not occupy all the places of power. The church does not dominate the various Inner Rings of social and political life—the smoke-filled rooms and conference tables where men labor under the delusion that they control the world. Christians do not necessarily sit on earthly thrones.

Yet, even if Christians were removed from every earthly throne, even if they were deprived of every place of worldly influence and power, even if deprived of all their property and wealth—none of this would diminish in the smallest measure the church's reign over all things. Compared with the heavenly dominion of the church, earthly dominion is paltry and impoverished, for it matters little that a man gain the whole world if in the process he loses his own soul.

Whether or not they presently gain the world, Christians have gained heaven. Whether or not they presently dominate society, Christians have been admitted to the true Inner Ring. Whether it appears so or not, in actual fact all things serve the church.

Dominion by Faith

"He's so heavenly minded he's no earthly good."

In recent years, that reproach has been on the lips of many Christians. They are understandably distressed by the condition of the world and by the church's apparent indifference and inaction. They insist, correctly, that Christians are responsible to act positively in society, and they want to motivate other Christians to take a more active role in pursuing earthly dominion.

But this reproach has a disturbingly unbiblical ring about it. Let's face it. Despite all the attempts to deny or qualify it, it remains a fact that the kingdom of God is a *heavenly* kingdom. Jesus called it the "kingdom of the heavens" (Matt. 4:17; passim, my trans.). He said that His kingdom is not of this world (John 18:36). Some scholars have argued that Jesus was saying that His kingdom was not *from* this world. Jesus was talking, they argue, about the *origin* of His kingdom not the *nature* of His kingdom.[11] But that argument misses Jesus' point. Origin determines nature. What is born of flesh is flesh, and what is born of Spirit is spirit (John 3:6). Men originate from the dust of the earth and so are earthly creatures. So also, whatever is born of heaven is heavenly. Jesus clearly taught that His kingdom was a heavenly kingdom, and this has been the almost uniform teaching of the church throughout the centuries.[12]

We must be careful, however, not to misunderstand the nature of heavenly things. In the Bible, heaven is not an airy-fairy, ethereal place. C. S. Lewis was closer to the truth when, in *The Great Divorce,* he depicted heaven as *more* solid than earth, not less so. Angels are not chubby toddlers or winged androgynes. Angels are terrifying creatures and meeting an angel is a life-shattering experience (Judg. 6:22; 13:22).

To say that the kingdom of God is heavenly, then, is not at all to detract from its reality or "solidity" or its importance to our earthly lives. Jesus taught that the heavenly kingdom has come to earth in His person and work. Under the influence of the heavenly kingdom, the earth is to be transformed into a temple-city that reflects the glories of the heavenly city of God.

Biblically speaking, a person can be of earthly good *only* if he or she is heavenly minded. To be earthly minded is to be a child of Adam (Col. 3:2). To be heavenly minded is to be a new creation, a reborn son of God, a co-heir with Christ (Col. 3:1). It means, quite simply, to have our minds directed to and filled with Christ. To be heavenly-minded is to love God with our whole mind and soul.

To put it another way, Christians exercise dominion on earth *only by faith*. As brothers of the Last Adam, called to rule in heaven and on earth, we Christians can rightly do so only if our eyes and hearts strain beyond the earth—"upward" to the heavenly throne of Christ and "forward" to His final coming and the perfected heavens and earth.

This is one of the main themes of the eleventh chapter of Hebrews. Faith is defined there as the "substance of things hoped for, the evidence of things not seen" (Heb. 11:1).[13] The man of faith is not ultimately guided by what he sees. He does not despair when he is confronted with adversity; faced with persecution, he does not shrink back (Heb. 10:38–39). He lives victoriously because his hope is set on things that have not yet happened. His stability is founded on something he cannot see. His attention is directed not to his earthly conditions, but toward an unseen heavenly reality. He is not obsessed with access to the various Inner Rings of earthly influence, but thankful for the privilege of access to God's presence. The man of faith, in short, is heavenly minded.

As we read through Hebrews 11, however, we discover that men and women of genuine faith are not hermits, sitting on mountaintops gazing at their navels or waiting for the rapture. Though they all endured hardship, the dominant note of the chapter is one of victory—an emphatically earthly victory at that. Hebrews 11 is more the "Hallelujah Chorus" than a Requiem. It is a shout of victory, not a dirge. By faith Joshua conquered Jericho; by faith kingdoms were vanquished; by faith the saints enforced righteousness; by faith many were "mighty in war"; by faith they "put foreign armies to flight." Even the political and military exploits of the Old Testament saints were expressions of faith: Joshua carrying out the ban against Jericho, Ehud thrusting his dagger into Eglon's immense belly, Samuel hacking Agag in pieces before the Lord at Gilgal. The blood of the battlefield as much as the blood of the altar is a testimony to the faith of God's people. The life of faith, you see, is not for the squeamish.

The heroes of the Old Testament moved history and ruled on earth precisely because they were looking for a heavenly city (Heb. 11:16). They were triumphant in holy war on earth because they were intent on unseen things in heaven. Though there is indeed an absolutely crucial distinction, there is in the Bible no separation between heavenly faith and earthly rule.

All this may seem highly paradoxical, but it is not. In fact, as G. K. Chesterton noted with respect to Jesus' statement that one must lose his life to save it, it is simple common sense. It is the way the world works. Only when we recognize our weakness and look for strength from the Lord do we become strong (Heb. 11:34).

Consider a few examples of how this works.

• The Bible describes heaven as a bank in which we should deposit our treasures (Matt. 6:19–21). This is not because earthly treasures are evil, or because earthly rewards are insignificant (Mark 10:29–31). We lay up treasures in heaven, Jesus taught, because heaven is a more secure place for our treasures to be. Heaven is a better long-term investment because there our "preferred assets" are invulnerable to the marauding of thieves and the decay of moth and rust. Earthly treasures are good, but heavenly treasures are better.

Storing up heavenly treasures, however, does not give us free reign to misuse earthly treasures. Quite the opposite. Jesus said that our diligence in the management of earthly treasures is a sign that we are fit to receive "true riches" (Luke 16:11). Moreover, we can confidently take risks with earthly treasures and even lose them all with joy, because we know that our true treasure is secure. Meditation on our heavenly treas-

81

ures—being heavenly minded—enables us to live like kings whether in prosperity or in poverty.

- Scripture tells us that our very lives are hidden with the exalted Christ in heavenly places (Col. 3:1–4). We can be indifferent about our lives. We can witness for Christ without fear, knowing that though our enemies can kill the body, they cannot snatch us from His hand. Indeed, as Luther pointed out, death and suffering are not only harmless, but actually serve us: to die is gain (Phil. 1:21). Because our lives are hid with Christ in God, we can boldly follow Christ's call to go onto a dangerous mission field or to mount a campaign to fight abortion or pornography.[14] If we are not heavenly minded, we may be too timid to risk our lives and reputations for Christ's sake. The earthly minded man would be too concerned with the loss of earthly comforts and privileges. If we are not heavenly minded, we will not live a victorious Christian life on earth.
- Finally, we can exercise *righteous* rule on earth only if we are guided by things not yet seen. The temptation to grasp for earthly power and fame, to enter some Inner Ring, often comes subtly. You have finished a pleasant lunch with a business associate, and as you are waiting for dessert, he proposes a deal. It is a big deal, just the break you have waited for, a deal that will catapult you to the top of your field. It involves some slight shady dealing, some fuzzy, ambiguous dishonesty, but you are quite sure you could discover a rationalization. If you are convinced that you shall stand before Christ's awful judgment seat—that is, if you are guided by things unseen—you will resist that temptation.

Conclusion

The gospel promises victory. God directs us to pray that His will be done on earth as it is in heaven (Matt. 6:10), and He promises to answer our prayers. One goal of Christ's rule and the rule of the saints is to transform the earth as the Spirit of God works through redeemed men. It is good for the righteous to be in positions of earthly influence and authority (Prov. 29:2; 29:12).

But *how* are we to accomplish this? Do Christians gain earthly dominion by scratching and clawing their way into the Inner Rings? Do Christians acquire earthly dominion by concentrating all their energies on acquiring earthly dominion? Is acquiring earthly dominion the chief end of man? To these questions, the Bible answers a thundering NO! On the contrary, the Bible teaches us that Christians will accomplish God's grand design only as they live by faith in the unseen things, only if they put heavenly things first.

No matter how many victories are won, therefore, the life of the Christian and of the church remains, as the Reformers knew, one of continual humility and patience, faithfulness and repentance. The church will never be at peace with the world and must never be immersed in it. The church's sufferings will never, this side of the Second Advent, come to an end. Though Christ will reign until His enemies are defeated, the world will always remain worldly, the flesh fleshly, and Satan satanic. No matter how pleasant this earthly city becomes, we must continually remind ourselves that we are citizens of a better city, whose Architect and Maker is God.

Cathedrals, to be sure, are far superior to catacombs, and Constantine is far preferable to Caligula. But we must repent as strenuously, and be as heavenly minded, in prosperity as in persecution. Victory has much to recommend it, but we must be forewarned that victory comes with its own peculiar temptations.

FIVE

$\blacklozenge$

The Torn Veil

Junk mail is, along with death and taxes, one of the trinity of certainties of modern life. Its inevitability notwithstanding, junk mail employs a charming variety of voices. Magazine publishers tend toward flattery, reminding me that I am not one of the slumbering masses. No, no. They offer inside information and intelligent analysis, because they know I'm not like that publican in the corner there.

Political junk mail, by contrast, thrives on terror. The issue at stake may be anything from art exhibits to violence on television to congressional hearings to the next election, but the frenzied tone is constant. Pockmarked with exclamation points, the cover letter announces, "Only *your* contribution can avert disaster! Give NOW!" Direct mailings are the shock troops of the culture war.

I am being flippant (if not funny), but there is a serious point here. Junk mail is one of the many media through which modern Americans are inundated with news—much of it bad. Television, newspapers and newsletters, and radio talk shows bombard us with information—much of it depressing. We have to absorb the bad news of the underclass, unrest in the Persian Gulf, the drug trade, abortion, militant homosexual advocacy, and the general decay of Christian standards.

The cumulative effect can be overwhelming. We can develop a combat mentality and begin to think that, in such extraordinary times, the ordinary rules and patterns of "normal" life no longer apply. We eat, drink, and sleep the *Kulturkampf;* we dream in exclamation points. Our enemies seem so powerful, so successful, so invincible that if we let down our guard for only a moment, we will have lost the battle. It seems as if the wicked are always at ease, as if we have been fools to keep our hearts pure, as if there is no Judge in heaven. We grit our teeth and persevere, but we run the danger of becoming burned out. Cynicism catches hold, then yields its place to despair.

Long ago Asaph contemplated the prosperity of the wicked—their fatness, their ease, their arrogance. He was troubled by their strength, ". . . until I came into the sanctuary of God; Then I perceived their end" (Ps. 73:16–17). From atop the temple mount, Asaph got a true perspective on the war raging in the valley below. It was only in the sanctuary that Asaph saw clearly the true end of the wicked. His cure for combat fatigue was a trip to the mountains—the temple mountains.

What Is a Sanctuary?

In both Greek and Hebrew, as in English, the words for "sanctuary" are related to the words for "sacred" and "sanctified." A sanctuary is a sanctified place or "holy space." We saw in chapter 2 that the Garden of Eden was the original earthly sanctuary. Both the tabernacle and temple were sanctuaries (Ex. 25:6; 1 Chron. 22:19), and the inner room, the Holy of Holies, was specially sanctified (1 Kings 6:16). The entire land of Israel was also a sanctuary (Ex. 15:17; Ps. 114:2); the holiness of the temple spread to the boundaries of the Holy Land.

Throughout Scripture, moreover, the "holy place" is, symbolically, the highest point and center of the world. Eden's sanctuary was planted on a mountain (Ezek. 28:13–14), and the temple was built on the mountain of the Lord's choosing (2 Chron. 3:1; Ps. 68:16). Along with the city of Jerusalem, the temple was pictured by the poets and prophets as the center of the world and the goal of the "pilgrimage of the nations." Because God had set His name there, Jerusalem was the "joy of the whole earth" (Ps. 48:2). In the latter days, Isaiah predicted, the nations would stream to the temple mountain to worship the Lord and to feast on His rich banquet (Isa. 2:2–4; 25:6–8). At the time of the restoration, all the nations would gather around the throne of the Lord in Jerusalem (Jer. 3:17). John saw a vision of the kings of the earth bringing their glories into the new temple-city (see Rev. 21:22–27).[1] Despite the later pretensions of the Romans, every Hebrew knew that all roads led to Jerusalem.

What makes a place holy? In the modern study of comparative religions and anthropology, a holy place is often defined as a place that connects heaven and earth, the sacred and the profane realms. A holy person is a "window to the sacred."[2] Scripture, however, does not use these terms. We find nothing in Scripture about an impersonal and abstract "sacrality." In Scripture, things are holy only insofar as they symbolize holy persons or have contact with God.[3] In the biblical world view, "sacredness" is always a personal quality.

Specifically, places become holy when God comes. Of course, God is everywhere at all times, yet the Bible teaches that God is specially present at certain times and in certain places. The Bible speaks of "holy ground" (Ex. 3:5) and of God "visiting" His people (Jer. 29:10; Luke 1:78). Throughout the Old Testament, God's special presence was marked by the visible "glory-cloud." This was the cloud that led Israel through the wilderness, as a token of His presence and protection (Ex. 13:22). The cloud was the whirring chariot, consisting of angelic beings, that Ezekiel saw by the brook Chebar (Ezek. 1).

The glory-cloud was closely associated with the various Old Testament sanctuaries. When the tabernacle was completed, the cloud filled the Holy of Holies (Ex. 40:34–38), and the same thing happened upon completion of the temple (2 Chron. 5:11–14). This cloud is also connected in Scripture with the lightsome Spirit who hovered over the dark waters of creation (Gen. 1:2; Deut. 32:11). In the sanctuary, God dwelled by the Spirit in visible glory, surrounded by His heavenly hosts.[4] Indeed it is the presence of the glory-cloud that made the sanctuaries holy places. Places are sanctified by the glory of God (see Ex. 29:43).

Biblically defined, then, *a sanctuary is a place where God is present in glory, and sacred things and persons are things and persons consecrated for service in the place where God is present in glory.*

The sanctuary not only was the place where the cloud came to rest, but was made according to the pattern of the glory-cloud. Moses was told to make the tabernacle and its furnishings according to the pattern he saw in the cloud atop Mount Sinai (Ex. 25:40; Num. 8:4; Heb. 8:5), and the blueprint of the temple was likewise copied from heavenly things (1 Chron. 28:20). The glory-cloud was God's traveling sanctuary, of which the Garden, the tabernacle, and the temple were copies. A careful study of Ezekiel's vision of the glorious chariot of God (Ezek. 1:1–28) will show, for example, its close similarity to his description of the "holy mountain" of Eden (Ezek. 28:12–19). One point of comparison must suffice here: the glory-cloud was filled with cherubim (Ezek. 1:5–14; cf. Luke 2:9, 13–14), and Eden's Garden, the tabernacle, and temple were likewise filled with images of cherubim (Ezek. 10; 28:14; Ex. 25:18–22; 26:1; 1 Kings 6:23–36). Sanctuaries, then, are places where God is present in glory and at the same time architectural representations of the heavenly dwelling place of God.

The book of Revelation is one of the best places in Scripture to learn about the sanctuary (Rev. 1:10; 11:19). Caught up by the Spirit into heaven, John witnessed a worship service. Twenty-four elders, four living creatures, myriads of angels, and finally the entire creation bow in worship before the Lord (Rev. 4–5). Later, it is in the heavenly sanctuary that the great multitude celebrates the marriage supper of the Lamb

(Rev. 19:1–10). In Revelation, the heavenly sanctuary is above all a place of worship.

This is entirely consistent with what we learn of the sanctuary in the Old Testament. The Israelites were allowed to offer sacrificial worship to God only at the central sanctuary (Deut. 12:5–14). They gathered there for their three annual feasts to eat, drink, and rejoice in God's presence (Deut. 14:22–29; 16:1–17). Psalm 68 describes the Lord's triumphant liturgical procession, as He makes His way to the holy place surrounded by singers, musicians, and maids beating tambourines. In the Old Testament, the sanctuary is the place where God's people gather for sacrificial and festal worship. The sanctuary is the place where God's people meet with their Lord.

When the people gathered at the sanctuary, they not only celebrated a feast with songs of praise, but also listened to the Word of the Lord (Deut. 31:9–13). Ezra the scribe read and explained the law to the people of the restoration at the Feast of Booths (Neh. 8). Meeting with God includes listening intently to every Word that proceeds from His mouth.

All Old Testament sanctuaries were restorations and glorifications of the Garden of Eden, the primal earthly sanctuary. Just as God met with Adam and Eve in the Garden, so also He was present in His glory at the tabernacle and temple. Just as Adam and Eve were to feast and rejoice in His presence in the Garden, so also the sanctuary was a festival center. The Garden, too, was the place where God spoke to His servants, just as the Word was spoken to the people at the sanctuary. The tabernacle and temple were provisional restorations of Paradise.

The Great Throng

For Americans, especially individualistic American Protestants, the word "sanctuary" calls to mind dark, dank, echoing cathedrals. "Sanctuary" is associated with "priestcraft," a word that cannot be uttered without a sneer. We have adopted what we think is a prophetic contempt for the sanctuary.

In the Bible, however, the attitude toward sanctuaries is very different. The sanctuary is not depicted as the center of merely external religiosity or of "ritualism." Though the prophets insisted that the physical presence of the sanctuary was no guarantee of God's favor, the sanctuary was nonetheless the heart of biblical worship, and worship was the very core of the lives of the biblical saints. The sanctuary was the object of their deepest longings and desires. In one of the most poignant of all the psalms, David wrote that his hunger and thirst for God was satisfied only in the sanctuary (Ps. 63:1–2). There the strength and glory of God were revealed (Ps. 96:6). Strong help comes from the sanctuary (Ps. 20:2). David wrote, "One thing I have asked from the Lord, that I shall seek: That I may dwell in the house of the Lord all the days of my life, to behold the beauty of the Lord, and to meditate in His temple" (Ps. 27:4). Levites were specially blessed, because dwelling in the temple courts meant they could draw near to God (Ps. 65:4). The sanctuary is the Inner Ring, the secret place where men meet the living God.

Many evangelical Christians today think that the really important kind of worship is private and individual. This notion is perhaps one of the definitive elements of evangelical Christianity. Many more books are written about deepening one's individual walk with the Lord than about worshiping God in the assembly of His people. Much more effort is spent thinking about and discussing the structure of one's "quiet time" than considering questions of the church's liturgy.

As we have seen, however, the Bible gives no indication of this kind of dichotomy. Biblical saints looked forward with intense eagerness to the public worship of God, to the public proclamation of His Word, and to the communal feasts of the sanctuary.[5]

This is true in the new covenant as it was in the old. Today Jesus Christ is the central sanctuary. Our hunger and thirst is no longer for a place, whether Jerusalem or Samaria, but for the One who "tabernacled" among us and in whom we behold the glory of God (John 1:14). His body is the temple of God (John 2:21). He is the supreme holy place, the radiance of God's glory (Heb. 1:3), where the fullness of God dwells bodily (Col. 2:9). He offers His flesh and blood for the sanctuary feast; He is the Word of God, and His words are Spirit and life (John 1:1; 6:63). All the patterns of the Old Testament sanctuary are fulfilled in Jesus. Wherever Jesus is, then, there is the "holy place" of God. Christians can enter the sanctuary anytime they approach Jesus in prayer. In the privacy of his or her closet, the Christian can enter the gates of Paradise.

Yet, the people of God still meet Him chiefly in the *assembly*. When the writer to the Hebrews encouraged his readers to approach the Lord with confidence, he immediately added a warning against forsaking the assembly of God's people (Heb. 10:19–25). Throughout the book of Acts, we rarely read of the early Christians in their private prayer closets (but see Acts 10:9), but frequently find them gathering to break bread (Acts 1:12–14; 2:1, 42; etc.). Certainly, Christians ought not neglect private worship and prayer, but private worship should not be separated from the worship of the church. Even in the new covenant, meeting God in worship is a *corporate* as well as an individual act.

The corporate dimensions of the sanctuary become clearer when we consider heaven as a sanctuary. Heaven is a holy place because the glory of God dwells there. Christians constantly live as citizens of heaven (Phil. 3:20). Yet, the New Testament teaches that Christians enter heaven in a special way when they assemble to offer their sacrifice of praise and to celebrate the new covenant feast. On the Lord's Day the heavenly sanctuary opens, and the church on earth joins with all the company of heaven, with the heavenly choir of angels and saints, to worship the Lord (Heb. 12:18–24). Indeed, when she assembles in Christ's name and Christ is present, the church not only enters the heavenly sanctuary, but actually is a sanctuary (1 Cor. 3:16–17). The glory of God, which dwells fully in Jesus, descended on the church on the Day of Pentecost (Acts 2) as it had descended on the tabernacle and temple. Because she is the dwelling place of the glorious Spirit, the church is the holy place of God.

Practically, then, Christians enter the sanctuary in a special way when they assemble as the church. It is in public worship that the Spirit-glory of God descends, as the triune God meets with His people and offers Himself to them. Jesus, after all, promised to be present in a special way not where one man calls upon Him, but where *two or three* gather in His name (Matt. 18:20).

Enter into My Rest

The Old Testament also closely associated sabbath rest with the sanctuary. Adam and Eve entered into God's sabbath rest when they appeared in the Garden on the first day after they had been created (Gen. 2:1–4). Keeping the Sabbath means not only refraining from work, but also worshiping the Lord in the beauty of holiness (Ex. 20:11; Lev. 23:3). Significantly, Moses' record of the plans for the tabernacle is bracketed by laws having to do with Sabbath-keeping (Ex. 23:12; 34:21). The plot of the book of Exodus moves from the unending toil of slavery to rest and worship at God's sanctuary (Ex. 1:8–15; 40:34–38). The temple was built only after David had gained rest from the enemies of Israel (2 Sam. 7:1–3). When the people of Israel were excluded from the sanctuary land of Palestine, God said He would not let them enter His "rest" (Ps. 95:6–11).[6] Throughout Scripture, rest is found in the sanctuary.

Rest in Scripture does not mean mere cessation of labor, but celebration and consummation of work. God did not merely cease working on the seventh day, but delighted in and celebrated His completed creation. Here again, Jesus Christ is the fulfillment of the Old Testament pattern. He has delivered His people from bondage to sin and offers rest to the heavy-laden (Matt. 11:28). In Him all of God's promises are yea and amen (2 Cor. 1:19–20). He has declared, "It is finished" (John 19:30). Jesus submitted Himself to death because of the joy that was set before Him (Heb. 12:2). Because Jesus has completed the work given to Him by His Father, He has entered into the celebration of that completed work. He has entered into the joy of sabbath rest. When we draw near to Jesus, we are entering God's rest. Our hearts are restless until they rest in Him who has ascended into the heavenly sanctuary.

The Kingdom of God and the Sanctuary

The Bible is a complex book. Consisting of sixty-six books written over several millennia, it describes a bewildering array of characters and events. The Bible seems especially complex and difficult to modern Christians, because, however hard we try to think biblically, we have been subtly but deeply influenced by modern philosophy and science. Often, even when we have rejected the explicit conclusions of science, we unconsciously adopt a scientistic mind-set. One example of this is our tendency to operate on the modern assumption that all ideas can be defined with infinite, scientific precision, and that concepts can and should be distinguished very sharply.

The more you study the Bible, the more you will find that it cannot be forced into this mold. Ideas and symbols in the Bible meld together, overlap, and stretch out in a thousand different directions. This is not to say that the Bible is irrational or unscientific, or that we cannot make any meaningful distinctions. But a modern reader cannot escape the sense that the Bible speaks a very different language than he learned in "Chem. Lab" or Philosophy 101. As theologian Vern S. Poythress has noted, the biblical world view acknowledges the reality of "fuzzy boundaries."[7]

Dutch theologian Herman Bavinck drew a distinction between pagan and biblical thought that may help to clarify this idea.[8] Bavinck said that modern (and ancient Greek) thinkers attempted to find the "essence" of a thing, that which makes a thing uniquely what it is, by *subtraction*. To discover the "essence" of a pencil, we subtract its color, its size, its shape—all of which may vary without changing the nature of the thing and all of which may describe something other than a pencil. (There might be a red apple as well as a red pencil, a six-inch slug as well as a six-inch pencil, etc.) When we have subtracted all the variables, what we have left is the "essence" of the pencil, what might be called "pure pencilness." (Of course, what we really have left is nothing at all.)

Scripture, by contrast, describes the essence of a thing by *addition*. Only when we know the fullness of a thing, all of its attributes, do we really know its uniqueness and "essence." God's "essence" is not some "bare minimum" of deity, or some "basic attribute" from which all the other attributes can be derived. Instead, the "essence" of God is the fullness of all His attributes.

All this probably sounds rather abstract, but keeping in mind the distinction between subtraction and addition will help us better to grasp the Bible's teaching on the kingdom of God. To know the "essence" of the kingdom, we should not try to reduce the kingdom to a few "basic" elements or attributes. Instead, if we wish to approach an understanding of the biblical theology of the kingdom in all its imponderable richness, we must see it in relation to other biblical themes.

Of Sanctuaries and Kings

Bavinck's point helps to explain why I have spent so many pages discussing the sanctuary in a book about the kingdom of God. That question might have already occurred to you. After all, modern Americans associate "sanctuaries" with priests and worship, not with kings and kingdoms. That is partly because of our secularized understanding of politics and religion, church and state. In traditional societies, by contrast, the king is considered a special representative of God. In medieval Europe, for example, when a man was anointed as king, he also became a priest. Indeed, the king was something more than a run-of-the-mill cleric; he was believed to have special charismatic powers. Even into the late eighteenth century it was believed that the touch of the anointed king of France had the power to heal. The person of the king was sacred. To attack the king was not mere treason; it was sacrilege.[9]

Conversely, medieval bishops were often kings in their own right. After the conversion of the barbarian tribes of Northern Europe, it was many centuries before the church was able to convince bishops to cease and desist from their military activities. At one time, the Vatican had the largest army and navy in Europe!

In traditional societies, then, kings are priestly and priests are royal. Similarly, in Scripture, priesthood and kingship are very intimately related. The king, like the high priest, was anointed with sacred oil (Ex. 28:41; 1 Sam. 9:16; 16:3, 12; 1 Kings 1:34; 19:15–16; Ps. 89:20). After Solomon's time, the king's palace was built near the temple on the mountains of Jerusalem as part of the same sanctuary complex (1 Kings 7:1). The kings of Israel provided sacrifices for the priests (1 Kings 8:62–66), and David even reorganized the Levitical priesthood (1 Chron. 24–26). Both the First and Last Adams are priest-kings as well.

Just as kings and priests are closely associated, and just as the temple and palace were closely situated in Jerusalem, so also the sanctuary and the kingdom are closely connected, and even, we might say, identical realities.[10] That may seem an unusual thing to say, but I believe that the parallel of the kingdom and the sanctuary is absolutely crucial to a correct understanding of the biblical teaching on the kingdom of God. What exactly does this connection mean?

The Cosmic "Bridge"

"Star Trek" fans will recall that Captain Kirk controlled the starship Enterprise from the area known as the "bridge." From the bridge, Kirk made decisions and issued orders. When there was trouble in the engine room, Kirk called Scotty to the bridge, gave him instructions, and sent him back to straighten things out. When an enemy attacked, Captain Kirk, Mr. Spock, and Dr. McCoy huddled together on the bridge to decide what to do, and their decision was broadcast throughout the ship from the bridge.

The book of Revelation shows that the heavenly sanctuary is not only a place of worship, but also something like a cosmic "bridge." God issues His declarations and decisions from heaven, and sends out angels and prophets to declare and execute His will. Horsemen ride out from heaven bringing war, famine, and death to the earth (Rev. 6:1–8). When the prayers of the saints arise before the heavenly altar, angels throw burning coals to the earth, producing thunder, lightning, and earthquakes (Rev. 8:3–5). Seven angels emerge from the sanctuary to pour bowls of wrath onto the earth (Rev. 15:5–16:1). From the sanctuary in heaven, Christ, the Lamb sitting upon the throne, breaks the seals and unfolds His plan for history.

John's description of the sanctuary as the place from which God rules is perfectly consistent with the Old Testament. The tabernacle and temple in the Old Testament were God's houses (2 Sam. 7:1–6). God lived in a tent when His people were living in tents, and God had a house built for Himself after He gave His people rest from their enemies in the land. Kings do not dwell in ordinary split-level or ranch-style houses. Louis XIV did not live in a bungalow, but walked through the astonishing hallways of Versailles and slept in its centrally located bedroom. Because God was the King of Israel, His houses were ornately decorated palaces.

Within each of God's Old Testament palaces, there were two rooms: the Holy Place and the Most Holy Place. For our purposes here, we need only to note the central features of the inner room.[11] Within the Holy of Holies sat the ark of the covenant, over which two cherubim stretched their wings. The Lord was enthroned above the cherubim, robed in royal glory (Ex. 40:34–38). It was in the inner temple that Isaiah saw the Lord enthroned (Isa. 6:1–5). The Most Holy Place was the throne room of the King of Israel (2 Sam. 6:2; 2 Kings 19:15; Pss. 11:4; 80:1; 99:1).

The Holy of Holies, the inner room of God's palace, was the "concentration point" of God's rule, His "cosmic bridge." Just as earthly kings make and declare their decisions from their inner throne rooms, so also the Lord of heaven rules from the sanctuary. God spoke His authoritative laws from His throne above the cherubim; Moses met with God at the sanctuary, and upon the sanctuary mountain of Sinai, to hear God's words and to deliver them to the people (Ex. 19:20–25; Lev. 1:1). It is no accident that the ark of the covenant contained the tablets of the Law (Heb. 9:4). In the tabernacle and temple, the Lord was enthroned as the covenant King.

God also executed covenant threats from His sanctuary. When the men of Beth-shemesh looked in the ark, God's wrath flared out and killed them (1 Sam. 7:19–21). Nadab and Abihu perished when they offered strange fire before the Lord's throne (Lev. 10:1–7). God not only spoke His Word from the sanctuary, but also enforced His Word. In the Most Holy Place, God was enthroned not only as the supreme legislator, but also as the Judge and executioner.

As the covenant King, God also distributed gifts from the sanctuary. The children of Israel were invited to visit their Father's palace to eat and drink in His presence and to meet with Him. As Augustine put it, the chief gift that the Lord gives to His people is Himself; our "chief and entire good it is to have Him and to be His."[12] The King of Israel gave Himself to His people at the sanctuary.

This Old Testament matrix, it seems to me, provides the background to Jesus' frequent statements about "entering the kingdom of God" (Matt. 5:20; 7:21; 18:3; 19:23–24; John 3:5; etc.). We saw in the first chapters of this book that the kingdom of God came when Jesus defeated Satan and ascended to the throne at the right hand of the Majesty on high. It is entirely proper to say that the kingdom of God is the rule of Christ over His church and over all things. But in the teaching of Jesus, the kingdom of God is also—mainly—a "place" that some "enter" and some do not. That "place" is the heavenly sanctuary, from which Jesus reigns as the Last Adam and Son of David, as the covenant Lord. To enter the sanctuary, where Jesus is enthroned in glory amid the hosts of heaven, is to enter the kingdom of God.[13]

Worship and Holy War

Entering the sanctuary, in other words, means entering the "cosmic bridge," what Vern S. Poythress calls the "control center of the universe." This insight immeasurably enriches our understanding of worship. Worship in God's Holy Place is not merely a matter of "R&R" in the presence of God. Worship is the exaltation of God as covenant King, our response to His kingship. As William Dumbrell explains, worship is the protocol for entrance into God's royal presence.[14] Worship is not to be taken lightly because in worship we enter the presence of the Majestic Terror, the God who is a consuming fire (Heb. 12:29).

The Old Testament speaks of worship as "appearing before God" (Ex. 23:17), a phrase that suggests an army assembled for inspection by its commanding officer. Each Lord's Day, the church militant is called together to be judged and evaluated. God tests us and our works. If we have built with hay or wood or stubble, our works will be burned up in the consuming fire of God's presence. If we have built with gold, our works will be purified (1 Cor. 3:10–15). In either case, worship at the palace of the glorious King of heaven involves purification and judgment.

Even more, worship is a chief way that we participate in Christ's rule over all things. Worship is not merely a "rest" from "normal war," but a central act of holy war. When Christ is enthroned on our praises, He becomes a terror to our enemies (Josh. 6; 2 Chron. 20). Heaven is both the place where we meet with the triune God in intimate fellowship, and the place where we sit upon thrones ruling all things. Sitting is a posture both of kings and dinner guests; during our worship in the heavenly sanctuary, we sit both on thrones to rule and at table for a feast. Heaven is the Inner Ring, a place of both intimacy and power. If we wish to conduct a biblical holy war, our first offensive is to lift up our Warrior-King on our praises.

Worship is not merely a means to realize God's kingdom. Worship is itself the first form of God's kingdom in the world. The prophets often pictured the coming messianic order in terms of the sanctuary and worship (cf. Isa. 2:2–4; Ezek. 40–48). For the prophets, the coming of the kingdom meant that the nations would gather on the temple mountain, to render tribute the heavenly King and to listen to His Word. Worship is not the only form that the kingdom of God takes on earth; but the assembly of the church is the kingdom's primary earthly form. Are you looking for the kingdom of God in this world? The kingdom of God is there where God's people gather around the heavenly throne to exalt the King.

Exiled from God

King Uzziah's reign was a resounding success. Like his father, Amaziah, he followed the ways of the Lord. Amaziah had heeded the law and the warnings of the prophets against alliances with the northern kingdom of Israel, and the Lord had given him success in his war with the Edomites.

Late in his reign, however, Amaziah had become proud. He returned from war with some Edomite idols among his booty and began to worship them. Then, he attacked the Israelite king Joash. That was a complete disaster. Joash captured Amaziah, took him to Jerusalem, smashed four hundred cubits of the city wall, and stole treasures from the temple and the palace. That angered many of the people of Judah, and they plotted against Amaziah until they finally captured and killed him at Lachish.

Though only sixteen when his father was killed, Uzziah learned his lesson. He saw what would happen if he turned from the ways of the Lord or if he stirred up the anger and resentment of the people. Under the guidance of Zechariah the priest, he followed the commandments of the Lord, and the Lord blessed him. He conquered the Philistines and built cities in their lands. He defeated the Arabians and the Meunites. The Ammonites brought him tribute, and even as far away as Egypt he was known and respected. He had an army of 307,500 well-equipped soldiers under 2,600 commanders. Uzziah was famous, strong, feared, and respected throughout the Near East.

But it did not last. Like his father, Uzziah became proud. And like his father, the proud Uzziah violated the priestly calling of the kings of Israel.

The Lord had made it very clear that only the priestly descendants of Aaron were allowed to enter the Holy Place to burn incense (Num. 16–17). Uzziah knew that, but he thought he was an exception. After all, he was king, and a great one. Surely, God would not deny him access to the golden altar in the Holy Place. Angered by the warnings of the priests, Uzziah marched into the temple to offer incense.

Because of Uzziah's presumption, God struck him with leprosy, permanently. In the Old Testament, leprosy made a person unclean, and therefore unfit to appear before the Lord. From that day forward, Uzziah was never allowed near the temple courtyard. He could not even stay in his palace, but lived the rest of his life in a separate house. He had grasped for a forbidden privilege and lost all privileges as a result. He had presumed to enter the inner courts of the Lord's house and was exiled completely.

Leprous Uzziah represents all men of the Adamic, old covenant order. Like Uzziah, Adam grasped for a privilege, an authority, that God had forbidden. Like Uzziah, Adam was punished through the removal of all his privileges and through his deliverance into slavery to Satan. And like Uzziah, Adam and his descendants became unclean, unwelcome in God's house, exiled from the Garden. Gradually, God restored some of the privileges Adam had forfeited. Under the Mosaic system the high priest was allowed to enter the Holy of Holies once a year to sprinkle blood on the ark (Lev. 16). But the people could not draw near into the Holy Place, much less the inner sanctuary. For all practical purposes, even the priests were cut off from the presence of God. Far from being able to enter into the fullness of God, when the glory-cloud settled over the Holy of Holies, the priests were *prevented* from entering (Ex. 40:34–38).[15]

Uzziah is a type of Adamic man: leprous, living apart, cut off from the house of God. God offers Himself and His blessing to His people in the sanctuary. But sons of Adam cannot come near to receive it.

Return from Exile

When Jesus died on Calvary, the veil of the temple was torn in two from top to bottom. This event is highlighted in all of the Synoptic Gospels (Matt. 27:51; Mark 15:38; Luke 23:45). Why is it so important?

To understand the meaning of the veil, we must again go all the way back to the Garden of Eden.[16] The Garden, as we have seen, was the original sanctuary, where God was specially present, where He spoke to Adam and Eve, and where they were to eat the fruit of the Tree of Life. When Adam and Eve sinned, however, they were cast out from the Garden of God and prevented from eating the fruit of the Tree of Life. Cherubim with flaming swords were placed at the entrance to the Garden to prevent Adam and Eve from returning (Gen. 3:24).

The cherubim at the entrance to the Garden were taken up symbolically in the architecture of the tabernacle and temple. As the entrance to the Garden was guarded by cherubim, so the way to the Holy of Holies was blocked by a curtain interwoven with cherubim (Ex. 26:31–35; 2 Chron. 3:10–14).[17] The veil was a reminder that the people of God were denied access to God's inner sanctuary. A torn veil, on the other hand, means that the way into the Holy of Holies has been opened.

The book of Hebrews explicitly tells us that the rending of the earthly veil mirrors the heavenly reality. The rent veil points to the fact that in Christ we now have access not to an earthly copy but to the true heavenly sanctuary. By hope we can enter through the veil because Jesus, the forerunner, has entered and has been installed as a High Priest after the order of Melchizedek (Heb. 6:19). We have confidence to enter the Holy Place with boldness because Christ has shed His most precious blood (see Heb. 10:20). We not only *hope* to enter the heavenly sanctuary in and through Christ, but we already have access to heaven. We actually enter the sanctuary by faith.[18]

Jesus had been, as it were, "rending the veil" throughout His ministry on earth. As he went from place to place announcing the coming of the kingdom, He also performed miracles, healings, and exorcisms (Matt. 4:23–24). He healed lepers (Matt. 8:3; 10:8; Mark 1:42; Luke 5:13), and a woman with an issue of blood (Matt. 9:20–22). He cast out *unclean* spirits (Matt. 10:1; Mark 1:23–27; 9:14–29; etc.). All these afflictions prevented people from drawing near to God (Lev. 13–14; 15:25–30; 22:16–24). When He cast out an unclean spirit, therefore, Jesus was not only defeating Satan but also cleansing the unclean and qualifying them to enter the sanctuary. Jesus' military campaign against Satan was simultaneously a cleansing of sinners. Jesus came not only as the Greater Joshua, waging holy war against His enemies, but also as a Greater Aaron, sprinkling defiled lepers.

What does the tearing of the veil have to do with the *death* of Christ? Again, we must understand this in the light of Genesis 1–3. Adam and Eve were cast from the Garden because of their rebellion against God and His law. Sin defiled them and made them unfit to appear in God's presence. If the children of Adam and Eve are to be restored to God's sanctuary and to God Himself, blood must be shed. There is no forgiveness, and no access to the sanctuary, without the shedding of blood (Heb. 9:22).

By His death, Jesus paid the price. The Last Adam suffered the penalty for the sins of the First Adam and of his children. Now that the blood of the perfect Lamb has been shed, the doors of Paradise swing open, the cherubim sets down his flaming sword, the veil of the temple is torn in two—and we are invited to draw near to God in His heavenly throne room. We are allowed into the inner sanctuary, where the living God offers Himself to us. We are bidden to enter the kingdom to enjoy the marriage supper of the Lamb.

The High Priest's New Clothes

The dividing of the veil not only symbolized the opening of the heavenly sanctuary, but also desecrated the temple.[19] Once the temple's veil is torn, and the Holy of Holies disclosed, the temple no longer fulfills its function of restraining people from the presence of God.

This negative side of the tearing of the veil was also symbolized in the tearing of the high priest's clothes. Clothes are symbolic of man's office and glory. The high priest's clothes in particular were "for glory and for beauty" (Ex. 28:2). God is robed in glory, and our clothes image His. We must reflect God's glory to enter into His glory; only those robed in glory can enter God's glorious presence. We cannot enter the wedding feast without a robe. For this reason, the high priest was expressly forbidden to rip his clothes (Lev. 21:10). Those who tear their garments put themselves in the place of lepers (Lev. 13:45–52). They become outcasts, unfit to enter before the Lord.

When the high priest Caiphas tore his clothes upon hearing what he thought was the blasphemy of Jesus (Matt. 26:65), he desecrated his high priesthood. In the presence of the true High Priest, he unconsciously prophesied that the Aaronic priesthood was superceded, just as he had prophesied that Christ must be the One Man to die for the people (John 18:14). Caiphas, the priest according to the order of Levi, did unconscious obeisance to the High Priest according to the order of Melchizedek (Heb. 7:9–10).

The tearing of the robes of the high priest is thus a parallel event to the parting of the temple veil. Both tell us that the earthly temple and its Levitical priesthood were wearing away and about to disappear. Both tell us that human's exile from God has come to an end, and that in Christ we can now draw near. Both tell us that the blessing of the kingdom lies within reach (see Luke 17:21),[20] and a new world order is being born.

Conclusion: The Keys of the Kingdom

On a superficial analysis, it might appear that the people with real power are the ones with diversified portfolios, prestigious titles, spacious offices overlooking Central Park. A personal jet, a direct line to the president, a limousine—these are the symbols of real power. Or so we think.

Deeper reflection, however, reveals that real power belongs to the fellow with the most keys. Think about it. Where would we be without those fellows with the keys? Without them, prisons would be sieves, office waste baskets would never be emptied, and the very theory of valet parking would be utterly nonsensical. Without the fellows with the keys, the world would crumble of its own weight.

The man with the right keys can get into the right places, and he can also keep other people from getting into the same places. The man with the keys has access to the file drawer, to the corporate vacation house, and to the laboratory with the red "Top Secret" sign flashing above it. Having the right key can be, we might say, the "key" to success, as well as a reward of success. Keys are suitable symbols of authority. It should not be surprising, then, that when Peter confessed that Jesus was the Christ, the Son of the living God, Jesus rewarded him with a set of keys, the "keys of the kingdom" (Matt. 16:19).

Few texts of Scripture have been as important in the history of the church as Matthew 16:13–20. During the Middle Ages and within the Roman Catholic Church today this text has been used to defend the supremacy of the pope. Here, it is argued, Jesus specifically gave Peter preeminence among the apostles and established the authority of the successors of Peter in the see of Rome. Too often, however, commentators, both Roman Catholic and Protestant, have focused on controversial aspects of this text and missed some crucial features.

It is important to recognize that Jesus' language here is highly unusual. We do not notice the oddity because we are used to thinking of the church as a building. The Hebrew word that is translated by the Greek *ekklesia* and the English

104

"church," however, means "assembly." Never in the Old Testament is the "assembly" said to be "built." Assemblies are "gathered," "assembled," "mustered," and "called together," but the notion of "building the assembly" never appears in the Old Testament.

Clearly Jesus was using an architectural metaphor. The assembly (church) will be *built*, upon the solid foundation of a *rock*. In short, Jesus was combining two different Old Testament images: the temple and the assembly (1 Cor. 3:16–17).[21] He did not predict that His church would assemble around or in a building, but that the assembly would itself *be* the building, constructed from living stones (1 Peter 2:5).

Biblical theologian Geerhardus Vos argued that in this passage the "kingdom of heaven" and the "assembly" (church) are identical:

> Peter receives the keys of the kingdom to bind or loose on earth. What he does in the administration of the kingdom here below will be recognized in heaven. Now this promise immediately following the declaration concerning Peter as the foundation rock of the church, it becomes necessary to assume that in Jesus' view these two are identified. The force of this will be felt by observing that in the two statements made the figure is essentially the same, viz., that of the house. First the house is represented as in [the] process of building, Peter as the foundation, then the same house appears as completed and Peter as invested with the keys for administering its affairs. It is plainly excluded that the house should mean one thing in the first statement and another in the second.[22]

What Vos misses in this passage, however, is that the house—which refers both to the church and the kingdom—is at the same time the new temple. It is *Jesus'* house that is under construction, and, since He is the Son of God, Jesus lives in a palace. He is the *Christ*, the anointed Son of God, the

Greater Solomon, the temple-building Son of David (Matt. 16:16). The authority that Jesus gave to Peter was, therefore, the authority to open and shut the doors of the temple, and generally to administer the affairs of King Jesus' palace. He was vested with the power to admit men to and exclude them from the sanctuary.

Isaiah 22:22 presents a very similar picture. There, the Lord threatened to cast down Shebna, the steward of the royal household and to invest Eliakim with all the duties of that office. Eliakim would receive an official robe and sash symbolizing his authority, and the Lord would set the key of the house of David on his shoulder, so that "when he opens no one will shut, when he shuts no one will open" (v. 22). The key in Isaiah 22 symbolizes the authority to administer the affairs of the *palace* of David. In the same way, the keys given to Peter were the keys to the palace of the Greater Son of David.

By extension, though the apostles play a unique foundational role in erecting the new temple (Eph. 2:20), the church as a whole has received the authority to bind and loose. Jesus promised in Matthew 18:18 that what the *church* binds on earth will be bound in heaven, the very same promise He had made to Peter. The church has been given the keys to the kingdom. The authority to bind and loose was given to Peter as the head of the apostolate, and it is given to the church that is built upon the foundation of the apostles and administered by the church's officers.

Practically, this means that the pathway into the heavenly sanctuary and kingdom of God lies through the church. The church is the assembly of God's people that is permitted to enter His kingdom, His throne room, His inner sanctuary. It is as the church that people draw near to the covenant King, to hear His Word, and to stand for inspection. God grants salvation, life, and communion with Him by the Spirit in the church. The church administers the keys of the kingdom. The sanctuary is locked to sons of Adam. If you want to get into the Holy Place, you need to see the fellows with the keys.

SIX

---◆---

The King's Table

Mephibosheth, son of Jonathan, son of Saul, was a pitiable figure. The son of a mighty warrior, and grandson of a king, Mephibosheth was lame. He had not been born lame. When he was five years old, his nurse dropped him, crippling his legs. Mephibosheth was an orphan. His father and grandfather had been killed while battling the Philistines on the slopes of Mount Gilboa on the same day that Mephibosheth was crippled.

More than that, Mephibosheth had the misfortune of being born into a fallen family. His grandfather, King Saul, had attained the highest pinnacle of Israelite politics and society, but by the time Mephibosheth was grown, the family had nothing. They were objects of ridicule. He had been brought to shame because of the sin of his forefather.

King David, however, had compassion on Mephibosheth. Because of the oath and covenant he had made with Jonathan, David spared his life. That in itself was an act of mercy. Politically, it would have been more sensible for David to have Mephibosheth, a member of a fallen royal house, locked up or killed. But David opted for clemency and spared the grandson of his life-long persecutor.

David, however, did far more than spare Mephibosheth. He also restored all of Saul's ancestral lands and even gave

107

Mephibosheth a place at his table. In the ancient world, a seat at the king's table meant a great deal more than regular sumptuous meals. It was also a place of honor, privilege, and power. At table, the king's friends whispered advice into the king's ear. Only the king's closest friends and advisors were allowed to eat and drink with him.

We are all Mephibosheths. Our father, Adam, sinned, and brought shame and misery to all his children. Adam, anointed to be God's prince, became His enemy. Like Mephibosheth, we are crippled. We deserve to die.

But the King, great David's greater Son, has had mercy on us, on account of the oath He swore to our forefathers (Luke 1:70–74). He has restored the land to His people (Rom. 4:13). He gives us a robe and ring, slays the fatted calf, rejoices over us, and listens to our humble advice (Luke 15:11–32). Despite our weakness, our ugliness, our sin, we are given places of privilege and honor. We are allowed to draw near and enter the King's throne room. We are made King's friends, and treated as His brothers. We are seated at His table.

We have seen that the coming of the kingdom means that Satan is defeated, and Christ and His people exalted to the right hand of the Father. The coming of the kingdom also means that the debt of sin has been paid and we can enter the heavenly sanctuary in Christ to commune with the triune God. In this chapter, we will see that by entering the sanctuary and kingdom of God we receive the gifts of the kingdom and the privilege of table fellowship with the King.

Power from on High

In Scripture, good kings not only establish justice when they ascend to their thrones, but also show mercy and give gifts. When Joseph became ruler over Egypt in fulfillment of God's promise to Abraham, he provided food for the entire world. When David became king over Israel, he showed mercy to the surviving members of Jonathan's household. The ideal king described in Psalm 72 is compared to "rain upon the mown grass, like showers that water the earth" (Ps. 72:6). Dew and rain are used throughout Scripture to picture the gifts of God descending from the heavenly cloud.[1] So also in Psalm 72, gifts and blessings flow like dew from the king to his people. It is fitting, then, that the ascension of Jesus is described in these same terms: "When He ascended on high, He led captive a host of captives, and He gave gifts to men" (Eph. 4:8).

These promised blessings are not merely IOUs that God will honor at some date in the distant future. Notice Paul's words: the Father through Christ *"has* blessed us with *every* spiritual blessing in the heavenly places" (Eph. 1:3, emphasis added). Though we have not received the fullness of heavenly blessing, we already enjoy the gifts that Christ has secured. We have already received a downpayment on the kingdom we are yet to inherit (2 Cor. 1:22; 5:5).

Spiritual Gifts

The Spirit Himself is the chief gift of the ascended King, of the Father and the Son (Matt. 7:11; Luke 9:13). This is what Peter told the assembled crowd at Pentecost. "[Christ] having been exalted to the right hand of God, and having received from the Father the promise of the Holy Spirit, He has poured forth this which you both see and hear" (Acts 2:33). The Spirit is Jesus' coronation gift to His people.

The Spirit is not only Himself a gift, but a bearer of gifts; He is the gift that gives a foretaste of all our future gifts. He is the "earnest" of our inheritance who guarantees that we will receive the fullness of the gifts that have been promised (2 Cor. 1:22; 5:5). God has confirmed His oath by giving His people a pledge of their future blessings now. All the blessings that Jesus has promised are available now through the Spirit of Christ. That is why Paul calls them Spiritual blessings.

Spiritual blessings are also called the blessings of the kingdom. The connection between the Spirit and the kingdom is very close. Jesus Christ, who is the kingdom incarnate, was anointed with the Spirit beyond measure (Matt. 3:13–17;

Luke 3:21–22). When Jesus cast out demons by the Spirit of God, it was a sign that the kingdom had come (Matt. 12:28; Luke 11:20). Paul said that the kingdom consists in righteousness, peace, and joy in the Holy Spirit (Rom. 14:17). When the apostles asked Jesus when He was going to restore the kingdom to Israel, He told them to wait instead for the Spirit to clothe them with power from above (Acts 1:6–8). The Spirit brought the power of the kingdom to the disciples, and the Spirit continually brings to us the power of the kingdom as well. When we are born again by water and the Spirit, we enter into the kingdom and begin to enjoy its power and life (John 3:5). Many of the gifts of the Spirit are also gifts of the kingdom: joy (Rom. 14:17), healing (1 Cor. 12:9; cf. Acts 3:1–10 and note the context), miracles, prophecy (1 Cor. 12:10), and peace (Gal. 5:22).

We have already seen that the kingdom exists wherever the exalted King is present among His people. Since Christ is now present by His Spirit (John 14:16–18),[2] we can also say that the kingdom of God exists wherever the Spirit of Christ is. The people who have entered and received the kingdom are those filled with the Spirit.

Throughout the Old Testament, moreover, the Spirit is present at the sanctuary. We have already seen that the glory-cloud of God is the visible presence of God through the Spirit; the Spirit hovered over the waters of creation, molding them into an orderly cosmos (Gen. 1:2).[3] This was the same cloud that settled on the tabernacle and temple, preventing the priests from entering (Ex. 40:34–48). In the new covenant, the cloud no longer prevents access. We are invited to enter into the fullness of the Spirit in His sanctuary, gazing with unveiled face at the mirror of God's glory (2 Cor. 3:18). At Pentecost, the Spirit descended not upon the Holy of Holies in Herod's temple, but upon the gathered disciples, the church of Jesus Christ. The new temple is not a building but a people. In this new temple, the Spirit distributes the gifts of the heavenly kingdom. When we assemble for worship, the Spirit refreshes us with the gifts of the King.

Through the Spirit the church has fellowship with the triune God. The Spirit of truth leads into all truth (John 14:17, 26; 16:13). He enables us to discern spiritual things, revealing to us the riches of God's wisdom and the deep things of God (1 Cor. 2:6–16). The Spirit opens the channels of communion and fellowship between God and man. Through the Spirit, we know God. To possess and be possessed by God, to know and be known, is the chief spiritual blessing of the kingdom.

The Gifts of the Kingdom

Car dealers frequently offer "package deals" as enticements to encourage consumers to buy. They promise a tape deck, a rear window defroster, or an automatic door lock—all at no extra cost. When you buy the car, you get all the "perks" besides.

In some New Testament passages, the phrase "kingdom of God" is used to refer to the "package deal" we receive in Christ.[4] By receiving Christ and fellowship with the Father through the Spirit, we receive all the "perks": "He who did not spare His own Son, but delivered Him up for us all, how will He not also with Him freely give us all things?" (Rom. 8:32). The kingdom is not only the "place" where we meet God, nor only the rule of Christ over all things; the kingdom is also the complex of blessings, the "package deal" we receive through the Spirit. When Jesus told His disciples to seek the kingdom above all, He was telling them to seek the blessings of the kingdom (Matt. 6:33), the heavenly treasures that are the chief treasures (Matt. 6:19–32). When Jesus compared the kingdom to a pearl of great price and to a treasure hidden in a field, He was referring to the inestimable value of the blessings we receive through and with Him—treasures of such absolute value that we must sell all we have to attain them (Matt. 13:44–46).

The Making of an Heir

The package deal of the kingdom, of which we have the down-payment by the Spirit, is a "grant" from Christ to the church

(Luke 22:29). The kingdom is a gift, our inheritance in Christ (Mark 10:25–27). To understand the gift of the kingdom more fully, we may consider the imagery of the inheritance.

It must be stressed at the outset that although one does not earn an inheritance, to receive an inheritance one must meet certain conditions, conditions that we cannot fulfill on our own. As sons of Adam we deserve to be permanently deprived of any share in the riches of the kingdom.[5] Adam was created to be the son of God—the heir of His Father's kingdom—but he was disinherited for breaking covenant. Through the sin of Adam, all were made sinners, and all came under condemnation of death (Rom. 5:12–21). Our ancestry is defiled; we come from the wrong side of the tracks. We can do nothing to qualify ourselves for the rich gift of the kingdom. If we are to receive the inheritance, our Father must qualify us as legitimate heirs. Like the kingdom itself, the conditions for our inheritance of the kingdom are gifts of God.

The Bible describes those conditions in a number of different ways. We receive the blessings of the kingdom only when through faith we are legally declared brothers and co-heirs of the true Son and Heir, Jesus Christ (Rom. 8:17; Heb. 2:11). The Father of Jesus must legally adopt us into His family. But through the Spirit, the Father does much more than that. To make us heirs, God not only grants us a legal right to the kingdom, but also causes us to be born again into the heir's family, "born not of blood, nor of the will of the flesh, nor of the will of man, but of God" (John 1:13). The Father not only adopts us, but also gives us new life.

It is fitting therefore that the Spirit who communicates the kingdom is the "Lord and giver of life." "Life," in fact, is often synonymous with the whole package of blessings of the kingdom; to "enter into life" is to "enter into the kingdom" (Matt. 19:17, 23–24). In John's gospel especially, "life" and the phrase "eternal life" refer to the same reality that the other evangelists call the "kingdom of God" (John 3:5, 16; 4:14; 5:21, 24; etc.). The Spirit communicates the kingdom, or life, because the Spirit communicates Christ, who is the Bread and

Tree of Life, who is, indeed, life itself (John 6:35; 14:6, 26, 28). The Bible teaches both that we must have new life to enter the kingdom, and that life is the central blessing of the kingdom.

To receive the inheritance of the kingdom, moreover, we must be cleansed. To enter into God's inner chambers where the Spirit distributes heavenly blessings, we must be washed by water and the Spirit (John 3:3, 5). To draw near to the old covenant sanctuaries, a person had to be ceremonially clean (Lev. 12–15). Unclean people and things were kept out of the tabernacle and temple. How much more does this same principle hold true in the new covenant. If no unclean thing could come near the copy, surely no unclean person can be brought into the true heavenly sanctuary.

Blood alone cleanses sinners and makes them fit to enter the presence of God in His throne room (Heb. 9:22). The old covenant washings and sacrifices, the writer to the Hebrews tells us, cleansed the flesh, but did not cleanse the conscience. The blood of bulls and goats did not take away sins. That is why, despite the bloody sacrifices of the Old Testament, the people could not draw near. They awaited a perfect sacrifice for sin, so that sins could be removed once-for-all by better blood. They awaited blood that could cleanse the conscience from dead works (Heb. 9:14). If men are to receive the blessings of the kingdom, they must first be forgiven of their sins (Matt. 18:23–35). Before we can inherit the gifts of the Spirit in the heavenly sanctuary of God, we must be cleansed by the blood of Christ.

But cleansing sin in not enough. Blank slates do not inherit the kingdom of God. Not only must sin be cleansed, but righteousness must be attained. The kingdom of God is given to the righteous, to the saints, to the glorious ones in whom the Lord delights. To enter the kingdom and receive its treasures, we must exchange our filthy robes for new robes of righteousness and glory (Zech. 3; Rev. 22:14). Like Jehoiachin, to sit at the king's table we need to have a change of clothing (2 Kings 25:27–30); we must be clothed with

Christ (Gal. 3:27).[6] Thus clothed, we can draw near to God with a clean conscience, know Him, and enjoy continual fellowship with Him. Reborn by water and the Spirit, washed in the blood of the Lamb, adopted into the Father's family, and clothed in Him, we can enter the inner sanctuary and receive the blessings of the kingdom.

In more common language, if we are to be heirs of the kingdom, we must be regenerated, adopted, forgiven, and justified.

All these conditions for entrance into the kingdom are symbolized and sealed in baptism. Those who receive the sign of baptism are legally entitled to receive the inheritance of the kingdom.[7] We are baptized into Christ's death and resurrection, which were for our justification (Rom. 6:1–11). By the Spirit, baptism also seals to us new life (John 1:33; 3:5; Acts 11:16) and cleansing (Matt. 3:1–11), and clothes us with Christ (Gal. 3:27). Baptism is a seal of our adoption. Through baptism, God seals us as sons, co-heirs with Christ of His kingdom. Having crossed through the baptismal waters, we enter the promised sanctuary land to enjoy its bounty.

The Beatitudes of the Kingdom

Jesus began His Sermon on the Mount by pronouncing blessings upon His people, which summarize the "package deal" that the Spirit grants to God's redeemed people in the kingdom. It is significant that there are eight Beatitudes. In Scripture, the number eight is associated with new life, the resurrection, the day of the kingdom, the beginning of the week of the new creation. An eight-fold blessing is a blessing that bursts out of the wineskins of the old creation and brings in the reality of the new. An eight-fold blessing is a kingdom blessing. In the Beatitudes, Jesus described the blessedness of those who have received and will inherit the kingdom.[8]

What are the Beatitudes or blessings of the kingdom?

- In the kingdom we receive *comfort* for our mourning. All tears are wiped away (Isa. 25:8; Rev. 21:4). Comfort means more than soothing; comfort means restoration, strengthening, and encouragement as well (2 Thess. 2:16–17). In the kingdom we receive comfort because in the kingdom God, the Comforter, gives Himself to us (Isa. 40:11; 66:11, 13; John 14:26).

- Inheriting the kingdom includes inheriting the *earth*. God's kingdom brings not only "spiritual" blessings, but material blessings. We have already inherited the earth because we are united to *the* Heir of all things (Rom. 4:17; 1 Cor. 3:21–23). Through history, Christ is ruling to give the earth to His people, and when He returns, His people shall inherit the renewed heavens and earth. In giving the earth to the saints for their inheritance, the Lord at the same time disinherits His enemies (Ps. 37:11).

- In the kingdom, our hungers and thirsts are *satisfied*. Proverbs 16:26 says that a man's hunger drives him. We are hungry beings, and life is a following of our hungers, desires, and drives. Jesus promises full satisfaction to those whose deepest yearning and desire is to see God's royal righteousness vindicated and established in the earth. In the kingdom, all our deepest desires find full satisfaction because in the kingdom we come face to face with the living God—the desire behind all our desires, for whom we pant and hunger (Pss. 17:15; 42:1–2).

- In the kingdom we find *mercy*. God is under no obligation to permit us to enter His holy kingdom. We are people of unclean lips, hands, and hearts. We owe an infinite debt that we can never repay. But God in His compassion has paid and forgiven the debt and because of His covenant mercies has given us the kingdom (Matt. 18:21–35). Without the gift of mercy, there would be no others.

- The kingdom is where we *see God*. Entering the kingdom means appearing before the face of the King enthroned between the cherubim (Ex. 23:14–17). Even now, though through a glass darkly, we can "see" God by faith. Gazing intently at the Lord who has become life-giving Spirit, we are transformed into His image from glory to glory (2 Cor. 3:12–18).

- Being in the kingdom means that we are called the *children of God*. We are adopted into His family and made brothers of the incarnate Son of the Father (Heb. 2:11). Our heavenly Father loves us, cares for us, protects us. Because we are children, we are heirs of God and fellow heirs with Christ (Rom. 8:17). Being children of God also means having authority to rule in and with Christ (John 1:12).

Laboring in the Vineyard

Samuel was one of the great saints of biblical history. His zeal for the Lord was unsurpassed. He was a prophet, priest, and judge, and his diverse ministry among the Israelites sparked a general revival. But Samuel, great as he was, had to be taught that God's ways are not the ways of a man. When Samuel was told to anoint a son of Jesse as king, he was certain that Eliab, Jesse's eldest, had been chosen. In fact Jesse's youngest, David, was the Lord's anointed (1 Sam. 16:1–13). Samuel had to be reminded that the Lord does not look on the outward appearance—Eliab's handsomeness or his stature or his strength—but upon the heart. God's choice of David was a reminder that the Lord chooses the foolish, weak, and base things of this world to confound the wise, strong, and admired (1 Cor. 1:27–28).

Throughout His earthly ministry, Jesus constantly taught and acted upon this revolutionary doctrine. He consistently emphasized that the poor of the land were the special objects of His preaching and ministry. He came preaching the kingdom to the oppressed poor (Luke 4:18). He promised the riches of the kingdom to those who are poor now, who mourn now, who hunger and thirst now, who are persecuted now (Luke 6:20–26). Publicans and sinners sat at table with Jesus (Matt. 9:10; Luke 15:1–7), and prostitutes entered the kingdom before Pharisees and scribes (Matt. 21:31–32). Camels have an easier time going through the eye of a needle than a rich man has entering the kingdom (Matt. 19:24). Jesus came to call not the righteous, but sinners to repentance (Mark 2:17). He came to flatten mountains and to raise valleys.

Jesus' call to the oppressed poor, the sinners, and the prostitutes was, it must be understood, a call to *repentance*. He preached the kingdom to the unrighteous in order to call them to a righteousness that surpassed the righteousness of the scribes and Pharisees. He promised true riches to oppressive tax-gatherers, but Zaccheus restored fourfold of all he had stolen (Luke 19:8). Jesus' ministry focused on the lowest strata of Palestine's society, but He ministered among them in order to change them. Heaven rejoices not over every sinner, but over every sinner who *repents*.

The kingdom is given to those who are lowly of heart, who humble themselves to receive mercy (Matt. 19:13–15). It is given purely of grace. God, as we have seen, baptizes us into the kingdom. But the kingdom is a *covenantal* gift: it not only brings the *promise* of abundant life, but also comes with a *demand* for righteousness and a threat of vengeance. Jesus brought this out clearly in his parable of the vineyard. There, the vineyard, representing the blessing of the kingdom, was taken from the unworthy renters and given to another people who would produce its fruit. This new people, the church, did not *earn* the kingdom of God; they became heirs by the grace of God. But the kingdom was a place of labor, a vineyard, in which the new people were to work to bring forth fruit pleasing to God. The church has not been given the gift of the kingdom to let it go to seed.

Nor does she receive the kingdom only to use its blessings purely for her own good. The church receives the gifts of the kingdom in order to bring forth fruit that pleases God. We receive the earth so that we can glorify and mold it into an image of God's heavenly temple-city. We receive comfort so that we can comfort others (2 Cor. 1:3–7). We receive mercy so that we can show mercy (Matt. 18:21–35). We see

God so that we can reflect His glory as lights in the world (Matt. 5:14–16). As those who have been rescued from the Jericho road, we are commanded to rescue others (Luke 10:25–37). Our baptism signifies not only our access to the gifts of the kingdom, but also our calling to lifetime, fulltime service to Christ. Baptism is not only an entitlement; it is an enlistment.

In a word, God's kingdom is a kingdom of righteousness.[9] The King requires total surrender (Luke 9:60–62; 18:29). Jesus said that our status and usefulness in His kingdom depends on our attention to the details of His law (Matt. 5:19), and He warned that our righteousness must exceed even the meticulous righteousness of the scribes and Pharisees. In fact, Jesus sometimes went further and said that righteousness is a condition of entrance into the kingdom (Matt. 5:20; 7:21; see 1 Cor. 6:9–10). Jesus did not teach that we could *earn* the kingdom, but He insisted in no uncertain terms that righteousness is a *necessary* fruit of the gift of the kingdom. If we wish to retain our inheritance, we must be faithful laborers in the vineyard, bringing forth the fruits of the kingdom.

Feasting in God's Presence

Throughout the Bible one particular royal gift is highlighted above all others—the gift of food. Melchizedek, the king of righteousness and peace, gave food and drink to victorious Abram (Gen. 14:18); Abram enjoyed bread and wine in a victory feast. When Joseph was raised to rule over Egypt, he fed the world (Gen. 41:57). David permitted Mephibosheth to eat with him (2 Sam. 9:13), and Nehemiah fed 150 Jews at his own table (Neh. 5:17).

The royal feast is one of the chief Old Testament images of the coming kingdom of God.[10] In the Psalms and the Song of Solomon, the marriage feast pictured the joyful fellowship of the heavenly King with His people (Ps. 45; Song 5:1). Proverbs 9 depicts the feast prepared by Wisdom, and Wisdom was understood to be a messianic figure. Ezekiel prophesied that King David would shepherd Israel and would feed her from his own hand (Ezek. 34:23). Isaiah described the messianic banquet that would take place on the mountain of the Lord. "And the Lord of hosts will prepare a lavish banquet for all peoples on this mountain; A banquet of aged wine, choice pieces with marrow, and refined, aged wine" (Isa. 25:6). Just as life was to be communicated to Adam and Eve through the fruit of the Tree of Life, so also the life and blessing of the kingdom is given in a feast.

Isaiah's prophecy that the messianic feast would take place at the mountaintop sanctuary of God was consistent with other Old Testament teaching about the sanctuary. Feasting is a central act in the corporate worship of God's people. The people of God assembled for the old covenant feasts at the tabernacle (Lev. 23; Deut. 14:22–29). The sanctuary was a place of feasting and joy, where the people of Israel were encouraged to eat oxen and sheep, and to drink "wine, or strong drink, or whatever your heart desires" (Deut. 14:26).

Of course, the sanctuary, as we have seen, was also where the people of God heard the Word read and explained. Word and feast ought not to be separated. The King speaks to His friends as they feast around His table. In light of this background, it is not surprising that the prophets would picture the fulfillment of God's kingship both as a feast at the sanctuary and as the spreading of the Word of God to the ends of the earth (Isa. 2:2–4).

The Feast of Life and Joy

Modern Christians often read the New Testament with little reference to the Old. Thus, when we read that Jesus again and again *fed* multitudes, we think that these are included in the Gospels merely to display Jesus' divine power. To a modern reader of the Bible, Jesus seems to be portrayed in the Gospels as a magician—a first-century David Copperfield.

When we view the Gospels with Old Testament eyes, however, it is evident that Jesus' feeding of the multitudes points to the fact that He is the promised messianic *King*. Feeding the people was a royal act, not a magic act. When Jesus fed five thousand men reclining on the green grass, He was showing Himself to be the promised David, the royal Shepherd who would lead His flock to pasture (Mark 6:30–44; see Ps. 23:5; Matt. 14:13–21; 15:32–39; Luke 9:11–17). The royal significance of these meals was not lost on the Jewish people. After one meal, "they tried to make Him king" (John 6:15). We should understand Jesus' association with the publicans and sinners in the same way. He showed His royal clemency by eating and drinking with the socially rejected (Mark 2:15–17; Matt. 11:19; Luke 15:1–2; 19:1–10).

Jesus made very clear the connection of the kingdom of heaven with the feast. He summarized the blessing of the kingdom as sitting at His table, feasting with Abraham, Isaac, and Jacob (Matt. 8:11; see Luke 14:15). Drawing on the Old Testament prophecies about the pilgrimage of the nations to the mountain of God (Isa. 2:2–4), Jesus said that men will come "from east and west, and from north and south, and will recline at the table in the kingdom of God" (Luke 13:29). The coming of the kingdom means that the nations of the earth will gather for a feast at the sanctuary. To inherit the kingdom is to enter into the joyous feast of God (Matt. 25:21, 23). Jesus described the kingdom as a wedding feast for a king's son (Matt. 22:1–14) and conferred the kingdom on His disciples in these words: "And you are those who have stood by Me in My trials; and just as My Father has granted Me a kingdom, I grant you that you may eat and drink at My table in My kingdom, and you will sit on thrones judging the twelve tribes of Israel" (Luke 22:28–30).

Receiving the kingdom involves not only enthronement, but also the privilege of eating with Jesus! With the apostles, we feast at the King's table, and sit judging the twelve tribes of Israel. We are given to eat of both trees of the Garden, the Tree of Life and the Tree of Judgment.

The kingdom feast that Jesus taught and enacted throughout His earthly ministry was "institutionalized" in the

Lord's Supper (Matt. 26:26–29; Mark 14:22–25; Luke 22:17–20; 1 Cor. 11:23–25). During the Last Supper, Jesus pointed to the connection between the Supper and the kingdom's feast (Matt. 26:29; Mark 14:25; Luke 22:18). The Lord's Supper is a foretaste of the joy and fellowship of the final wedding feast that Christ's people will enjoy when the Bridegroom returns. Every time the church celebrates the Supper of the Lord, Jesus is there as our host and guest. Every time the church celebrates the Lord's Supper, the future kingdom is manifested in the present, and through the Spirit the kingdom's power and life comes to us.

Jesus is present not merely as guest or as host. He is present as the very food that we eat. He is the bread from heaven come down for our nourishment; His flesh is true food, His blood true drink (John 6:41–65). His flesh satisfies all our hungers, and when we drink His blood we shall never thirst. The bread that we break in the Lord's Supper is a participation in His life-giving body, and the wine that we drink is a participation in His blood (1 Cor. 10:16). In the kingdom feast, Jesus Christ, the kingdom of God made flesh, gives Himself to His people as heavenly food. Because we feast upon Christ, we have life—the life of the new creation that has begun in Christ. We have no life in ourselves, but must receive life from Christ through the Spirit (John 6:63). Through the bread and wine, we receive Christ Himself and become bone of His bones, flesh of His flesh (Eph. 5:30, KJV).

It is true, of course, that the Lord's Supper refers back to the Cross. Too many Christians, however, treat the Supper as a somber recollection of the pain and suffering of our Savior. The emphasis in the Bible and in the early church was very different. The Supper is a recollection not only of the suffering of Christ, but even more of the results of His suffering and death. The Supper recalls the Cross because it is through the sacrifice of Christ that we enjoy the life of the kingdom. The Cross is not a symbol of suffering only, but also of victory. Jesus crushed Satan's head by His death. When we proclaim the Lord's death in the Lord's Supper, we are proclaiming His triumph over sin, death, and hell. The feast of the kingdom is, like Abraham's, a victory feast.

The early Christians understood this well. An anonymous sixth-century hymn exults:

> At the Lamb's high feast we sing
> Praise to our victorious King,
> Who hath washed us in the tide
> Flowing from his pierced side;
> Praise we him whose love divine
> Gives his sacred blood for wine,
> Gives his body for the feast,
> Christ is Victim, Christ the Priest.
>
> Mighty Victim from the sky,
> Pow'rs of hell beneath thee lie;
> Death is conquered in the fight,
> Thou has brought us life and light.

Rejoicing at the feast, we taste of the heavenly gift and the powers of the age to come (Heb. 6:4–6). Given the Spirit to drink, we become, as Ambrose put it, inebriated with the Spirit (1 Cor. 12:13; Eph. 5:18).[11] The Spirit grants the Beatitude of the kingdom in the feast:

- At the feast mourners are comforted (Isa. 25:6–8; Jer. 16:5–7).
- At the feast the hungry are filled.
- At the feast the pure in heart see God (Ex. 24:9–11).
- At the feast the peacemakers sit as the King's sons at His Table.
- At the feast, our inheritance—the earth, this world of eating and drinking—becomes a foretaste of the kingdom of heaven.[12]

Given the biblical emphasis on the feast of the kingdom, the lack of practical and theological attention given to the

Lord's Supper by contemporary evangelicals is little short of astounding. If anything is clear from the Gospels, it is that for Jesus the kingdom is a place of feasting. Yet, many who talk and write about the kingdom completely ignore this crucial dimension of Jesus' teaching. Some look for the future millennial reign of Christ. Others talk about the kingdom in connection with social and political action. Still others concentrate on the power of the kingdom manifested in "signs and wonders" and the charismatic gifts. But many neglect the very dimension of the kingdom that was evidently central for Jesus Himself: the kingdom of God is a feast.[13]

In biblical perspective it is no exaggeration to say that the central act of the kingdom of God, and the most basic form of the kingdom in this world, is the sacramental feast of the people of God within God's heavenly throne room, a feast that symbolizes and provisionally realizes the future feast of the consummation. Unless we keep the feast, we will not enjoy the blessings of the kingdom.

Conclusion: The Eucharistic World View[14]

Kenneth L. Myers has argued that the distinction between sacred and profane is symbolized in the Lord's Supper. Eating bread and drinking wine at the Lord's Table is not the same as eating a Whopper at the Burger King. The Supper transforms us in a way that the Whopper does not. Every time we celebrate the Lord's feast, we show that there is a wide difference between the sacred realm of the kingdom of God and the profane realm of the world.[15]

Myers is certainly correct to focus on the Lord's Supper. Our views of the Supper crystalize and summarize our entire world view. Irenaeus insisted against the Gnostics that his theology agreed with the eucharistic practice of the church, and the Eucharist agreed with his theology.[16]

But Myers draws precisely the wrong conclusion. Clearly there is a difference between the royal banquet of bread and wine and the paltry burger; there is indeed a difference between the King of Kings and the Burger King. At the same time, there is an equally obvious similarity: both are *meals*. Jesus did not, after all, invent an entirely new activity to symbolize the kingdom in this world. The central act of the kingdom could have been something really "spiritual," like chanting a mantra or channeling or meditation or navel-gazing. But Jesus instituted that most common of all human activities— eating and drinking—to symbolize the kingdom and to communicate life to His people.

The Lord's Supper thus teaches that the "sacred" is *not* something alongside of the "profane." The kingdom is not a reality running parallel to and occasionally intersecting life in this world. The kingdom is not even something "supernatural" added to the "natural" life of this world. Against all these, the Eucharist teaches that it is precisely *this* world—this material, physical world of eating and drinking—that is the "matter" of the kingdom of God. The kingdom is, ultimately, *this world* transfigured by the Spirit.

In the Supper, normal bread and normal wine are used. But these normal, "profane" elements become in the Eucharist a means of communion with God, a means of strengthening our union with Christ and of communicating the life of the age to come. The Eucharist in fact discloses to us the purpose and ultimate destiny of the entire creation—that the creation was made to reveal God, to be a means of knowing and communing with Him. The Eucharist teaches that *this* world is to be redeemed, transfigured into the kingdom of God. The bread and wine of the Eucharist are the "firstfruits" of the transformed creation.[17]

The Eucharist thus reveals the "sacramental" character of all of creation and all of life. The Whopper is not the same as the bread and wine, but the Whopper is, like the royal feast, a gift of God that becomes a means of life by the power of the Spirit. Calvin observed that in itself bread has no power to give life; we live only by the power of the Spirit.[18] In itself, the Whopper is a warmed-over lump of dead cow flesh pressed between a baked mixture of dead grain, topped with dead tomatoes and limp lettuce. Only the Spirit can "resurrect" dead meat and make it life for us. The Eucharist in a special and dramatic way points to our dependence upon the Spirit of Christ in the totality of our lives. Thus, the Eucharist shows that even the common meal is from God, that even the Whopper is "good," and can be "sanctified [i.e., made holy] by means of the word of God and prayer" (1 Tim. 4:4–5).

The Eucharist also teaches that the kingdom is not something enjoyed in isolation. Some have supposed that Jesus' saying about the kingdom of God being "within" was an encouragement to introspection and isolated meditation (Luke 17:21). That translation is itself open to serious question. Regardless of the meaning of that verse, Jesus' teaching about the kingdom feast leads to an entirely different conclusion, for a feast is necessarily a communal affair. The kingdom of God is realized in this world not only or even mainly in our own individual striving for holiness and piety, but in the church gathered at the Lord's Table.

Geoffrey Wainwright, upon whose *Eucharist and Eschatology* I have relied throughout this chapter, has noted that the Eucharist involves a biblical doctrine of progress:

> The eucharistic celebration does not leave the world unchanged. The future has occupied the present for a moment at least, and that moment is henceforth an ineradicable part of the experience of those who lived it. . . . When God has visited a receptive people in the eucharist, men have been made more righteous, the peace of God has been more firmly established among them, and the Holy Spirit has brought an ineffaceable experience of joy to their hearts. . . . the kingdom of God has come closer with each eucharistic celebration.[19]

The Eucharist points toward the goal of all creation and history—the eschatological wedding feast—and, if faithfully celebrated, brings that goal nearer to full realization. On the other hand, if the gift of the kingdom is offered to an unreceptive people, God intervenes to judge (1 Cor. 11:29–32). Either way, the celebration of the Eucharist leaves its inevitable mark on the world.

The Eucharist, finally, also teaches that our present experience of God's presence and blessing is incomplete. We have *tasted* that the Lord is good, sampled a bit of the heavenly gift; we have entered into the sanctuary (Heb. 6:4–6). But we are not yet filled. Like eating popcorn, the Supper just makes us want more. The taste makes us long all the more for the consummation of the promise, when we shall see God face to face, know even as we are known, and sit with Him at His table in the eternal kingdom of heaven.

SEVEN

◆

After the Feast

Human life is pregnant with analogies to biblical truth. As we saw in chapter 6, the character of our daily meals is brought to light by a consideration of the Lord's Supper. The analogy works the other way too. We can understand the Supper better by thinking about our common meals.

Each day begins with breakfast, which gives energy to undertake our day's work. Each day ends with dinner, a meal of enjoyment and rest, during which we reflect on and celebrate the day's achievements and are comforted concerning the day's disappointments.

Just as the whole day is bracketed by food, the whole workaday life of the Christian is circumscribed by the feast with the King at His Table. The Supper is a weekend meal, a time to celebrate the week's accomplishments, to offer the fruits of our labors to Him, to give thanks (Eucharist) to God for His good gifts, to hear His promises afresh.

But each week also begins (or should begin) with a feast at the Lord's Table. Just as Adam and Eve were allowed to eat of the Tree of Life in the Garden to empower them for their work, so also the Christian is empowered for his week's work by the food and drink of the Lord's Supper. Once we have been admitted to the sanctuary and feasted on the heavenly bread and wine, once we have heard the King's commandments repeated, He sends us out again, back to the world, back to work.

This liturgical pattern suggests that our participation in the Supper of the kingdom should have some effect on our work. But what precisely is that effect? Does the Christian's access by the Spirit to the gifts of the kingdom make him more effective in his work? More successful? Does a Christian have any "cultural" superiority to his pagan neighbor? What is the relationship between our eating and drinking with Christ and our calling to build an earthly replica of the heavenly kingdom?

The Kingdom and the "Dominion Mandate"

Our answers to these questions depend largely on how we define our terms. So, let us begin with a definition. As used by most theologians, the word "dominion" highlights men's interactions with one another and with creation, as well as all the products of man's creative labors. Products of dominion include buildings and books, cars and congressional reports, ideas and IBM PCs. "Dominion" activities include architecture and the arts, scholarship, science and technology, economics and business, politics, and so on. Since there is no elegant adjectival form of "dominion," I will use the words "culture" and "cultural" to describe this whole range of activities. Culture also includes more abstract realities as institutions, attitudes, habits, world views, and such small concrete realities as gestures, symbols, signs, etc.

Man is a cultural creature in the sense that his life is by creation design intertwined with these various kinds of pursuits. Culture is inescapable. No one lives in a culture-free zone. Men and women are constantly forming, preserving, or destroying culture. Culture is, as Henry Van Til put it, a "secondary environment." Not only do men form cultures, but in significant ways culture forms men.

If all that seems too technical and abstract, let me offer this simpler definition. In this chapter, I will generally use "dominion" and "culture" to refer to workaday activities and the products of those activities. "Dominion" is what we do Monday through Friday (or Saturday). To "take dominion" means simply to work, to engage in those activities connected to your calling, whether it be construction, scholarship, sales, horticulture, management, or whatever.

The Dominion Mandate and the Great Commission

The Great Commission is acknowledged by nearly all Christians to be closely connected with the kingdom of God. When He commissioned the apostles to make disciples of all nations, Jesus was commissioning them to preach the gospel of the kingdom to the furthest corners of the world, to call men to repentance and faith in Jesus Christ.

Some have suggested that the Great Commission is a republication of the original "dominion mandate" given to Adam (Gen. 1:26–28). The two are certainly related, but I believe it is more accurate to say that the dominion mandate sets the context for the Great Commission. The Great Commission *assumes* that the dominion mandate is still in force. There was no need whatever for Jesus to "republish" the cultural mandate, because humanity never stopped forming cultures.

Instead, the Great Commission addresses sinful humanity's propensity to form corrupt, perverse cultures. When people turn from the living God to sin and idolatry, it affects their work. They continue to interact with the creation, form cultures, and produce cultural objects, but they do so in ungodly ways. When men abandon the Creator, He delivers their societies to darkness, ignorance, and chaos (Rom. 1:18–32). They feast at the table of demons and go out to form demonic worlds.

The Great Commission instructs the church to call sinners to abandon their ungodly cultural pursuits and to pursue godliness in their cultural pursuits. When people respond with faith and repentance to the preaching of the gospel, they are not delivered from culture. They continue to be cultural creatures, but now they are regenerate cultural creatures. They become cultural creatures who know the truth that sets them free, who have access to God's life and His banquet, who love, worship, serve, and obey the Creator rather than the creature. The Great Commission calls men to abandon the table of demons and invites them to the feast of the kingdom. By feasting on Christ, they are conformed to His image, and return to the world, like Moses, reflecting His glory.

Redemption and Dominion

In a certain sense, only redeemed men and women can obey the cultural mandate. Adam was not, as we have seen, simply required to rule the earth, but to rule the earth *obediently* and *for God's glory*. Adam's kingly work was to be done in submission to God's kingship. The dominion mandate, understood in its complete scope, is priestly as well as royal; the dominion mandate will not be fulfilled until the world has been subdued to *God*. From this viewpoint, access to the kingdom meal leads to the fulfillment of the dominion mandate in a very direct sense. When men are translated into the kingdom, they turn to God in worship and offer their cultural products to Him as tribute. When they heed His Word, feed on Christ, and are conformed to Him, they work more righteously. When men turn to the Lord, they begin for the first time to exercise true dominion—obedient, priestly dominion.

Generally, however, the dominion command is understood as primarily a royal, cultural activity. How does entrance into the sanctuary relate to the royal mandate? Does conversion improve a person's ability in cultural pursuits? To put it baldly, are Christian painters better painters than non-Christian painters? Will a Christian businessman be a better businessman than a non-Christian? Are Christian physicians better than non-Christian physicians? Does eating at the Lord's Table on Sunday make us better workers on Monday?

Again, our answers depend very much on how we understand the questions. In a very obvious sense, the answer to all these questions is no. If you could not play the violin before your conversion, you should not expect to be able to play it afterward. If you did not understand (or enjoy) Shakespeare before your conversion, it will be just as difficult afterward. If you did not have a green thumb before your conversion, you should not expect to have a lush garden after you become a Christian.

Cornelius Van Til used the illustration of the buzz saw to explain the difference between the regenerate and the unregenerate. The unbeliever's problem is not that the saw blade—representing his reason, his senses, his artistic or technical skills—is dull. His blade may be razor sharp. The problem is the blade setting. It makes magnificent, finished cuts—at the wrong angle. Likewise, the unbeliever constructs magnificent philosophical systems—on fundamentally false premises. His problem is not a lack of rational or technical skill. It is his inherited sinful flesh, and his actual unbelief, rebellion, and sin. As Van Til put it, his problem is ethical, not metaphysical. Conversion does not make the blade sharper; conversion sets the blade back at the correct angle.

The Blessing of God

Yet, in another sense, entrance into the kingdom and access to the sanctuary do improve a person's cultural abilities. Those who have eaten and drunk with the King at the beginning of the week will be made more righteous by the Spirit and will also be more skillful workers throughout the week. Those who listen to the Word of the Lord, and obey it, build superior cultures. The God who designed the world instructs us in Scripture how to live in it. Those who are obedient are building cultures as God intended them to be built. After all, if your saw blade is set properly, you are apt to make better bookshelves.

That is true, first of all, because a Christian is under the blessing of God, and this blessing extends to the Christian's workaday pursuits as much as his Lord's Day worship. In an ultimate sense, the cultural products of a Christian are more valuable than the non-Christian's because they are more valuable to *God*. God accepts the works of the believer in Christ and so is pleased with them in a way that He is not pleased with even technically superior products from a non-Christian.

Unbelievers are under the wrath of God in every area of their lives. They are in a state of living death; they are walking corpses (Eph. 2:1). Everything they touch and make carries the stench of the grave. The Proverbs tell us that "the way of the wicked is an abomination to the Lord, but He loves him who pursues righteousness" (Prov. 15:9). Evil plans are abominable to the Lord (Prov. 15:26), and the heart of the wicked is only evil continually (Gen. 8:21). The unbeliever is accursed in all his ways, but, through Christ, all the ways and works of the righteous are pleasing to the Lord.

For example, though the Tower of Babel might have been, on narrowly architectural grounds, superior to the tabernacle, it was far inferior to the tabernacle if both are considered in their widest context and meaning. The tower was an expression of rebellion—a magnificent expression perhaps, but an expression of rebellion nonetheless. By contrast, the tabernacle was constructed in obedience to God's blueprint, having been made according to the heavenly pattern. God was (for a time) pleased with the one, but He immediately destroyed the other. There is an ethical and religious dimension to all our cultural work and works. God is the standard of value, and a "good" cultural product in an ultimate sense is what pleases Him.

The Cultural Superiority of Christian Culture

Let us lay aside "ultimate" perspectives for a moment. While "good" is defined by the Lord, it is also true that cultural pursuits have their own internal standards. These internal standards are not ethically neutral; they too must be consistent with Scripture. But when speaking of cultural products, we usually don't have these ethical dimensions in mind. Normally, when we talk about good paintings, good music, good scholarship, or good novels, we mean paintings, music, works of scholarship, and novels that meet relevant artistic or academic standards. A good novel is one written with technical proficiency, in which the multiple variables (plot, setting, character, imagery, etc.) conspire to form a coherent whole. A good historical study is one that is thoroughly researched, accurately presented, clearly written, and so forth. Though there is a basic ethical dimension to all cultural activities and products, this is not the only dimension.

The Christian can readily admit that, by the grace of God, even monstrous people can produce and have produced paintings and music and novels of breathtaking skill and beauty, and saints certainly have produced monstrosities. There appears to be no necessary or direct link between saintliness and cultural skill.

Yet, the Christian West has produced a culture—literature, buildings, paintings, sculpture, political systems, scientific and technological advances—that at the very least rivals and in many respects far surpasses other cultures. The Hagia Sophia and Chartres Cathedral are surely as architecturally magnificent as the Taj Mahal. Of course, great artistic creations are notoriously difficult to compare. But in the areas of science and technology, economics, and politics, the superiority of the Western achievement is today too widely acknowledged to require argument here.

The question, then, is whether the political and technological superiority of the West is a product of Christianity or of historical "accident"—superior climate, favorable geography, a richer gene pool, or whatever. This is in part a historical question. I believe, however, it can be argued theologically that, other things being equal, Christian individuals and nations will, by virtue of their commitment to Christ and their access to the gifts of His kingdom, be culturally superior to non-Christian individuals and nations. While the links between saintliness and cultural achievement may not be obvious, automatic, or direct, in the aggregate and over the long run the links will manifest themselves.

In order to illustrate this hypothesis, allow me to present several detailed individual "portraits."

• Suppose a businessman is converted. In an obvious sense, his working skills as a businessman have not automatically improved. He still has the same training and skills in management, forecasting, and marketing as he had before his conversion. Nonetheless his faithfulness to God will make him a better businessman. He realizes that God expects his "yes" to be "yes" and his "no" to be "no," and he begins to acquire a reputation as a fair dealer. He treats his employees respectfully and sympathetically, and their personal affection to him makes them work harder. After sitting through a series of sermons on the prophecy of Malachi, moreover, he becomes convinced that, like Abraham, he should tithe if he is to accept bread and wine from the Greater Melchizedek (Gen. 14:17–20). He learns that the businessman who does not tithe is foolish. On the other hand, God has promised to bless tithing (Mal. 3:8–10). Other things being equal, a tithing businessman is a better businessman than a nontithing businessman. A nontithing businessman has not taken account of the most important economic factor in the business climate: God.

• Suppose an English professor is converted. Does his conversion make him a better scholar? In one sense, no. He still has the same reservoir of knowledge, the same linguistic skills, the same trained sensitivity to the nuances of meaning in a literary text. But in another sense the faithful Christian English professor will be superior *as a scholar*. Because he seeks to govern his mind by the Word of God, he will resist nihilistic and fundamentally stupid literary fads and will not waste his time pursuing what he knows to be barren theories. Because he is a Christian, he will know instinctively that radical deconstructionism is a dead end and Derrida a pretentious phony, and he won't be shocked to learn that De-Man was a Nazi. The Spirit will give him boldness to say so, and he will seem prophetic to his colleagues. As he absorbs the Bible, he will begin to understand the patterns and archetypes that God has built into the creation, patterns and archetypes that are reflected in the literary texts that he studies as a scholar. He will begin to have a better understanding of those works as he begins to share the thought-world of the authors.

• Suppose a physician is converted. Again, she will have no more technical skill after her conversion than she had before. If trained as a orthopedist, she will not suddenly be able to practice obstetrics. On the other hand, being a Christian will make her a superior physician in a number of ways. As she studies her Bible, she will learn that God is the One who heals, and she will begin to recognize the limited power of medical technology. As she draws nearer to the Lord, she will learn more and more that her patients are not machines, and that they are more than bodies. She will begin to see that physical illnesses sometimes have moral and spiritual causes. She will treat her patients as distorted images of God. Because that is the truth about her patients, she will be more effective as a physician. She may become convinced that socialized medicine is another pretension of the messianic state, and she will oppose the system on both professional and moral grounds.

• Suppose an assembly line worker becomes a Christian. As with the others, there is an obvious sense in which he will not be a better worker after his conversion. Yet, because he goes to a church that practices weekly communion and is serious about church discipline, he is motivated to make every effort to get along with people. When he has an argument with a co-worker, he takes him aside to work things out. Realizing that he has been stealing his employer's time, he stops taking the extra ten minutes on his lunch break and even offers to make restitution by working several hours of free overtime. Instead of concentrating on protecting himself, he tries to help his fellow workers do a better job—giving encouragement or nudging them when they slack off. His supervisor begins to see him as a potential shift supervisor.

These portraits, of course, show only one side of the picture. But they suggest that the faithful Christian worker will do things that the non-Christian may not do. Because the Christian worker lives under God's blessing and strives for obedience on the job, his work will be better than it would have been had he not been a Christian.

All this does not, of course, necessarily imply that the Christian businessman, scholar, or physician will be more "successful" by contemporary standards. The tithing businessman's cash flow may actually decline; the English professor may be denied tenure; the physician may lose patients who expect a quick fix for their pain; and the assembly line worker's fellows may resent his chances for advancement. But their conversion will, in an important sense, make them more effective in their vocations than they would have been otherwise. Eating with the King every weekend changes people.

The Cultural Failure of the American Church

Some will doubtless respond to this argument by appealing to the empirical evidence of our times. Look at all the horrid stuff that Christians produce, a skeptic will say. Look at all the horrid Christian art, listen to the horrid Christian music, watch all the horrid Christian movies. Another might say, Christians are notoriously unreliable, lazy, and sloppy in their work. How can anyone say that Christians are culturally superior?

Two responses are possible. First, not all converts take their faith seriously. An English professor or physician who makes a profession of faith, but who never cracks his Bible or attends worship, cannot expect his faith to affect his vocation. Not all churches, moreover, teach the whole Bible, practice church discipline, celebrate communion frequently. Some sectors of the evangelical church have for decades neglected cultural matters or declared them "worldly." In this climate, it is not surprising that lay Christians have not tried to work out the implications of Christian faith for their vocation.

American evangelicals, moreover, have generally cut themselves off from the intellectual and cultural treasures of

Christendom, to their own great loss. The appalling state of Christian "culture" is probably the result of an ingrained anti-intellectualism, hostility to history and the arts, and anticultural pietism—that is, the product of an unbiblical teaching and practice. Evangelical culture has come to its present condition because the church has failed to teach that there is any connection at all between the kingdom of God and culture. Christian culture is in disarray because the church has completely separated the sanctuary from the workplace, the Lord's Table from the workbench, the feast from the job.

Second, there is not, it seems to me, much to admire in contemporary non-Christian culture. The church may have no Bachs, but the world has little to boast about. Is contemporary Christian music worse than Madonna or Billy Idol?

The Meaning of Progress

Can these same arguments be applied to entire nations? Will nations that are permeated by Christianity, in which the majority of people or the leading minority have access to the table of the King—will such nations be culturally superior to non-Christian nations?

Again, there is a very obvious sense in which the answer is no. Traditional Chinese culture—in its art, architecture, philosophy—was more highly developed than the more Christian cultures of Latin America and Africa. Any number of similar examples might be offered. And, of course, cultural progress is not the primary effect of the permeation of the gospel into a culture. The primary effect is ethical transformation. As more and more people in a nation submit to King Jesus, and enter His kingdom to hear His Word and feed on His flesh and blood, they will turn from their idols and from their sin. Nations will learn of God's ways, and will devote themselves to worshiping and serving the King of heaven and earth. Christian nations will become devoted to God, will obey His will, and will pursue justice and peace in human relations. Cultures transformed by the kingdom will be more like the heavenly kingdom as they do God's will on earth as in heaven.

But will progress in righteousness lead to, say, scientific and technological progress? Historically, it is undeniable that cultures that have been deeply permeated by the powers and truth of the kingdom have progressed in these ways. Indeed, some scholars, such as Stanley Jaki, attribute the West's technological and scientific superiority to the influence of the Christian world view.

The reason for this is not hard to find. Christianity is the truth not only about God, but about the world. Christian scientists know that the world is not a machine, not divine, and not eternal. Knowing these truths makes them better scientists. A society in which most of the scientists know these things will develop superior science and technology to a nation where the "scientists" think the world sits on the back of a turtle. Freed from the burden of seeking infallibility in the creature, Christians philosophers should be better philosophers than their pagan counterparts, and so a Christian people will produce better philosophy.[1]

Outside of Christ, all men are slaves to sin and Satan. They believe Satan's lies not only about "religious" matters, but also about the world. People under Satan's dominion are duped into believing the absurd theory that the world just sprang into existence, and they teach their children the same foolishness! As the Word is proclaimed and as men and women are freed from the dominion of Satan, they turn from lies to the truth. And, knowing the truth about the world, they are better equipped to subdue and rule it in a technological and cultural sense.

Conclusion

However closely related they might be, we must be careful not to *identify* technological and cultural progress with the growth of the kingdom. Every event of history has its place in the history of the kingdom, but it is not always possible for us to see how particular events fit into that history. It may be that what is called "progress" is, in reality, something very different.

The ambiguities of technological (or other) progress are best illustrated in modern medicine. Is it progress for physicians to be able to fertilize eggs in a petri dish and to plant them in a woman's uterus? Is it progress to be able to transplant beating hearts from one body to another? Is it progress to be able to use the tissue of aborted fetuses to cure Alzheimer's disease?

Our answers to these questions depend on whether we consider these acts to be ethically permissible. If they are permissible, then certainly these new capabilities represent progress. If they are not permissible, then these new capabilities represent ghoulish tinkering and idolatrous pretension. What comes disguised as the voice of an angel of progress may in reality be the echo of the ancient temptation, "You shall be as gods."

EIGHT

◆

The People of the Kingdom

One of the recurring settings in fairy tales, myths, and other literature is the labyrinth. Sometimes the labyrinth takes the form of a forest, as in Hansel and Gretel. In other stories, the maze is a dungeon crawling with vicious monsters. In Umberto Eco's *The Name of the Rose*, the library is a labyrinth. (Take a moment to think about that, especially if you love to read!) Whatever form it takes, however, the labyrinth is a place of fear and confusion, a place that must be escaped. Stories often turn on the hero's ability, or inability, to find his way out of the labyrinth.

Books are in some ways like labyrinths. If you have been diligent enough to read this far in this book, you will have had a sense of wandering through one "room" after another. For a while we considered one hall of God's palace, stopping to admire the furnishings, and then we moved on to the next room. The specific point of similarity between a book and a maze is the fact that the reader does not know where he is heading. He innocently steps in the front door, but realizes after a few moments that he is not sure where the exit is, and he may begin anxiously to doubt whether or not he will ever get out.

Yet, if you have been careful to follow the bread crumbs that have been dropped along the way through the maze of

141

this book, you will have noticed that our consideration of the heavenly realities of the kingdom has invariably led toward the same destination, and you will have begun to find the way out.

As we followed the passageway leading from Satan's defeat and Christ's exaltation, for example, we were led to consider Christ's reign over His people. Our perusal of the open sanctuary led us into the new temple. We lingered momentarily at the King's Table to take note of His guests. As we have moved from room to room, we have stumbled again and again over the same obstinate fact. In every case, our examination of heavenly realities led us ultimately to an earthly reality. You can exit this book only by the west door. If this book is a labyrinth, the central room, where the treasure is hidden, is the church.

Kingdom and Church

It has been said that "Jesus announced the kingdom, but ended up with the church." Jesus hoped, it is said, to establish a wonderful new order of things, but His efforts were frustrated. Paul picked up the shattered pieces of Jesus' dream, rearranged them, and the church was the disappointing result. Generations of Christians gradually sucked the life from the church, reducing her to a static, lifeless institution, far inferior even to the charmingly unpredictable charismatic assemblies of Paul's day. Later generations bottled up the Spirit that Jesus had tried to release.

Though evangelical Christians would surely reject this historical reconstruction, something like this attitude toward the church is not unusual. In theory, many evangelicals believe that the church is something of an afterthought, a "parenthesis" between God's dealings with the true earthly object of His love—the people of Israel.

In practice, many treat the church as a more or less helpful addendum to the Christian life—if, that is, one can get free on Sunday mornings. The church is an aid to devotion, like rosary beads or a crucifix. If it makes you feel closer to God, fine. If not, well, one can surely be a Christian without being a member of the church. For all the professed religiosity of Americans, comparatively few believe that regular association with a specific group of people is a necessary and central part of a genuinely Christian life. Fewer still think of the church as an institution with real authority over her members; ask any pastor who has tried to enforce discipline, and he will show you his scars. The fact that evangelicals who are serious about the church feel compelled to flirt with Rome and Constantinople suggests that something is terribly amiss in the evangelical world.

The biblical view of the church is far different. The apostles could not have imagined anyone living the Christian life outside the church. Outside the church was the "world," the system still under the dominion of Satan and sin. Only in union with the body of Christ could one be united to Christ Himself. Baptism into Christ's death and resurrection was understood to be simultaneously an incorporation into the fellowship of believers, and at the Lord's Table the saints participated together in the Savior's life-giving body and blood. Submission to Christ meant submission to the leaders He had installed (Eph. 4:11–16; Heb. 13:17). The New Testament everywhere assumes that membership in the church is normal and normative.

The church, moreover, was no afterthought. One of Jesus' main aims in His First Advent was to gather a *people,* to begin building His church, His worshiping assembly (Matt. 16:13–20), to gather His "little flock" (Luke 12:2). And He intended this people to be organized as an institution, with designated rulers and definite procedures, a particular form of worship and life (Matt. 16:13–20; 18:15–20). The erection of the church was one of the essential features of the new order of things that Jesus called the kingdom of God.[1]

What Is the Church?
It will be helpful before going further to define "church." That is not as easy as it might sound. The church, of course, is people, not buildings or programs or bureaucracies. But that

definition of the church simply begs the question, *Which* people? Historically, a distinction has been made between the "visible" church and the "invisible" church; the "visible" church consists of those whose names are on the membership rolls of some local congregation, while the "invisible" church consists of those whose names are written in the Lamb's Book of Life. This is a helpful distinction because it reminds us that not everyone who professes Christ will be welcomed into the eternal kingdom, and that the local membership rolls are not identical to the Lamb's rolls (Matt. 7:15–23).

But the distinction between "visible" and "invisible" can also be misused. That happens when Christians try to discern who is a member of the "invisible" church, and who is not— a futile exercise that can lead to an attitude of suspicion disguised as piety. Some Christians are rather like a man going through mid-life crisis who dreams of a perfect woman to replace his aging wife; the concept of a perfect "invisible" church is used to rationalize abandonment of what is, to all appearances, a sagging, wrinkled "visible" church.

Nowhere, to be sure, do the New Testament writers flinch from a full acknowledgment of sin and turmoil within the church. The apostles would no doubt have grimly nodded if told of some wit's suggestion that the church is like Noah's ark: if it weren't for the rain outside, you couldn't stand the stench inside.

Yet, in the Bible the "visible" church is addressed as if it were identical to the "invisible" church. The "visible" church is described as the spotless virgin bride of Christ, the temple of the Holy Spirit, the harmonious body of Christ (Eph. 5:25–30; 1 Cor. 3:16–17; 12:4–31). When Paul addressed the Ephesian church, he addressed the whole church, not some super-spiritual elite, as the elect (Eph. 1:1–11). All members of the "visible" church were counted and treated as saints, as Christians.[2] Besides, as it has been said, the "visible" church is, in the last analysis, the only one we've got.

In this book, then, I am using "church" almost exclusively to refer to the living, breathing, all-too-visible (and audible) body of baptized sinners that gathers for worship every Sunday morning in the Baptist (or Presbyterian or Anglican or Catholic) church on the corner.[3] I will also use "church" to refer to the sum-total of all those throughout the world who gather somewhere to confess the name of Jesus Christ as Lord, to hear His Word, to celebrate (however infrequently) the sacrament of His Table, along with their children.[4] In this book, however, I am not using "church" to refer to the eternally elect. As I have defined her, the church is certainly a mixed multitude. Yet, though fully aware that the church has "false sons in her pale," in this book I will, like the apostles, count and treat the church as the elect people of God.

This chapter explores some of the relationships between the kingdom and the church. That is a highly complex issue, and I make no claim to have treated it exhaustively. I suggested in the first chapter that the new people of God is one "feature" of the new world order, the new creation, that the Bible calls the kingdom of God. In this chapter, I will further refine that formulation. Interspersed with a historical perspective on the people of God is an exploration of the relationship between the kingdom and the church under several headings: the church as the people that possess and will inherit the kingdom; the church as the new temple; the church as the bride in a new covenant with the King; and the church as the mother of a new kingly race.

A Tale of Two Cities

Why did God make woman? Puzzled men from every age have asked that question in one form or another. In the movie version of John Updike's *The Witches of Eastwick*, Jack Nicholson's devilish character suggested hopefully that woman is a disease; if that were the case, he manically mused, there might be some chance for a cure.

However damaging to the male ego, the Bible's answer is clear: God made woman because "it is not good that man should be alone." God created Eve to help Adam accomplish his commission to subdue and rule the earth (Gen. 2:18–25). Adam and Eve were to work together to fill the earth, and to construct an earthly city that reflected the heavenly city of God. The original agents of earthly dominion were a man and his wife. In covenant with the Lord and with one another, they were to pursue their calling.

God did not, of course, mean for Adam and Eve to accomplish this task by themselves. He also told them to "be fruitful and multiply, and fill the earth" (Gen. 1:28). Ruling the earth presupposed multiplying and filling it. When Adam and Eve's children had grown, they were to find spouses of their own and form separate households, from which they were to pursue their particular callings (Gen. 2:24). God intended Adam and Eve to begin to produce an entire race of rulers to share His rule over the creation.

The human race was to work as in harmony to accomplish God's purposes,[5] but this unity was not to be uniformity. Men and their households were to cooperate with one another, but God did not intend for all people to live together in one place or to adopt the same way of life. Just as the earth was created with diverse resources (Gen. 2:11–12), so also even sinless men would have had diverse tastes, gifts, plans, ways of doing things—and this diversity was fully a part of God's plan. As each man left his father and mother to cleave in covenant to his wife, a new household, a new center of dominion, was to be created. These households would eventually join together in cities and nations blanketing the whole earth, ruling and subduing the earth to the glory of God.

Not a single megalopolis, but many earthly cities were to result—all of them diverse replicas of the infinitely rich archetypal city of God. God intended the human race to praise Him with a symphony of harmonious voices, not in a monotone. God surrounds Himself with a rainbow, not a grey cloak. God, we trust, delights in Gothic architecture as well as Romanesque; He is pleased with baroque as well as classical music; His people were governed not only by judges, but later by kings. Like the triune God Himself, the human race and the culture it created was to be a diversity-in-unity, and a unity-in-diversity.

The Divided Race

Sin, and God's judgment on sin, disrupted the realization of this plan. God had created a unified human race, but because of sin it was divided. Not only was the human race divided, it was in conflict. Since Adam, the seed of the Serpent has waged an unremitting war against the seed of the woman (Gen. 3:15). As Paul makes clear, the Seed of the woman is Jesus Christ. In a secondary sense, all who are united to Him are the seed. Thus, because of the sin of Adam, the race that was intended to transform the matter of creation into a replica of the heavenly city occupies two antagonistic cities. Instead of harmony and concord in the midst of diversity, the human race is divided into two opposing armed fortresses.

Scripture teaches several important facts about this conflict within the human race:

- The conflict between the two races within humanity is *radical;* it goes to the root. The conflict does not have to do primarily with culture or politics or taste; the main conflict of history is not between conservatives and liberals, or between America and the world. It is not so superficial a conflict. This conflict has to do with the heart. Indeed, as Solzhenitsyn says, the conflict is carried on in every heart; even the Christian remains a son of Adam.
- The conflict is *comprehensive.* At every point and at every moment, the seed of the Serpent contends with the seed of the woman. At every point, the two are in a state of cold or hot warfare. There is what theologians call an "antithesis" between the two races of the human race.
- The division is *eternal.* Sin irremediably disrupted the human race. When Christ returns to bring the conflict finally to an end, the human race will remain divided between those who are cast into the lake of fire and

those who are invited into the wedding feast of the Lamb, between the sheep and the goats, between wheat and tares (Matt. 25:31–46).

The radical division and conflict within the human race appeared very early. The history of fallen man began with an act of fratricide: Cain rose up and killed Abel his brother. The reason for Cain's envy of his brother is noteworthy: the issue was worship, liturgy (Gen. 4:4–5). This is always the basic issue that divides one part of the human race from the other. Cainites served and worshiped idols; Sethites worshiped the living God (Gen. 4–5). As Augustine explained, the two cities are distinguished by their different objects of love—either self or God. Though the conflict among the races of the human race is comprehensive, it centers on the issue of worship.

Even sinful men, however, retain a created desire to produce a unified race and a unified city. God made from one blood all nations under heaven; all are descendants of Adam. Men "naturally" hope and strive to restore the Edenic unity of the human race. From the Tower of Babel to the United Nations to recent fantasies of a "New World Order," people have expended themselves to restore the unity that sin dissolved. But sinners generally seek to *impose* uniformity upon one another, rather than pursuing harmony. God intended diversity, and sinners produce conflict; God intended unity under His law, and sinful men impose uniformity on each other.

Hence, on the plains of Shinar, in direct violation of God's command to fill the earth, rebellious men gathered to build a city "lest we be scattered abroad over the face of the whole earth" (Gen. 11:4). God's judgment on Babel underscores the fact that only God can heal the breach within the human race. When sinful humans seek to reunify on their own terms, they end in confusion. When they gather themselves together against the Lord, He disdainfully scatters them (Gen. 11:6–9; cf. Ps. 2). But God still holds out the promise that the harmony of the human race will one day be restored.

A Peculiar People

Haste makes waste, said Aesop. And, in some situations, haste can be deadly. A physician's hasty diagnosis or a surgeon's impatient incision can do irreparable harm. Like a skilled physician, God deals with sinners patiently. To avoid harming the patient, He gives people no more power or responsibility than they are able to stand. We have already seen several times how God gradually restored and fulfilled the creation order of His kingdom. Even though Adam sinned, God still intended for his descendants to be sons of God. But God did not immediately permit Adam's children to sit on thrones, or to reenter the sanctuary.

So also, God did not immediately reunify the human race. Instead, after the calamitous events at Babel, God began to gather from the human race a separate race, from the peoples a peculiar people, from the nations a holy nation (Gen. 12:1–3; Ex. 19:5–6). As God protected sinful men from His holiness by erecting a tabernacle, so also He protected them from their own folly by erecting boundaries between His chosen people and the other nations of the earth. God isolated Israel from the nations by such symbolic boundaries as the food laws, laws concerning dress, and the law of circumcision.

At the same time, however, Israel was to be an instrument for the reunification and redemption of the human race. From this race would come a New Man, and through Him a new humanity that would embrace all peoples. It is significant that God began the process of re-creating the human race with a man and a woman: Abraham and Sarah. Abraham was a new Adam, who through his household was to extend his dominion over the Promised Land. In Abraham's descendants through Isaac, God began to accomplish in miniature His plan for all humanity and all history.

This new human race was called, first of all, to be a nation of priests. Wherever he travelled in the land, Abraham built altars (Gen. 12:8; 13:4, 18; 22:9). Later, Israel was set apart preeminently as a worshiping community, a people whose reason for being was to honor and obey the King of heaven, a people redeemed from slavery to worship the Lord exclusively (Ex. 19:1–6; 20:1–3).[6] Like Adam, Israel's first priority was worship.

It was fitting that, as a new humanity within the human race, Israel should also be a nation of rulers. She was not only a priestly nation, but also a nation of kings—a royal priesthood. Though Abraham did not inherit the land, he did gather vast riches and commanded an army of over three hundred men that defeated the Canaanite kings of the time (Gen. 13:2; 14:14). Through Isaac, the Lord promised Jacob that his descendants would multiply and rule among the nations (Gen. 27:27–29; 28:2–4). Even during her captivity in Egypt, Israel was fulfilling her calling as a new race, multiplying throughout the land (Ex. 1:7).

But Israel fulfilled her royal calling most fully after she was delivered from captivity in Egypt. Under Joshua, she conquered the Canaanite peoples, and after the conquest, Israel divided the land among her tribes, each family receiving a parcel of the Promised Land to till as its own garden. David extended his dominion over surrounding nations (Ps. 18:43), and Solomon received tribute from foreign rulers (1 Kings 10:1–10). Israel's royal calling was not confined to her kings. The entire nation could sing that the Lord "subdues peoples under us, and nations under our feet" (Ps. 47:3). Israel was an Adamic race, a race that inherited the land promised to them and ruled over it under God's direction.

By fulfilling God's purposes for mankind, Israel was to be a model of what all nations and the whole race were intended to be: a unified people worshiping the Lord, living in obedience to Him, and ruling the earth to His glory. The global scope of Israel's ministry was embedded in the original promise to Abraham: "In you all the families of the earth shall be blessed" (Gen. 12:3). Everywhere in the Old Testament, the nations are called to follow the example of Israel by worshiping and serving God, and submitting themselves to His good commandments (Pss. 22:27–28; 46:10; 47:8; 67:3–4;

100:1–2; 117:1). Isaiah prophesied that in fact the nations would someday stream to a new Zion (Isa. 2:2–4). Israel existed not for herself, but for the world.[7] She was a type of the kingdom and an instrument for its establishment.

Though we frequently fail to notice it, God's people did serve as a model to other nations under the old covenant. Throughout the ancient world, kings paid obeisance to the Lord of Israel. Pharaoh acknowledged that Joseph's wisdom was from God (Gen. 41:39), and Joseph married the daughter of what must have been a converted Egyptian priest (Gen. 41:45).[8] The Queen of Sheba praised the Lord for His mercy to Israel in raising up a king like Solomon (1 Kings 10:9), and all the earth sought audience with the most wise king (1 Kings 10:24). The Ninevites repented under the preaching of Jonah (Jonah 3:5–10), and after living like a beast for many days, Nebuchadnezzar finally humbled himself before the Lord (Dan. 4:28–37). Israel actually served as God's instrument for turning the human race to homage and obedience to the King of all the earth.

Cain and Abel Revisited

Despite these examples of faithfulness, the history of Israel was frequently one of failure. She did not live up to God's requirements. Already during Solomon's reign, she had begun to turn from her exclusive devotion to the Lord (1 Kings 10:14–11:8). Immediately after Solomon's death, the kingdom of Israel was torn into northern and southern kingdoms. Because of the harshness of Rehoboam, the new human race, like the old, became divided and was often in civil war (2 Chron. 10:12–15). Called to be the peculiar people of God, Israel became instead a mirror of the divided human race. Instead of worshiping the Lord, Israel turned to idols. Though called to be a royal nation, Israel was eventually reduced to slavery.

The southern kingdom of Judah remained faithful to the Lord for a time. Many of the priests and Levites fled from the northern kingdom of Jeroboam when he prohibited them from serving the Lord (2 Chron. 11:13–14). Meanwhile, Jeroboam set up high places where the people of the northern kingdom worshiped satyrs and golden calves (2 Chron. 11:14). As with Cain and Abel, the division within Israel centered on worship. Over time, however, Jerusalem became as corrupt as her sister Samaria (Ezek. 23), and God sent both kingdoms into exile as a punishment for their idolatry (2 Kings 17:7–18). Like Cain, both were spewed out of the land.

The prophets of the exile, however, held out hope for the reunification of the divided people. Dry bones would take on new life (Ezek. 37:1–14). The stick of Judah would be tied together with the stick of Joseph or Ephraim, and the Lord would make them "one nation in the land, on the mountains of Israel" (Ezek. 37:15–23). Under the leadership of Ezra and Nehemiah, this promise of restoration was literally fulfilled. But the prophecies of a resurrected and reunited kingdom pointed beyond the restoration of the people of Israel to the land, to a time when a new David would shepherd the Lord's people forever (Ezek. 37:24–28). Jeremiah likewise looked forward to the restoration of the people of God to their pasture to fulfill the Adamic commission to be fruitful and multiply (Jer. 23:1–4).

Clearly, the prophets looked forward not only to the coming of the Messiah, but to the re-creation of the people of God. Part of their hope for the coming kingdom was a hope for a renewed, reunified Israel, an Israel that would remain faithful and would rule among the nations (Isa. 49:6, 23; 55:1–5).[9] The prophets looked forward to a transfigured Israel, the full reality of which Old Testament Israel was a shadowy type.[10]

The Kingdom Transferred

As I write, Thanksgiving is still two weeks away. Yet, already the Walmart up the street is full of Christmas trees, blinking lights, illuminated Santas, snowmen, angels, and who knows what else—all of which has been on display for at least a month. Even Peanuts' Charlie Brown laments the commercialization of Christmas. More seriously, even when the basic facts of the Christmas story are recalled, their significance is lost in a flurry of sentimentality. Tell someone that Christmas has everything to do with God's remedy for human *sin,* and you'll get, at best, a blank stare; at worst, random violence.

The wise men have become part of commercialized Christmas lore. At the Walmart, the illuminated wise men are displayed right next to the blinking Santas. Like all the features of the biblical Christmas story, the significance of the wise men's search for the Christ is completely lost. In Matthew's gospel, in fact, the wise men play an almost tragic role. When the wise men arrived in Jerusalem asking for the king of the Jews, "all Jerusalem was troubled" (Matt. 2:3). Imagine, the city of the great King was *troubled* at the thought that the Messiah had been born! The Gentile magi sought the newborn Messiah to worship Him, while the same news drove the king of Israel into a murderous rage.

Matthew 2:15 ("Out of Egypt did I call My Son"—Hosea 11:1) connects the flight from Bethlehem with the Exodus of Israel from Egypt. But this verse seems out of place. Matthew applies this prophecy to Jesus' flight from *Israel,* not to His later return from Egypt to Nazareth (vv. 19–23). Matthew's point is that Israel had become like Egypt, troubled at the announcement of deliverance. Herod had become a Pharaoh, ready to commit mass infanticide to secure his throne against a supposed rival. He had acted, as it were, as an angel of death, slaughtering the "firstborn" of the "Egyptians," while "passing over" the true Israel who had fled to safety—in Egypt!

The story of the wise men provides a preview of the conflict that dominated much of Jesus' earthly ministry. Jesus, Son of Abraham and Son of David, was an Israelite of the Israelites. He came as the Messiah to proclaim the kingdom to the Jew first, and then to the Greek (Rom. 2:9–10). But the Jewish leaders and people, like Herod and the city of Jerusalem, resented and rejected Him. Jesus came to His own, but His own did not receive Him (John 1:11). Israel had become like the seed of the Serpent (John 8:44) seeking to kill the Seed of the woman; she had become like Cain rising up against One greater than Abel (Heb. 12:24).

As time went on, Jesus' teaching became more and more preoccupied with the Lord's rejection of the Jewish people in response to their rejection of His Messiah. A clear statement of this theme is found in the parable of the vineyard in Matthew 21:33–46. The men renting the vineyard mistreated the owner's servants and killed his son. As a result Jesus said, "The kingdom of God will be taken away from you, and be given to a nation producing the fruit of it" (v. 43). The rebellious renters would be crushed to powder by the stone of God's kingdom (v. 44; see Dan. 2:34–35, 44–45). The Pharisees, Matthew notes, realized that Jesus was speaking about *them* (v. 45).

In the Old Testament, the people of Israel enjoyed the privileges and blessings of the kingdom in a preliminary, typological form. Though they did not enjoy the fullness of the kingdom, to them belonged "the adoption as sons and the glory and the covenants and the giving of the Law and the temple service and the promises" (Rom. 9:4).[11] But because the Jews rejected the incarnate Word, all these privileges were removed from the Jews as a people and given to a new people, who are now obligated to produce abundant fruits. All the privileges and blessings of the Old Testament Israelites now belong to the Christian church, which consists of Jews and Gentiles.[12]

Though astute students of the Old Testament such as Simeon recognized that the Messiah was coming as a light to the Gentiles (Luke 1:32), many in Israel apparently looked for the restoration of the national glory of the reigns of David and Solomon. It was inevitable that the early Christians, claiming to be the fulfillment of Israel's calling, would meet vicious opposition from the Jews. Indeed, the New Testament cannot be understood without the recognition that the church was making precisely this claim. Like the conflict between Cain and Abel and between Judah and Israel, the conflict between Jews and Christians centered on a question of worship: Should Jesus Christ be acknowledged and honored as Lord?

This conflict is a major theme in nearly every book of the New Testament:

- One of the main points of the book of Acts was to explain and defend Paul's ministry among the Gentiles (Acts 28:25–28). Peter's dealings with Cornelius (Acts 10–11) and the Jerusalem Council (Acts 15) are both concerned with the application of Mosaic Law in the new world order of the kingdom. The turning from the Jews to the Gentiles is symbolized by the geographic movement of the book from Jerusalem to Rome.[13]
- The early chapters of the book of Romans are preoccupied with the questions, Who is the true Jew? and "What benefit does the Jew have? (Rom. 2–3). Later in the same letter, three chapters are devoted to an explanation of how God's promises to Israel can be reconciled with the unbelief of the Jews (Rom. 9–11).
- The book of Galatians is a challenge to the Judaizers, the party of the circumcision.
- The epistle to the Hebrews was written to Jewish converts who were in danger of reverting to Judaism. More generally, Hebrews is a defense and explanation of the new covenant order out of the Old Testament.
- The book of Revelation is largely concerned with Christ's judgment on the temple and nation of Israel.[14]

From this viewpoint, the church's relationship to the kingdom can be described this way. The church is the new Israel, the people that now possesses and will inherit the kingdom, that is, the "package deal" of covenant privileges and blessings promised to God's people throughout the ages.

Not One Stone upon Another

From the beginning of the ministry of John the Baptist, the preaching of the kingdom included not only a promise of mercy and life, but also a warning of judgment. John warned,

"The axe is already laid at the root of the trees," ready to cut down all the trees that do not bear good fruit (Matt. 3:10). Isaiah had written that God would wield the "axe" of Assyria against the vine that He had planted in the land, the people that produced rotten fruit (Isa. 10:5–19). Similarly, John was warning not of eternal judgment, but of an imminent temporal judgment on Israel. This warning lent intense force to his call to repentance. There was no delay of judgment here. Judgment, an essential aspect of the coming of the kingdom, was as imminent as the kingdom itself. As the prophets foretold, the coming of the new order of the kingdom would be preceded by a day of terrifying judgment (Isa. 2:12–22; 35:4; Jer. 51:25; Ezek. 7:1–27).

Jesus took up the same theme of imminent judgment. After instructing His disciples on the duty of self-denial, He warned that the "Son of Man is going to come in the glory of His Father" to judge every man according to his deeds. The timing of this catastrophic "coming" was not left in doubt: "Truly I say to you, there are some of those who are standing here who shall not taste death until they see the Son of Man coming in His kingdom" (Matt. 16:28). Jesus was clearly warning of a judgment that would occur within the lifetime of some of the disciples. Vengeance for the Jews' attack on all the prophets from Abel to the Greater Abel was going to be exacted from the generation that witnessed the coming of Jesus (Matt. 23:37–39; Luke 11:47–51).

Jesus' fuller explanation of the coming judgment is recorded in Matthew 24 and its parallels in Mark 13 and Luke 21. Of the temple, He warned that "not one stone here shall be left upon another, which will not be torn down" (Matt. 24:2). He predicted tribulations, false prophets and false Christs, and signs in the heavens—all of which would occur before the generation of His disciples had passed away (Matt. 24:34). These were prophecies not of Christ's Final Advent, but of His coming judgment upon Jerusalem. When Jerusalem, the center of God's rule under the old covenant, was destroyed, the entire order of the old world collapsed. The destruction of

Jerusalem and its temple, which occurred in A.D. 70, was in a very real sense the end of the world (Matt. 24:29–31).[15]

This is why Christ's visitation in judgment is called the "coming of the Son of Man in His kingdom." It was the final revolutionary act in Jesus' establishment of His new world order. By His death, resurrection, and ascension, Jesus had already achieved a revolution in the heavens. With the destruction of Jerusalem, Jesus accomplished a revolution on earth. The new people of God was separated finally and completely from the prototypical nation of Israel. During the early history of the church, the new people of God was barely distinguishable from the Jews. Christians worshiped and met at the temple (Acts 3:1, 11; 5:12); they were considered by outsiders to be a sect of Judaism, analogous to the Pharisees or Sadducees (Acts 24:14). When the temple was destroyed, the newness of the Christian church became clear. When the old covenant types were overthrown, the new covenant realities emerged from the shadows.

Destroy This Temple

Throughout history, conquerors have recognized the symbolic and political significance of art and architecture. Until recently, paintings and statues of Marx, Lenin, and Stalin were found everywhere in Moscow. Saddam Hussein's image is (for the moment at least) inescapable in Baghdad. Buildings and other architectural monuments have often served the same purpose. In 1806, Napoleon began to build the Arc de Triomphe in Paris, which still stands as a reminder of the glory that was once France.

We find a similar pattern reflected in the Bible. The reason, however, is not political, but religious; because it is the Lord who has won the battle, His victorious people erect a monument not to their own glory, but to His.

In keeping with this, the spoils of Egypt were dedicated to the tabernacle (Ex. 12:35–36). After Joshua had conquered the land of Israel, he set up the tabernacle at Shiloh (1 Sam. 1:3). Because the Lord had given the victory, the booty of the conquest was His and was kept in His tent (Josh. 6:24; 7:1–26). When David completed the conquest of Jerusalem, he brought God's throne, the ark of the covenant, into the city (2 Sam. 6:1–19), and his first desire was to build a house for the Lord (2 Sam. 7:1–2). Though David was not able to build the house, he did gather the materials that Solomon later used (1 Chron. 22:2–16). Whenever a biblical figure was successful in holy war, he erected a sanctuary, using the plunder gained from his conquest.[16]

Similarly, Jesus Christ, having conquered Satan, began to construct his new temple from the spoils of His holy war. After His ascension, He continued to battle against all who opposed Him—in particular, His satanic Jewish enemies (John 8:44). James B. Jordan explains, "During the years A.D. 30 to 70, the Church spoiled the Old Covenant, the temple and the synagogue. During this time, the Church was established as God's new and final house."[17] From the plunder of His vanquished enemies, the remnant of the Jews, Jesus began constructing His new temple, the church (Matt. 16:13–20; 1 Cor. 3:16–17).

The destruction of Jerusalem was, therefore, not merely an act of judgment, but also the birthpangs of the coming order of the kingdom (Matt. 24:8). It was a ringing out of the old and a ringing in of the new. Out of the labor of A.D. 70 was born a new, transfigured temple, the fulfillment of Ezekiel's spectacular visions (Ezek. 40–48). God prepared Israel as a vessel of wrath in order to show His riches to the church, the vessel of glory (Rom. 9:22–23). When the Deliverer came out of Zion to take away sins, Israel was reborn (Rom. 11:25–32).[18]

Just as the destroyed temple of Jesus' body was transfigured by resurrection, so also the destroyed temple of Jerusalem was transfigured into the full reality of the church, which is the fullness of Him who fills all things in every way (Eph. 1:23). With the destruction of Jerusalem, the true temple of the Holy Spirit was revealed in her glory. With the destruction of the Jerusalem temple, the kingdom came.[19]

The Bride of Christ

Comparing a woman to a building would probably seem like an insult. To say that a woman is built like a "brick house" hardly connotes femininity. In the Bible, however, such comparisons are not unusual. Solomon compared his beloved's neck to "the tower of David built with rows of stones, on which are hung a thousand shields, all the round shields of the mighty men" (Song 4:4). Whatever our modern sensibilities, such comparisons were considered complimentary in ancient times.

Generally, when the Bible talks about a woman-building, it is talking about the church. The church is the temple of God (1 Cor. 3:16–17), and she is also the bride of Christ (Eph. 5:22–33). John described the New Jerusalem sanctuary descending from heaven as a "Bride adorned for her Husband" (Rev. 21:2). In relation to God, the church is both temple and bride.

Jesus claimed to be the Bridegroom come to earth to deliver His bride and to consummate His marriage in a wedding feast (Matt. 9:14–15; 25:1–13; John 3:29; Rev. 19:1–10). Jesus' description of Himself as the Bridegroom grows out of Old Testament symbolism of the relationship between the Lord and His people (Isa. 54:5; 62:5). Despite the loving gifts the Lord had bestowed on Israel, however, she had become an adulterous wife, lusting after strangers rather than devoting herself to her Husband (Ezek. 16:32). Hosea's enduring love for an adulterous woman symbolized the Lord's enduring love for idolatrous Israel (Hos. 2:1–7; 3:1–5).

From this perspective, the destruction of Jerusalem can be understood as the Lord's divorce of adulterous Israel. Jesus came not only to deliver the Virgin remnant, but also to send away the adulterous nation. Jeremiah 3:1–10 describes the Lord's judgment on Israel as a divorce. The Lord says that Israel, who has left her first Husband (the Lord) cannot return to Him without defiling the land (Jer. 3:1). Here the Lord is applying the divorce law of Deuteronomy 24:1–4 to Israel. Under that law, it was abominable for a wife to return to her first husband. For Israel, the very act of repentance would further defile her. How was she to repent? How was Israel ever to be restored to her Husband?

Paul gives the answer in Romans 7:1–3. There the apostle writes that a woman is freed from her marriage covenant by the death of her husband. When her husband dies, she can marry another man. Paul was describing how God delivered His faithful bride from her dilemma, how God can be both just and the justifier of those who have faith in Jesus, how God could both divorce and remarry Israel. When Jesus Christ, the Husband of Israel, died, Israel was freed to marry with a new husband. But Jesus not only died, but also rose again. He is not only the first Husband, but the second as well (Rom. 7:1–4). Similarly, as we have seen, Israel herself died and rose again in the judgment of A.D. 70. The resurrected bride can therefore lawfully remarry her resurrected Husband.

The New Covenant

The covenant is the common element between marriage and Israel's relationship to her Lord. Marriage is explicitly described as a covenant in the Old Testament (Mal. 2:14). To say that the Lord was the Husband of Israel was, therefore, a vivid way of saying that the Lord had entered into a covenant with His people.[20]

Thus, when Jesus called Himself the Bridegroom, He meant that He is the Head of a new covenant. Having divorced His unfaithful bride, Jesus, the crucified and now ascended Husband, has entered into covenant with His new bride, who died and rose with Him. Jesus, the New Adam, has formed a new household with the church, the new Eve, and together they rule the earth. This new covenant was sealed with the Husband's blood and celebrated in the communion of the marriage feast, the Lord's Supper (Matt. 26:28).

We saw in chapter 3 that the new Davidic dynasty is not a replacement of the old, but a transformation of it. The same is true of the new covenant in relation to the old. It is not as if God changed His mind about how He would structure His relations with His people. God still makes promises, requires obedience, and threatens sanctions against the disobedient. The new covenant is simply the old covenant transformed by the death and resurrection of the covenant Head, Jesus Christ.

Our Husband thus still expects His bride to be faithful, to keep herself pure, to prepare herself for the feast of the consummation. The new covenant, like the old, includes demands and threats as well as promises. Indeed, the new covenant brings greater responsibilities. The writer of Hebrews made precisely this point when he reminded his readers that those who sinned against the Mosaic Law were stoned without mercy on the testimony of two or three witnesses. "How much severer punishment do you think he will deserve who has trampled under foot the Son of God, and has regarded as unclean the blood of the covenant by which he was sanctified, and has insulted the Spirit of grace?" (Heb. 10:29). In the new covenant, as in the old, the Husband is jealous of His bride's loyalty and devotion (Ex. 34:14).

To whom much is given, much is required. The new covenant brings greater responsibilities and more severe sanctions because it offers better promises. As described by Jeremiah, the new covenant promises precisely what the children of Israel, and all children of Adam, lack (Jer. 31:31-33; cf. Ezek. 36:22-32). God promises that through Christ the new covenant people will be a faithful people. The new covenant answers to the problem of disobedience and idolatry. Under the new covenant, sinners are enabled by the Spirit to worship and obey the Lord. Under the new marriage covenant, the bride will not be an adulteress, but a virgin (2 Cor. 11:1-3). The coming of the kingdom means that God has begun to gather a *faithful* people.

The church is thus not only the people that possess and will inherit the blessings of the kingdom. The church is also the Bride that joyfully submits to the easy yoke of her Husband, who is the covenant King.

Because the church is the people in covenant of King Jesus, the church herself may be called Christ's kingdom. Peter described the church with a phrase borrowed from Old Testament descriptions of Israel: a "royal priesthood" (1 Peter 2:9–10). By His blood, Jesus has redeemed His people, and made us a kingdom of priests (Rev. 1:6). In several of Jesus' parables of the kingdom, He described the kingdom as a community of men (Matt. 13:41). Because the church submits to the rule of her King, the church is the kingdom of Christ.[21]

Children of the Freewoman

The church is not only the bride of Christ, but also the mother of believers.[22] Indeed, it is precisely as the bride of Christ that she is our mother. Because the bride is one flesh with Christ, she produces children unto God. Like Sarah, the church, though barren in herself, gives birth by the Spirit to children of the promise (Gal. 4:21–31). Though a harlot in herself (Ezek. 16), in Christ, the church is accounted a virgin. Like Mary, she is overshadowed by the power of the Most High and gives birth to brothers of the Lord (2 Cor. 11:2–3; Heb. 2:11).

There was an obvious element of judgment in Jesus' turning from the Jews to the new Israel. At the same time, the Bible teaches that the typological kingdom was never intended as a permanent arrangement. One of Paul's main points in Galatians 4 was that physical descent from Abraham never was a guarantee of inheritance of the promise. Most of the members of Abraham's household were not in fact blood relatives. The Lord set apart and gave special protection to the household of Abraham until the Seed appeared. God intended, moreover, for Abraham's Seed to be a blessing to all nations (Gen. 12:1–3). God always intended that the nations should come to worship at His mountain and live in obedience to His Word (Pss. 46:10; 47:1–3; etc.). From the beginning, God had elected the children of the freewoman to be His people.

But here as elsewhere, the reality exceeds the types and shadows. Though the Old Testament prophets predicted that the Gentiles would turn to the Lord, their prophecies often assumed that the nation of Israel would remain central in God's plans. The Gentiles would worship the Lord, but they would certainly travel to Jerusalem to do so!

The New Testament discloses something so surprising that Paul sometimes referred to it as a mystery and admitted that it had been hidden from past generations. The Gentiles would not only turn to the Lord, but by faith would also be admitted fully, together with believing Jews, into the privileges of the new covenant (Col. 1:26–27; Eph. 3:4–6).[23] In Christ, the two have become one new man, and the dividing wall has been broken down (Eph. 2:11–15). Through faith, all— whether Jew or Gentile—are sons of God, baptized and clothed with Christ so that "there is neither Jew nor Greek" (Gal. 3:23–28). Formerly afar off, they have been brought near by the blood of Christ and grafted into the tree. The mystery is not that the Gentiles are saved; Gentiles were saved in the old covenant. The astounding revelation is that the Gentiles have become part of the priestly people, building blocks of the new temple of God, admitted with the priestly nation into the sanctuary (Eph. 2:11–22).

The reconciliation of Jew and Gentile in one body has global implications. It is as revolutionary an event as the destruction of the temple. Paul said the enmity was abolished and the wall destroyed so that there would be *peace* (Eph. 2:14–15). "Peace" was one of the key prophetic descriptions of the coming messianic age. Isaiah said that the rule of the Prince of Peace would be marked by ever-increasing justice and peace (Isa. 9:6–7), and prophesied of a new heavens and new earth characterized by harmony and joy (Isa. 65:17–25). Zechariah foretold of a humble king who would "speak peace to the nations" (Zech. 9:9–10). These prophecies of peace find their initial fulfillment in the reconciliation of Jew and Gentile in the Christian church. The healing of the breach between Jew and Gentile is the seed and pledge of the healing of the breach among all nations.

The kingdom comes with the promise of peace on earth (Luke 2:14), but that peace is possible only in Christ, and

Christ's peace becomes manifest first in the church. Within the church, and only within the church, is the division and conflict that originated with Cain and Abel remedied. The United Nations cannot bring peace, nor could all the frantic diplomacy or stern threats of a thousand presidents. Only the Prince of Peace can bring peace. It is only when the nations come to the new temple to worship the Lord and hear His Word, only when the Lord judges among the nations and renders decisions for the peoples, only when the nations are born again from our mother, the church—only then will the nations begin to beat their swords into ploughshares and their spears into pruning hooks (Isa. 2:2–4). The peace of the kingdom comes to reality through the work of the church, as the nations are formed into diverse but harmonious replicas of the city of God.

The church is called to reconcile not only all nations, but all social classes. In Christ, and in His body, there is neither Jew nor Greek; neither is there bond nor free, male nor female, for all are one in Christ Jesus (Gal. 3:28). There is only one body of Christ (Eph. 4:4–6), and Christ is not divided (1 Cor. 1:13). The rich should consider himself poor in Christ, and the poor should consider himself rich. The freeman is a bondslave of Christ, while the slave has been liberated.

Paul did not mount an abolitionist campaign or press for an Equal Opportunity Act for noncitizens. But within the church, a new kind of community was formed, one in which each man and woman, regardless of lineage or tax bracket, was an organ of a body. The church is not a conglomeration of atom-like "individuals," but a *body*, in which each member is gifted with a unique dignity, purpose, and function. In the church the less honorable members receive greater care and honor. The church is called to be a community in which each member uses his or her particular gift for the building up of the whole body; each member is to serve the common good. The church is a community dominated, in a word, by *love* (1 Cor. 12–13).

Conclusion

Out of our mother, the church, then, is born a race of new Adams and Eves, reborn by water and the Spirit in order to fulfill the original mandate of Adam to worship and obey God and to share His rule over creation. The reconciliation of Jew and Gentile is the seed of the re-creation of a new human race within the human race. Jew and Gentile have in Christ become one new *Adam*. The people of the kingdom is not merely a fulfillment of the Mosaic order of things, or of the Davidic kingdom. The church is the fulfillment, the coming into fullness, of the Adamic order. In the church, we find the purposes of God for humanity beginning to be fulfilled. She is the continuing creation of a new humanity in the midst of humanity. In the church, as Irenaeus put it, "God has re-formed the human race."[24]

The pouring out of the Spirit at Pentecost illumines the fact that the church is the fulfillment of the Edenic order. Filled with the Spirit, the apostles spoke in tongues, undoing the confusion of Babel. The people of God were reborn at Pentecost as a new race united not by political coercion, but by the one Spirit of God. As the Spirit hovered over the waters of the first creation, so at Pentecost the fullness of the Spirit was poured out upon the church. United to Christ by the Spirit, the church is the beginning of the new creation.

Roman Catholic historian Christopher Dawson echoed Irenaeus when he wrote that "Christianity it not to be identified either with ethical idealism or with metaphysical intuition. It is a creative spiritual force, which has for its end nothing less than the re-creation of humanity. The Church is no sect or human organization, but a new creation—the seed of the new order which is ultimately destined to transform the world."[25]

165

NINE

✦

On Earth as It Is in Heaven

Sunrise is one of the most dramatic times of day. The black curtain of night is slowly drawn back, revealing a dimly lit stage full of ready players. Pink, orange, and red streaks drape the sky as the peak of the sun comes over the horizon. Trees and houses, indistinct and ghostly presences before dawn, begin to take on familiar, comforting shapes. The sun warms and brightens the dark world.

Sunrise provides a helpful analogy to the relation of the church and kingdom to the world. Christ is the true Sun of Righteousness (Mal. 4:2), the Light of the world, and His light shines through His people (Matt. 5:14–16). The church is the earthly mirror of the glory of Christ. What the sun is to the earth, she is to the world. If the light of the church is dim, the world will suffer in darkness and fear, ignorance and death. When the light of the church burns brightly, the world is filled with the light and life of the kingdom that is yet to come.

The world is not and will never be the church, just as the earth is not and never will be the sun. The world will never be as radiant with the glory of God as is the church. In itself, indeed, the world is darkness, uncomprehending of the Light. But with the coming of the Sunrise from on high (Luke 1:78), and the shining of His light through His city, the world is lighted and is transformed into an image of the heavenly kingdom. Though the world cannot be God's kingdom in the same way that the church is, the world can, however dimly, reflect the glory of the kingdom that shines through the church.

A careful balance must therefore be maintained when we speak about the mission of the church. Some, forgetting that the church exists for the life of the *world,* have tended to limit the cosmic scope of her mission. Others, forgetting that the *church* exists for the life of the world, have tended to displace the church from her central place in the plan of God. To maintain a proper balance, we must remember both that the church has a *mission,* and that it is the *church* that has a mission.

Till Justice and Peace Embrace

In order to understand the mission of the church, it is important to know something about God's purposes in establishing the kingdom. What was the Father seeking to accomplish when He sent His Son into the world? Why did Christ revolutionize heaven and earth to establish the new world order of the kingdom? Should we think of Christ's coming as a rescue operation in which a few helpless victims are pulled here and there from the rubble? Or should we think of Christ's coming as a construction project, intended to build and create a new world?

First and foremost, the Last Adam established His kingdom for the same ultimate purpose that He does all He has done: to bring glory to His Father (John 4:23–24; 17:4–5; 1 Cor. 15:24). In this, the Last Adam stands in complete contrast to the First Adam. Adam's sin was to seek wisdom and dominion apart from submission to God. He put dominion before worship, seeking to be like God without first acknowledging that he was not God. But the Last Adam sought above all to worship and honor the Father. Christ's kingship serves His priesthood; He reigns in order to render tribute to His Father.

Jesus also established the kingdom to bring His people into the life of eternal communion with God (John 17:3). He defeated Satan to deliver His people from bondage to sin and death. Having ascended to heaven, He poured out the Spirit that clothes His people with power and fills them with life and joy. He is building His church to perfect the saints and to enable them to persevere to the end and so inherit a crown of eternal life. Christ established the kingdom to save His people and to secure for them eternal fellowship with the triune God.

Salvation in Scripture involves more than deliverance from sin and death, however. Salvation is not only negative, but positive; it implies not only the destruction of sin, but a new creation of righteousness leading to life. Man was created as a liturgico-cultural being, a priest-king. Salvation restores communion with God, and with that communion comes a complete fulfillment of the image of God. By His death and resurrection, Christ has made His people to be a kingdom and priests (Rev. 1:4–6), new Adams and Eves called to worship Him and to mold the creation into an image of the heavenly temple-city. Jesus established the kingdom to bring people to worship, serve, and obey Him in all they do, so that they would do His will on earth as in heaven (Matt. 6:10). He established the kingdom so that the life of men on earth might reflect the life of the angels in heaven, so that heaven and earth might come to resemble each other ever more closely, so that they might be ever more closely joined.[1]

Though the kingdom was established primarily for the Father's glory and the salvation of His people, the kingdom inevitably exerts its influence on the world in time and space, in real history and among real nations. Christ established His kingdom so that, through His people, He could bring all nations and the entire creation under His sway.

The gospel of the kingdom, then, is something more than a message of personal deliverance from hell. The gospel is not only the good news of individual salvation, but also the good news that in Christ a new creation has begun (2 Cor. 5:17).

As William J. Dumbrell has expressed it, "To say . . . that the gospel is Christ crucified, or Christ dying for sins is correct: but we need to put the further question, 'with what in view?'. On this question the Pauline evidence . . . is unequivocal. Christ crucified is the architect of the new creation, the new Adam, the Image."[2] The establishment of the new world order of the kingdom was not a rescue operation, but the beginning of a cosmic construction project.

Many Old Testament prophetic passages bring out the cosmic, global effects of the Messiah's coming. While it is true that prophecies of the messianic kingdom should not always be understood literally, it is clear that the prophets predicted that the rule of the Christ would bring untold blessing to all nations and to the entire creation (Gen. 12:1–3):

- In Psalm 72, the Messiah, a Greater Solomon, is said to reign not only over His own people, vindicating the afflicted and saving the needy (vv. 2–4), but also "from sea to sea, and from the River to the ends of the earth" (v. 8). As Sheba brought tribute to Solomon, the nations will bring tribute to the Christ (vv. 9–11). He causes the righteous to flourish like trees, and brings forth an abundance of peace (v. 7). Throughout the world He delivers the oppressed (vv. 12–14). The messianic King rules to make the howling waste into a Garden, to bring the nations to worship the Lord (vv. 16–17).
- In Ezekiel 34:20–31 the Lord promises to install His servant David to feed and shepherd His flock (vv. 23–24). The rule of the New David transforms the land: wild animals are eliminated (v. 25); showers of blessing are poured out (v. 26); the trees and the land yield an abundant harvest (v. 27); Israel's enemies no longer threaten her (vv. 28–29). All this—a veritable restoration of Paradise—results from the enthronement of the new Davidic King. In this way, the Lord shows the world that He is with Israel (v. 30). Jesus is that Good

Shepherd, the Greater David, whose rule brings blessing to all the families of the earth (John 10).
- In the prophecy of Isaiah, the suffering and death of the servant of the Lord (Isa. 53) lead to a restoration of the people to their land, a new Exodus, and the re-creation of the heavens and the earth, where the nations will live in harmony with one another (Isa. 65:17–25). Through the ministry of the Anointed One, the Lord causes righteousness and praise to spring up before the nations (Isa. 61:1–11).
- The Old Testament Jubilee provides a useful perspective here as well (Lev. 25). Under the Jubilee laws, non-Israelite residents of Israel had to return their land to the descendants of the original Israelite settlers every fifty years. Only the holy people could live permanently on the Holy Land. Drawing on Isaiah's prophecies, Jesus announced the beginning of the favorable year of the Lord in His sermon at Nazareth (Luke 4:16–21). He came to inaugurate the cosmic Jubilee, the restoration of the land to the sons of God.

Clearly, the coming of the Messianic kingdom not only brings glory to the Father, not only secures forgiveness and life for God's people, but also transforms the world. Christ's kingdom has as its goal nothing less than the re-creation of the cosmos and the healing of the nations. Jesus established His kingdom to bring the creation to its appointed goal.

The Growth of the Kingdom
Scholars have debated for centuries about how to interpret Jesus' parables. Teachers in the early church made an effort to find significance in each detail, while twentieth-century scholars tend to take a "minimalist" approach, claiming that each parable makes only a single overall point. Recently some scholars have begun to call for a moderately allegorical approach.

Without trying to resolve this question, it seems reasonable to assume that the images that Jesus used to explain the

171

kingdom were not randomly selected. It is not insignificant that Jesus compared the kingdom to a wedding rather than a funeral. It is no accident that He compared the kingdom to a pearl rather than a lump of coal, and to a feast rather than a fast. Nor is it accidental that Jesus frequently compared the kingdom to a "seed" that "grows" (Matt. 13:24–32; Mark 4:26–29).[3] In Mark 4:26–29, Jesus made the significance of this imagery plain. The seed of the kingdom grows, though the one who planted it does not know how. This is also implicit in Daniel's vision of a stone that grows into a cosmic mountain. Stones do not grow of themselves; only God can out of stones raise up children unto Abraham (Dan. 2:35, 44–45; Matt. 3:9).

In some sectors of evangelical Christianity today there is a lot of talk about "building" the kingdom of God. But Jesus *never* talked about building the kingdom. He instead used organic images, emphasizing that the kingdom *grows*. Jesus' reason for using the seed image was evidently to stress that the growth of the kingdom is God's work. Just as the farmer does not make his seeds grow into wheat, so also we do not make the seed of the kingdom grow.

This does not mean, however, that we sit back and just wait for the mountain of the kingdom to fill the earth. Christians are fellow-workers with Christ in His kingdom (Col. 4:11). Though the kingdom's growth happily does not depend on our feeble efforts, we are nonetheless called to make our feeble efforts.

When it comes to evangelism, every Christian would certainly agree with all this. We cannot just sit back and wait for the Father to translate men and women into the kingdom of His beloved Son. Christians are clearly called to participate in the growth of the kingdom in this sense. In the parable of the sower, the seed that grows up into the kingdom is the Word of God (Matt. 13:19). Similarly, the book of Acts talks about the growth of the kingdom as the "spreading," "growing," and "prevailing" of the Word of God (Acts 6:7; 12:24; 19:20). The kingdom grows as the powerful and living Word of God spreads. And *we* spread it. Of course, God does not need us to spread His Word. Yet, though He alone brings the harvest, He calls us to plant and water the seeds of the kingdom (1 Cor. 3:6–7). As Calvin said, God has freely chosen to exercise His rule and spread His Word through the instruments of men.

Christians are colaborers in the kingdom when they proclaim the gospel. Whenever the gospel is proclaimed, the seeds of the kingdom are sown. Whenever the gospel is proclaimed, men and women are called and enabled to abandon vain idols to worship and serve the living God, invited into the heavenly sanctuary to feast with the Bridegroom, and gathered into the church. When the gospel is sown on good soil, the fruits of the kingdom spring up.[4] In preaching the gospel and leading others to repent and believe, Christians share in the extension of God's kingdom.

But the growth of the kingdom's influence in the world is not merely a matter of increasing numbers of saved people or of increasing numbers of congregations. That kind of growth is basic, but the kingdom grows in another sense as well. The kingdom grows as righteousness is established in the earth, as God's will is done on earth as it is in heaven (Matt. 6:10). It grows as the purposes of Christ's reign are realized, as the nations flow to Zion to worship the Lord and hear His Word, as peace and justice are established, as Christ through His church molds the matter of creation into a earthly temple-city that is a replica of the heavenly city of God. The kingdom grows as the original purposes of God's creation are brought to fulfillment. And the church participates in the growth of the kingdom in this sense as much as it does in the area of evangelism.

The church, as a colaborer with God, is called to nothing less than world conquest, world construction, in the widest possible sense. She is called to labor by God's power to bring every man, woman, and child into the life and under the dominion of the kingdom; to work to see that every institution in every nation conforms itself to Christ's commandments; to bring every thought into captivity to Christ (2 Cor. 10:5). Her mission is to see that every human being brings every created thing into service to God, so that the Adamic commandment in both its royal and priestly dimensions is fulfilled. So, the church has a *mission,* and what a mission!

As we noted above, however, it must be equally stressed that it is the *church* that has this mission. Recall my definition of the church from chapter 8. "Church" is not just a codeword for "individual believers." Individual believers do, in their various callings, help to fulfill this global mission. Some of the ways in which individual Christians fulfill this mission have been examined in chapter 7. But by "church" I mean the organized body, the "institution," marked by the Word, sacraments, and discipline.

In order better to understand how the *church* goes about bringing the world into submission to Christ (or, if you prefer, how the light of the church dispels darkness and illumines the world), we need to recall the various features of the kingdom that we have examined in the preceding chapters. These should not be understood, however, as sharply distinct parts of the church's mission, but rather as various perspectives on the mission of the church:

- The coming of the kingdom means that Christ has defeated Satan in holy war; the mission of the church is, from this viewpoint, to *continue the holy war.*
- The coming of the kingdom means that the saints are seated on heavenly thrones; the mission of the church is to exercise *Christian dominion* on earth.
- The coming of the kingdom means that the heavenly sanctuary is opened; the mission of the church is to *offer spiritual worship in God's presence.*
- The coming of the kingdom means that we are invited to eat the heavenly feast at the King's Table; the mission of the church is to *keep the feast,* to *invite the world to share the joy of the feast,* and to *speak to the King on behalf of the world.*

174

• The coming of the kingdom means the gathering of a new people of God, under a new covenant; the mission of the church is to *pursue unity and peace* and to *make disciples of the nations* through baptism and teaching.

In the remainder of this chapter, we will examine each of these perspectives on the mission of the church in turn.

Continuing the Holy War

In the autumn of 312, the Roman emperor Constantine was camped with his army near Rome. During the previous summer, he had conquered the north of Italy, and now he was on his way to Rome to unseat his last rival, Maxentius, and to take sole possession of the Western Empire. As the sun began to set one afternoon during the army's encampment, a cross of light appeared in the sky, with the inscription, "Conquer by this." Constantine ordered his troops to paint crosses on their shields. A few days later, he defeated Maxentius at Milvian Bridge spanning the Tiber River at Rome. The Roman and Christian worlds were never the same.[5]

Even Eusebius, Constantine's wildly admiring biographer, was skeptical of this story, and modern scholars are much more so. Whatever the truth of the incident, however, it captures two important biblical insights emphasized by the early church. For the early Christians, the cross was a sign of conquest, not of defeat. Athanasius rejoiced that the gospel of the Crucified was driving away demons, turning vicious barbarians into peaceful worshipers of God.[6] Other church fathers exulted in the triumph of the martyrs, who, like Christ, gained victory through their suffering unto death. The early church took Jesus at His Word when He said of His death, "Now judgment is upon this world, now the ruler of this world shall be cast out" (John 12:31).

Second, Constantine's vision symbolized the early church's belief that Christians were to participate in the war whose decisive battle was waged on the mountain of Calvary.

Satan has already lost the decisive battle, and with it the war. Jesus' victory is assured, but the war continues. Now, however, the battle is not between Jesus and Satan directly, but between the dragon (and His hosts) and the woman, between Satan and the church. Jesus continues to wage holy war against the kingdom of Satan, but now He fights *through us* (Rev. 12:7–17). As Irenaeus described it, Satan was "biting, killing, and impeding the steps of man, until the seed did come appointed to tread down his head." That Seed of the woman, Jesus Christ, came to "bind 'the dragon, that old serpent,' and subject him to the power of men."[7] Satan is subject to the God-man, the Last Adam, and also to those who are united to Him. By faith, we overcome Satan and his demons.

Even during Jesus' earthly ministry, His followers participated in the holy war. Jesus sent out His apostles with instructions and power to proclaim the kingdom of God, to heal, and to cast out demons. The success of their mission prompted Jesus to rejoice that He had seen Satan fall from heaven like lightning (Matt. 10:7–8; Mark 3:14–15; Luke 10:17–20). After Pentecost, the Spirit-filled apostles continued the same campaign (Acts 16:16–18; 19:8–20). The disciples of Jesus are still called to wage unending war against Satan and his seed, working out on earth the exorcism that Jesus had decisively accomplished in heaven.

Fighting Satan can sound overly pious and pietistic, but the scriptural view of holy war involves more than struggling to subdue the sin rooted in our own hearts (though it does involve that). Battling Satan also means opposing his slaves wherever they may be found, whether in the statehouse, the corporate office, or the pulpit. As more and more people are delivered from the kingdom of darkness into the kingdom of God's dear Son, the kingdom of Satan loses power (Col. 1:13). As the plans and programs of Satan's slaves are thwarted, the purposes of God's kingdom are realized on earth, and God's will is increasingly done on earth as in heaven.

The Weapons of Our Warfare

With the rawest kinds of satanism rising throughout the nation, it is crucial to ask how the church wages war against Satan. At this point, it is essential to remember the distinction we noted in chapter 1 between "normal war" and "holy war."[8] According to James B. Jordan, holy war always has several characteristics. First, all holy war is a war unto the death. Like Israel's, the holy war that Jesus wages through us is a war of utter destruction (Ex. 23:23), destruction unto life or unto death. If Christ's enemies do not repent, they will be buried in the rubble of Jericho; if they turn, they will find compassion. Like Christ's own war, moreover, the church's holy war is offensive, not defensive; the church is commissioned in the power of the Spirit to trample down the gates of hell. The church is called to storm the dragon's lair to plunder him.

But she does not wage holy war with carnal weapons. Jericho did not fall by sword or battering ram; Joshua's weapons were priestly trumpets, the ark, and faith. Contemporary satanism will not be defeated with legal or political weapons, important as they are. Satan's power over men is not broken when his activities are declared illegal; Satan's yoke is broken only when his demons are driven out by the finger of God (Luke 11:20). The darkness of the human heart can be dispelled only by the light of the gospel. Holy war is primary because holy war attacks evil at its very source. Weapons of normal war may be used to head off some of Satan's schemes, but only the gospel of the Seed of the woman is powerful enough to crush Satan's head.

In holy war, the church's chief weapons are those of her Master; her armor is the same as His (Isa. 11:1–5; Eph. 6). She fights with spiritual weapons that are powerful to destroy idolatrous speculations and bring every thought captive to the obedience of Christ (2 Cor. 10:3–6). She fights evil spiritual forces with the weapons of truth, righteousness, the gospel, faith, salvation, and the Word of God (Eph. 6:10–20). Through her prayers, her acts of righteousness and mercy, her witness and proclamation of the Word, her faith, and the power of the Spirit, Christ puts demons and demonic men to flight.

Jesus defeated Satan by suffering and dying. For the church, too, suffering is a weapon against Satan. We conquer Satan insofar as we deny ourselves and daily take up the cross to follow Jesus, insofar as we are daily *dying* in union with Him (Matt. 16:24–26). If we seek to save our lives, to throw off the cross, we have no hope of winning the victory. Marching under the banner of the cross, we conquer.

The Dominion of the Church

As we have seen, the coming of the kingdom means that the saints are, in Christ, seated in heavenly places, enthroned in fulfillment of the dominion mandate. Heavenly dominion over sin and Satan is the basic form of dominion for the individual Christian. But the Bible teaches that the saints have dominion on earth as well as in heaven (Rev. 5:10). Heavenly dominion is over "spiritual forces of wickedness in the heavenly places" (Eph. 6:12), but by exercising this heavenly dominion, the church rules also on earth. The rule of the church over the demons is not only subjective and spiritual, but has objective historical consequences.

Jesus came down from the Mount of Transfiguration to find His disciples trying to cast out a demon—unsuccessfully. Jesus' response is worth noting. He did not say that the disciples lacked the power to cast out demons. He did not apologize to the disciples for expecting too much. He did not excuse them in any way. On the contrary, He was *angry*. He placed all the blame on their unbelief and inaction. If the demon was not cast out, it was the disciples' fault, not Jesus' or the Spirit's: "This kind does not go out except by prayer and fasting" (Matt. 17:14–21).

Alasdair MacIntyre has said that today the barbarians are not at the gates; they have been ruling over us for some time. Carl F. H. Henry and Charles Colson have suggested that we are entering a new dark age. If evil, satanic men are riding the high places of the earth, it is not because there is any flaw in the gospel. If our world has become demon-possessed, it is not because Jesus lied about His victory over Satan. If ominous clouds fill the darkening sky, it is not because of any lack of power in the Spiritual weapons of our warfare. If Satan is alive and well on planet earth, it is because of our unbelief, our prayerlessness, our cowardice, our unwillingness to fast from the pleasures of this life. If we are entering a dark age, it is because of our lack of training in the weapons of spiritual warfare, or because we have become too enamored of carnal weapons. If righteousness is not prevailing on earth, it is only we Christians who are to blame.

Because the church is enthroned in heaven, she has the authority and power to exorcise a demonized world. If we faithfully use the spiritual weapons given us, the "satans" of our day will be crushed under our feet (Rom. 16:20).

Binding in heaven

One way in which the saints exercise their heavenly authority on earth is through church discipline (1 Cor. 5–6). Knowing that they would someday judge the world and even angels, Paul argued, the Corinthians should have realized that they were competent to judge "matters of this life" (1 Cor. 6:1–6). The future rule of the saints is manifested in the world when the saints purge the wicked from among them.

Church discipline is not merely a practical necessity, a part of the efficient management of a social institution, or an effort to ward off chaos and maintain some semblance of decency and order. Church discipline is a prelude to and anticipation of the eschatological rule of the saints over the world and the angels. It is a primary visible form of the rule of the saints.

The right to exercise discipline in the church is the highest privilege that God has yet given to man. Civil governments, though they can serve the kingdom, are of the earth, earthy. Church discipline, by contrast, is an earthly manifestation of

179

the heavenly rule of the saints. With his sword, the civil ruler administers the wrath of God (Rom. 13:1–7), but nowhere does the Bible say that the civil ruler's decisions have standing in the court of heaven. His sword is a dim shadow of the sword wielded by the Lamb. To the church alone Jesus made the promise, "Whatever you shall bind on earth shall be bound in heaven; and whatever you loose on earth shall be loosed in heaven" (Matt. 18:18).

Paul said in 1 Corinthians 5:12 that the saints have no business judging outsiders, but only those in the church. That seems to imply that though the saints rule the church, they do not yet rule the world. But that is too facile a conclusion. Paul went on to say that those outside the church are judged by God. By purging the wicked man from their midst, the Corinthians were turning him over to the judgment of God and binding him over to Satan (1 Cor. 5:5, 13).

The church has authority to turn men over to the wrath of God or to admit them into the sphere of mercy and life. The life that the world seeks comes from the Spirit who has been poured out in the church, and the saints, equipped with the keys of the kingdom, are the guardians of the treasure. By denying an unrepentant world access to the King and His banquet, the church is signing the world's death warrant. When the world turns to God in faith and repentance, the church opens her doors and welcomes the strangers into the inner sanctuary. The church ministers life, or, withholding life, is a savor of death. The church has authority to determine whether the world will live or die. The saints rule the world by serving as doorkeepers of the King's palace.[9]

But to Serve

The present rule of the saints on earth takes forms other than church discipline. Here, as everywhere, Christ is our example. Christ ascended to His throne as a reward for His obedient and self-sacrificing service, and He demands that we empty ourselves as well (Phil. 2:5–11). The saints, then, do not rule by domination, or by scratching and clawing for legal privileges or for access to the Inner Rings of earthly power. Jesus said that whoever wishes to be great must become servant of all.

In Christ, to lead *is* to serve. Husbands rule their wives by loving them as Christ loved the church—that is, self-sacrificially (Eph. 5:22–33). The Proverbs tell us that it is by love that a king secures his throne. Elders in the church are to rule, but not in the way that the world rules (Heb. 13:17; 1 Peter 5:1–4). When the people of God minister in works of mercy and justice, their light shines and the world is brightened (Isa. 58:6–12). The ones who inherit the kingdom are those who have sacrificed themselves in serving others (Matt. 25:31–46). Even if the church is forced to worship in catacombs, away from public view, she is visible in the world performing ministries of mercy. Christians exercise earthly dominion by loving their neighbors as themselves.

Service is not a *means* to earthly dominion. It is not as if we serve our neighbor so that we can gain sufficient influence and opportunity to dominate and exploit him. For the Christian, service is the *form* of dominion. This is because Christian dominion, even on earth, is not primarily cultural or political, but spiritual. The church rules by leading the world to faith and repentance, by sacrificing herself, by letting her light shine so that men will turn to glorify the Father in heaven (Matt. 5:14–16). The reign of the church follows the example of John the Baptist: "He must increase, but I must decrease" (John 3:30).

The Service of the Sanctuary

A study of the various words for "work" and "service" in the Old Testament shows that both are used mainly to describe the work of the Levites and priests (2 Chron. 24:12). They are supremely the "servants of the Lord" who stand by night in His sanctuary (Ps. 135:1–3). If service is a basic Christian form of dominion, it can also be said that worship of the heavenly King, being the central act of service, is central to dominion.

181

In a certain sense, God alone wages holy war; Israel's part is simply to stand firm at the Red Sea to watch the Lord's deliverance (Ex. 14:13). Yet, at the same time, the church plays an important role in God's rule over the earth. She exercises dominion by rendering homage to her Lord; she rules as she humbles herself before God. We become kings by first being priests.

Worship is not, as we have seen, merely rest and recuperation; it is the first act of the holy war. As we exalt the heavenly king on our praises, He fights on our behalf (2 Chron. 20). It is in response to our prayers that He sends His fiery judgment to the earth (Rev. 8:3–5). Singing the imprecatory psalms, the church calls God to intervene to protect her and to destroy her enemies. When the church prays that God will not hear the prayers of her enemies (Ps. 109:1–13), she closes the world off from its source of life and blessing. The church's liturgical pronouncements in worship, like her declarations of church discipline, bind and loose on earth (1 Cor. 5:4). Through the words that she speaks to her Lord in worship, the church participates in His rule of the world.

The Priority of Repentance

When the church pleases God by her worship and obedience, God blesses her. He promises to bless those who bless the sons of Abraham, and to curse those who curse them (Gen. 12:3), a promise that today applies to the church (Luke 10:16; Gal. 4:28). When the church faithfully goes about her business of serving God and humanity, she can be confident that the Lord will scatter and confuse all who oppose her (2 Chron. 20). When the church is faithful, the fear of the Lord descends upon her enemies (Acts 5:1–11). In His letters to the seven churches of Asia Minor, Jesus said in many different ways that He would reward His faithful people with authority and power (Rev. 2–3).

Conversely, when God's temple is defiled by idolatry, the glory departs and the house is left desolate, a haunt for jackals and owls (Ezek. 8–10). When the church plays the harlot and her Protector abandons her, she is in danger of being raped, plundered, and brought to shame. Only when the Spirit is driven out do seven demons come to inhabit a man (Luke 11:24–26). It was not because of the power of the Philistines that they were able to capture the ark; it was because of the faithlessness of Eli and his sons. It was because of the idolatries and adulteries of the priestly nation that she came to be called Ichabod (1 Sam. 4:1–22).

The problems that the church faces today are not, then, first of all a product of the world's hostility. The world is always hostile to the church. The problems are rather the result of her failure to be pleasing to her Lord. The church is in danger not of the world's wrath, but of God's. As Eliot said, it is when we will not worship the jealous Lord that we have to pay our respects to Hitler and Stalin.

The world's attacks on the church, then, are not overcome primarily by direct counterattack. The church's first response to legal attacks must not be legal; her first reaction to slander must not be self-defense. The church's first response to the world's hostility must always and ever be abandonment of idols and repentance toward God. Her first response must always and ever be to return to exclusive devotion to her Lord.

Filled with the Spirit

The importance of worship in the church's mission comes into sharper relief when we recall what we have said about the Spirit and the sanctuary. In the sanctuary we "enter into" the Spirit and are filled with His power. In the sanctuary we are transformed from glory to glory by the Lord who is Spirit (2 Cor. 3:12–18). In worship, the Spirit remakes us.

In the Bible, when the Spirit descends, someone usually gets hurt.

- When the Spirit came upon Jephthah, He defeated the Ammonites (Judg. 11:29–33).
- When the Spirit of power came upon Samson, he went out and killed someone or something: a lion (Judg.

14:5–6), thirty men of Ashkelon (Judg. 14:19), or a thousand men with a donkey's jawbone (Judg. 15:14–20).

- When the Spirit came upon King Saul, he gathered the people and slaughtered the armies of Nahash the Ammonite (1 Sam. 11:1–11).
- Jesus received the Spirit at His baptism immediately before entering into combat with Satan (Matt. 3:13—4:11). Jesus was not anointed with the Spirit of God so that He could retreat to the mountains, or so that He could sense God's presence. The Spirit was given to empower Him in combat.

We have received the same Spirit, and for the same reason—to empower us to fulfill the mission God has given. The Spirit was not poured out so that the saints could experience warm fuzzies, or so that they could "fe-e-e-el so-o-o go-o-o-od." He was and is given to empower God's people for holy war. The Spirit was poured out once-for-all at Pentecost, but He continues to come every Lord's Day. As God's people are filled with the Spirit each week in the worship of the sanctuary, they are restored after the image of the heavenly Man, and empowered to wage holy war with Spiritual weapons. Week after week, the Spirit hovers over the church and re-forms her into an ever-new creation. Week after week, the Spirit is poured out afresh through Word and sacrament, creating a new Israelite militia, an army without number (Ezek. 37:10, 14).[10]

The River from the Sanctuary

In Ezekiel 47 the prophet envisioned a river of water flowing from the glorified sanctuary. The water from the temple becomes deeper and deeper, flowing to the sea. Trees spring up on its banks, fish come to life in the waters, and the river turns the seawater into fresh. The trees along the banks of the river remind us of the Tree of Life in Eden and in Revelation, whose leaves are for the healing of the nations (Gen. 2; Rev. 22).

The sea is often an image of the nations, and a purified sea pictures the conversion of the nations to God. All of these images suggest the re-creation of the land, the restoration of Paradise, the fulfillment of God's purposes for creation.

A key element of this vision is the source of the river: it flows from the sanctuary. The river of life flows from the throne of God. The renovation of the world, which is one of the goals of Christ's kingdom, does not start by a takeover of the thrones of earthly monarchs. If we want to turn this corrupt world into a replica and anticipation of the heavenly city, we do not begin at the statehouse. The renovation of the world begins in the King's sanctuary. The re-creation of the world begins around the throne.

Keep the Feast

Jesus described the kingdom as a wedding feast (Matt. 22:1–14). A king's son was getting married, and the king invited his most honored subjects to the wedding. But they refused. The king would not have his feast empty, so he sent his servants into the highways and byways to invite all into the feast. Though this parable is primarily concerned with Jesus' conflict with the Jews, it is appropriate to see in this parable a picture of the evangelistic work of Christ and His church.

Thinking about this parable from that perspective helps us better understand the goal of evangelism. Notice that the invitation of the king's servants is not, "Receive the king" or "Pray a prayer" or "Walk the aisle." They invite the strangers to a feast! Evangelism takes place when King Jesus' servants (His priests, the saints) invite whoever will come to the wedding feast of the kingdom. Evangelism is eucharistic![11]

Notice also that the invitation is extended to those inhabiting the highways and byways. The aristocracy had their chance to come to the feast, but they blew it. The King's servants are to invite *particularly* the lame, the blind, the halt, the outcasts to the feast. The church is especially to extend her invitation to the homeless, the hungry, the naked, those who are sick and in prison. These are not merely to be tolerated at the King's table, but, like Mephibosheth, they are to be honored guests (James 2:1–9).

Advisors to the King

In the ancient world, the king's table was a place not only for sumptuous banquets, but also for consultation and decision making. At the king's table, his closest advisors gave counsel to the king. At the feast, the king promulgated his decrees (Est. 1:7, 10; 7:1, 8–10). The royal word was proclaimed at the feast.

In Luke 22:29–30, Jesus said His kingdom feast would likewise be an occasion for decision making and judgment. In the new covenant, since all of God's people are prophets, members of His inner council, they sit at His table to give counsel and advice to the King (Gen. 18:22–33). Together with the King, they pass judgments from the banquet table. Again, we see that the church, whatever the appearances, already rules the world. The King listens to His bride's advice and enforces the decisions that she makes at the wedding feast.

In this way the church acts as a mediator for the world. Jesus Christ Himself is, of course, the Mediator between God and humanity (1 Tim. 2:5; 1 John 2:1). But as His people, united to Him by faith, the church also acts as a mediator, a fact most clearly seen in her responsibility to pray for all people (1 Tim. 2:1–4). Through intercessory prayer at the King's Table, the church mediates before God on behalf of those unwilling or unable to pray for themselves. The church, in its worship, shares in the mediating activity of her Head. As children of Abraham, the church pleads with the King for mercy and for justice. And the King listens.

Enter into Joy

Before the church can invite the world to the feast, she must of course keep the feast (1 Cor. 11:25). Simply keeping the feast is at the heart of the church's mission in the world, because at the feast the members of the church partake of the one loaf, and are formed into one body, a body whose joy and love shines into a sad and cold world (1 Cor. 10:17).

C. S. Lewis once wrote that a truly Christian society would be "a cheerful society: full of singing and rejoicing, and regarding worry or anxiety as wrong." Lewis may have over-stated his point, but the point is well taken. Christian society, a society permeated with the life of the kingdom of God, is joyful society. As Chesterton pointed out, contrary to the common caricature of Christianity as a religion of killjoys, pagan Rome took itself far more seriously than the Christian empire that replaced it.

Along similar lines, sociologist Peter Berger has suggested that, since biblical religion takes a transcendent view of human history and institutions, it "refuses to take with ultimate seri-ousness the solemn dramas of the social world." Knowing that earthly kingdoms are destined to rise and fall, Christians can regard the apparent chaos of human history without despair, and even with joy. In Berger's phrase, the consummation of the ages "will be of the nature of cosmically comic relief." Eliot notwithstanding, the world ends with neither a bang nor a whimper. The world ends with laughter—the laughter of a wed-ding feast. We must beware of taking our efforts too gravely, for, as Chesterton said, "Satan fell by force of gravity."

Since the late 1970s, Christians have, quite properly, be-gun to engage in a large-scale political and cultural war with humanism. Thus far most efforts have been deployed in po-litical, educational, ecclesiastical battlefields—in short, on the institutional front. These efforts are in themselves quite proper and necessary. But we must avoid the trap of thinking that ex-tending the kingdom of God is a matter of exchanging one grim set of grey institutions for another.

Instead, the kingdom is a spiritual leaven that permeates existing structures—eventually changing the structures to be sure, but meanwhile suffusing all with the light, joy, right-eousness, and peace of which the kingdom consists. Even cat-acombs can ring with praise, and cathedrals can become empty shells, silent as tombs. The restoration is not complete when we have rebuilt the shattered walls of the dance hall: we must begin to dance. To talk of the kingdom as something to be "built" is indeed of limited usefulness. The point is not merely to remodel the living room; the point is to *live*. The kingdom is not the living room; it is not so much the structure as the *life*, new life, joy, peace, feasting in the presence of the Lord who is Spirit. The kingdom is not so much something to be built, but something to be tasted, something to be celebrated, something to be enjoyed.

Restoring this understanding of the kingdom, and embodying it in practice requires a restoration of the feast of the kingdom, the preliminary taste of the Final Supper of the Lamb. It would be wrong to think of restoring the feast of the kingdom as simply one more "technique" for the spiritual improvement of the church. The issue is much deeper than that, for the gathering of the people of God for the royal feast is not a means to establishing the kingdom. In a profound sense, the feast *is* the kingdom in its present form. In the most basic sense imaginable, serving the kingdom of God today means restoring the joy of the Eucharist to its central place in the life of the church.

The Great Commission

Like the original cultural mandate to Adam and Eve, the commission of the Last Adam is hard to take in. Jesus, the resurrected Son of David, commissioned His twelve timid disciples to go out from Jerusalem into Judea and Samaria and to the ends of the earth, not merely to proclaim the message of the kingdom, but to make disciples of the nations, to bring all the nations under the easy yoke of Christ. We can take this commission seriously only because the One who has been given all authority in heaven and on earth has promised to be with us to the end of the age (Matt. 28:18–20).

The Great Commission is clearly a kingdom commission. Jesus issued His orders after assuring His disciples that He had received all authority and power in heaven and on earth.

In His resurrection, Jesus had entered into the first stages of His glorification. He had become the Firstborn of the new creation, the firstfruits of the transfigured universe. Against this background, Jesus gave marching orders to His troops, orders that involve nothing less than bringing the nations under the rule of the Word of Christ.

The Seal of Baptism

The work of the church is to expand the new human race in the midst of the human race. Jesus said that the church was to do this by *"baptizing* them in the name of the Father and the Son and the Holy Spirit, *teaching* them to observe all that I have commanded you" (Matt. 28:19–20, emphasis added).

Notice that Jesus did not tell His followers to make disciples of the nations by "gaining decisions" or "making converts." Instead, Jesus said that we make disciples, first, by baptism. Baptism certainly implies that a choice has been made. Before baptizing the Ethiopian eunuch, Philip asked if he truly believed in Jesus from the heart (Acts 8:37). Before baptizing the jailor and his household, Paul and Silas explained the gospel to him (Acts 16:19–34). Discipling the nations certainly involves calling people to make a decision to turn to Christ in faith.

But baptism is more than a "spiritual birth certificate," a nice little ritual that reminds us of the really important thing—our inner conversion. On the contrary, the Scriptures treat baptism as the turning point in a person's life. When Paul appealed to the Romans to offer themselves up as instruments of righteousness, He reminded them not of their conversion, but of their baptism (Rom. 6:1–11).

Baptism not only assumes that a commitment has been made. Baptism is itself a commitment, an oath-sign. When one is baptized, he takes an oath that he will be the Lord's. Baptism is what theologians call a "self-maledictory oath." To take this kind of oath is to declare that one will keep his word even if it costs him his life. Baptism is a symbolic martyrdom and commits us to be martyrs, witnesses to the death of the things we have heard and seen. Baptism is not a "nice little ritual," but a solemn oath taken in the presence of God.

Moreover, when the Lord baptizes us, He claims us as His own possession. Though the Bible does not directly use the term to describe baptism, throughout the history of the church baptism has been called a "seal." Circumcision was a seal (Rom. 4:11), and, since circumcision is fulfilled in baptism (Col. 2:11–12), it is appropriate to call baptism a seal.

But what is a seal? What does it mean to be "sealed" by baptism? The Greek word had several different connotations. It referred to the brand that a shepherd put on his sheep, or to the tatoo that marked a soldier as a member of a particular regiment, or to the sign placed upon a slave. When we were sealed with baptism, we were marked as God's property, His slaves, His soldiers.

One Body, One Baptism

A seal, it should be noted, always has corporate dimensions. A branded sheep becomes a member of the flock, a sealed slave a member of the household, a tattooed soldier a member of the regiment. So also baptism inducts us into the fellowship of the church. The church is the disciplined regiment of holy warriors, the household of God, the flock of the Good Shepherd. Because of our baptism into the church, we are under the protection and care of our Master. A shepherd protects and feeds the sheep that bear his seal, as a master does his own slaves.

Baptism therefore points to the unity of the church. An aspect of the sevenfold expression of the church's unity (Eph. 4:4–6), baptism not only marks us as the Lord's possession, but also commits us to the other members of the body. The baptismal vow includes a promise to pursue the peace and unity of the church. Individual Christians do this by striving to live at peace with one another, by loving one another deeply from the heart, by scrupulously dealing with conflicts with their brothers, by daily encouraging one another to love and good works (Matt. 5:23–24; 18:15–20; Heb. 3:13).

Churches—local churches and denominations—are also obligated to pursue unity. Indeed, one of the basic dimensions of the church's mission is to display the love of Christ before the world. Jesus prayed that the church would display her unity before the world "that the world may know that Thou didst send Me" (John 17:20–23).

The contrast between Jesus' requirements and the current state of the church is alarming. In America, the church is deeply fragmented. Competition rather than love often dominates interchurch relations. The church, like Old Testament Israel, has become a mirror of the darkness of the world. Is it any wonder that the world is filled with chaos and violence?[12] If we wish the nations to be discipled, to be brought to worship and obey King Jesus, we must diligently pursue the implications of our "one baptism."

The Lord's promise of protection to His flock, in short, comes with obligations. A sheep that strays from the Shepherd's fold is in danger. A freeman can travel where he will, but a slave that flees has robbed his master. A civilian that acts like a civilian is quite within his rights, but a soldier that acts like a civilian is AWOL and subject to court-martial. So also, a Christian sealed by baptism is obligated to persevere in the way of the Lord, to continue to submit himself to his Lord, to fight on His behalf, and to pursue the welfare and peace and unity of the church. And if he fails in his obligations, he will be subjected to judgment.[13] Baptism is a covenant sign and brings not only promises, but demands and threats, as well.

Baptism and Discipline

When Jesus told the disciples to "baptize," He also implied that they were to establish churches and church discipline. Jesus' commission was not that the apostles should go about randomly baptizing everything that breathed. By baptism, converts come under the authority of Christ, exercised through the church's leaders (Matt. 18:15–20; Heb. 13:17). Discipling the nations thus involved setting up churches to enforce the law of Christ among those who had been marked with the seal of baptism. As masses of men and women respond to the gospel and are baptized into and disciplined by the church, righteousness springs up from the earth, and the earth becomes more and more like the heavenly city.

The church has historically understood her discipline as a means for the healing of the nations. During the medieval period, the church enforced the Truce and the Peace of God; she used her discipline to force kings to work out their conflicts peacefully.[14] In the modern world, the church, despite her many failures, has been a protector of many oppressed by totalitarian regimes. Through her discipline, then, the church not only prepares individuals for the heavenly kingdom, not only enforces righteousness among her members, but also shapes Christian nations.

Teaching Them All Things

The second of the church's tools for the discipling of the nations is teaching. The church's work of instruction does not end at the baptismal font; indeed, at that point it has only begun. Once the nations arrive at the Lord's mountain, they are to be instructed in His ways (Isa. 2:2–4). This teaching is to be done in the context of a disciplined community of baptized believers.

The apostles were commissioned to teach the nations everything that Jesus commanded. That means teaching the whole Bible, and it means applying the whole Bible to the whole of human life and thought. As John M. Frame has forcefully written, "Our God, through his word, desires to rule *all* aspects of human life—not only our worship and evangelism, not only what is usually described under the headings of personal and social ethics, but simply *everything*."[15]

Preachers proclaim the kingdom of God, calling all men everywhere to repentance and faith. Those who respond in faith are to be baptized, brought under the authority of Christ and His church, and admitted to the banquet table. Within the church, they are to be taught all that Christ has commanded. In this way, the nations become obedient worshipers of God, and the world is transformed into an image of the heavenly kingdom.

Conclusion

Nearly everyone, I suppose, has had the experience of trying something for the first time and finding it astonishingly simple. Perhaps it was learning to swim; after years of thrashing about in the water, suddenly you could float. Perhaps it was learning to drive a car, or operating a word processor, or replacing a belt on the washing machine. After these kinds of experiences, we are left asking ourselves, "Is that all there is to it? Can it really be so simple?"

That is the feeling we have about the church. She has been given a mission of global conquest. As Rudolf Schnackenburg has explained, "Through the Church Christ wins increasingly his dominion over all things and draws them ever more powerfully and completely beneath himself as head. . . . the Church's mission is necessary and willed by Christ to bring the world of men and with this the whole of creation under his rule."[16] One cannot conceive of a more astounding project.

And yet, as we examine the "tools" that the church has been given to accomplish this mission, we are prompted to ask, "Is that all there is to it?" Surely there has to be more to the church's arsenal of weapons for world conquest than worship, baptism and the Lord's Supper, church discipline, preaching the gospel, teaching, prayer, and service. Surely God expects the church to be doing more in the real world than that! We are inclined to think that God has provided us with a sharp rock for a construction project that requires power tools. We seem to have been given muzzle-loaders in a war that demands nuclear capability.

The church is a mystery. Though she is an "institution," she is more than an institution. She is the assembly of the Father, body of Christ, the temple of the Spirit. Because the church is a mystery, she is grasped only by faith.

Likewise, the church undertakes her mission, and fulfills her mission, only by faith. In ways that we cannot fully understand, the mere presence of the church affects the world for good or ill. In mysterious ways, the public worship and feast of the assembly of God bring nearer the consummation of the kingdom of God. In ways that go beyond human comprehension, the preaching of the gospel has creative power. If we cannot understand precisely how this takes place, it is not because it does not take place. It is because the church, even in her mission of world conquest, is required to walk by faith, not by sight.

TEN

✦

Into the Political Arena

It was 1988. A presidential election year. The last year of the Reagan era. The first year of a still-undefined period of American politics. The year we would take over the county Republican party.

"We" were a group of politically naive Christians, whose only common bond was a sense of impending danger to America and a judgment—in my case, highly qualified—that a Pat Robertson presidency would be an improvement. Somewhere along the line, someone decided that the way to promote a Robertson presidency was to take control of the local Republican party apparatus.

The plan worked wonderfully. When we met to elect delegates to the county convention, our precinct was stacked with evangelical Christians, who voted as a bloc and generally rode roughshod over the party regulars. All through the county, Robertson delegates flexed their muscles and won precincts. When the dust cleared and the cries of protest subsided, we had won a great victory.

Or so we thought. When we arrived at a local high school for the county Republican convention the following month, we—mostly Robertson delegates—were told that our credentials had been challenged. We were directed down a long hallway and told to wait until called. Hours passed. Meanwhile, in the gymnasium the party regulars were calmly moving through the convention agenda. Though elected as delegates, we were never seated, and the county went for Bush.

Not surprisingly, this experience lent itself to cynicism. My cynicism about the good-old-boy party system was matched, however, by my discomfort with our own tactics. We barged in and, without experience or any real understanding of what we were doing, claimed the party as our own. That experience left me asking whether Christians are forced to abandon Christian virtues to succeed in the political arena. It left me asking how my conduct in the political process could be made consistent with my Christian profession. It left me wondering about the relationship between the kingdom of God and politics.

Defining the Questions

In this chapter the relationship between the kingdom of God and politics will be explored from two different directions. First, we will examine the influence that the kingdom of God has on politics. What political difference, if any, does it make if the men and women involved in the political process have access to the gifts of the kingdom and strive to live in obedience to the King? What influence should the church as such have on political life? Second, we will examine what effect political action has on the growth of the kingdom. Is it biblical to speak about "building" the kingdom through political action? Does political action have any influence at all on the advance and growth of the kingdom? If so, what is the nature of that influence?

Before exploring these precise questions, it is important to provide some definitions. The word "politics" can refer either to "political order" or to "political action" and can carry other nuances as well. Because of the ambiguity of "politics," I have used more specific terms throughout this chapter. "Political order," however, is itself ambiguous. It can be narrowly or broadly understood; it can mean either the order of a governing apparatus ("Constitutional procedures") or something like "social order." In this chapter, I am using "political order" in its broader sense to refer to the entire socio-political structure of a political entity such as a nation, state, city, county, or whatever.

I am also using "political action" in a broad sense that encompasses acts by private citizens (such as directly or indirectly influencing legislation or public policy, promoting the election of a particular candidate, or appealing one's rights before a civil court), as well as the legislative, judicial, or administrative/executive acts of public officials.

Before turning to the question of politics specifically, we should recall the general conclusion concerning the relationship of Christianity to social and cultural life. I have found few statements to rival the profound reflections of Georges Florovsky.

> Man was created by God for a creative purpose and was to act in the world as its king, priest, and prophet. The fall or failure of man did not abolish this purpose or design, and man was redeemed in order to be reinstated in his original rank and to resume his role and function in the Creation. And only by doing this can he become what he was designed to be, not only in the sense that he should display obedience, but also in order to accomplish the task which was appointed by God in his creative design precisely as *the task of man*. As much as "History" is but a poor anticipation of the "Age to come," it is nevertheless its actual anticipation, and the cultural process in history is related to the ultimate consummation, if in a manner and in a sense which we cannot adequately decipher now. . . . The destiny of human culture is not irrelevant to the ultimate destiny of man.[1]

Christ's revolutionary establishment of the kingdom is intended to restore man to his original vocation, and to enable him to fulfill his original task of forming the matter of creation into a city that would reflect and anticipate the heavenly, eschatological city of God. In what follows, we will attempt to answer the question of what role political action plays in the completion of this task.

Politics and the Fruits of the Spirit

Charles Colson has frequently cited a quotation that he attributes to Martin Luther, to the effect that it would be better to have a competent Turk than an incompetent Christian for a king. In an obvious sense, Colson has a valid point. No one wants to be ruled by an incompetent, whether Turk or Christian. As I have pointed out in chapter 7, there is an undeniable sense in which being translated into the kingdom of God will not affect one's cultural or political life. If you did not understand political strategy before your conversion, it's unlikely you will become a Lee Atwater. If you were not a persuasive public speaker before your conversion, it's improbable that you'll be transformed into a Patrick Henry.

The Bible does teach, however, that the God-fearing political leader is superior to his pagan counterpart *as a political leader*. This is true, first, in the ultimate sense that a godly political leader pleases God. God works all things for his good and favors him. Righteous rulers therefore bring blessing to the people: when the righteous triumph, the people are glad (Prov. 28:12; 29:2). A city rejoices when the righteous prosper and the wicked are trampled down (Prov. 11:10).

Citizenship in the kingdom affects political action in more specific ways as well. In our day, for example, politicians are expected to be self-confident and to express that confidence in their campaign rhetoric.[2] From a biblical perspective, however, such statements must be condemned as vain, prideful, and foolish. Pride, moreover, comes before a fall (Prov. 16:18). Pride, in fact, is incompatible with true wisdom (Prov. 11:2) since the fear of and submission to the Lord is the root and ground of knowledge (Prov. 1:7). Proud nations and kings are condemned and stripped of their power (Ps. 2:10–12). Nebuchadnezzar is the most conspicuous biblical example of the political dangers of pride (Dan. 4:28–37), but he is by no means the only example (2 Kings 19:20–37; Isa. 10:12–14; Rev. 13:1–2; 19:19–21). Paradoxical as it may sound in a culture that assumes that political success requires ruthless self-assurance, the Bible presents humility as an essential *political* virtue.

The same can also be said of the other fruits of the Spirit and of the kingdom (Gal. 5:22–23). *Love,* the willingness to sacrifice for the good of others, is essential to the shepherding and ministerial role of the statesman (Ps. 78:72; Rom. 13:4). A good ruler acts out of genuine concern for the welfare of the people, not out of a lust for power or glory. Similarly, Solomon exhorted his son, the prince, to practice *kindness* in order to gain the favor of the people (Prov. 1:8; 3:3), and it was Rehoboam's refusal to show kindness that precipitated the division of the northern and southern kingdoms (1 Kings 12:1–15). Without *self-control,* the exercise of power degenerates into tyranny, luxury and excessive debt, and manipulation.

These truths hold not only for elected officials, but for all politically active Christians. Since the ultimate goal of all our doing is to glorify God, political tactics that suppress the fruits of the Spirit and dishonor Christ are ultimately counterproductive. Our only real duty is to honor Him; if He is pleased with us, He will give us political victory (if He so wishes). This is not to say that Christians may not act decisively and firmly in the political arena, or that we may not use the tools of politics in the pursuit of godly justice, or that we may not express strong disagreement and indignation with injustice. Indeed, Christians may and must do all those things. The point is that Christians are never free to live after the flesh. Politics is simply one arena in which Christians are to manifest the fruits of the Spirit.

Politics, indeed, cannot achieve its proper ends without the leavening influence of the kingdom and Spirit of God. The collapsed Communist regimes of Eastern Europe were case studies showing the political consequences of pride, envy, and greed. They provide a grim illustration of politics consciously divorced from the Word and kingdom of God.

Humility, love, self-control—all the fruits of the Spirit of God—are prerequisites for long-range political stability because Christ rules in heaven to cast down the proud and to raise up the humble to thrones. Unless kings and judges kiss the Son, they will eventually be dashed by His rod of iron (Ps. 2:10–12). Ceaucescu was a victim not merely of the rage of the Romanian people, but ultimately of the rage of the Lamb.

One can, of course, like Cain and Lamech, attain a certain kind of political "success" through pride and violence. One can attain a certain stability by terror, or by technical administrative excellence. But one cannot achieve justice and peace, true political order, without the leavening power of the kingdom. The world cannot be formed into an image of the heavenly city unless the Spirit has hovered over the waters.

The Church and Political Order

With little fear of contradiction, I can state that Christians unanimously agree that the Bible teaches a form of separation between church and state. The civil magistrate may not usurp or suppress the distinctive functions of the church: the preaching of the gospel, the administration of the sacraments, and the exercise of discipline. Contrary to the popular mythology, throughout his time as pastor of the Reformed church in Geneva, John Calvin fought to free the church from civil controls, particularly to prevent civil officials from interfering with church discipline. Such challenges to the state's totalitarian pretensions has always been a mark of renewed vigor within the church. On the other hand, it is none of the institutional church's business to employ the distinctive weapon of the state, the sword. The Western conception of church-state relations has taken various forms, but there has been a general agreement that the church should not exercise direct political power.

This does not imply, however, that the church's distinctive activities have no influence on politics, or that the church has nothing whatever to say to the state. The issue in debates among Christians about church-state relations is the form that the church's political influence should take. As I have argued, the church's main role in the world, and its main political role, is to produce a race of godly men and women through its teaching, worship, and discipline. The church also influences politics by offering prayers for all in authority. The church is most effective not by becoming a political lobbyist, but by being the church.

A church obedient to Christ's command to teach all of His commandments will, however, have a significant effect on political views of its members. One of the great deceptions of the modern world is the belief that the state can solve all social problems. Suppose a woman laboring under that deception is converted and joins a faithful church. She will begin to see the folly of her earlier opinion. She will learn that Christ alone is the Savior of the world. She will learn of the effects of sin on political life. She will learn that statism is ultimately a form of idolatry. She will, in short, begin to develop a very different perspective on politics in general, and this will lead her to change her positions on specific issues as well. If she was a radical feminist, she will begin to see that the Bible teaches something very different about womanhood. If she was pro-abortion, she will learn that the Bible teaches that abortion is murder.

Unfortunately, too many churches today do not teach the whole word of God. They do not teach their members that the Bible presents a comprehensive world view or that it provides wisdom on contemporary questions. Throughout American history, the Bible has been central to the political life of the nation. If it is no longer so, it is because the church long ago abandoned her calling to teaching all that Christ has commanded. It would be wrong, of course, for a pastor to preach on political issues every Sunday. But a pastor who never addresses the political issues of the day from the Word of God is unfaithful to the Lord of the church.

What Would Ambrose Do?

The church also affects political events through its discipline. The current political situation affords many illustrations of the church's failure on this score, but the example of Bill Clinton is by far the most appalling. President Clinton has already proved himself to be the most pro-abortion president in American history. He has not merely acquiesced to a Supreme Court decision, but, by his executive orders issued in January 1993, has actively aided and abetted legalized murder. It is also becoming clear that Clinton is the most pro-homosexual president in history. Not only has he appointed a number of known homosexuals to his administration, but he has worked strenuously as president to overturn the military's ban on open homosexuals.

Despite pursuing policies that are clearly contrary to Scripture, Clinton remains a member in good standing of a Southern Baptist church. A group of Southern Baptists in Arkansas has disavowed his actions, but there has been no effort by the denomination at large to take formal disciplinary action against him.

Lest I appear unduly partisan, I must add that there are doubtless scores of church-going Republican congressmen, senators, state legislators, and governors who advocate positions contrary to Scripture yet receive no censure from their church. There are also many professedly Christian politicians who are in fact free-lance Christians, accountable to no one and out fellowship with the church.

All of which brings to mind a not-so-obvious question: What would Ambrose have done? Ambrose of Milan (c. 340–97) was a churchman's churchman. He is perhaps best known as the bishop whose preaching and energetic apologetic efforts led the brilliant but confused young philosopher Aurelius Augustinus to embrace Christianity. If Augustine is the father of the Western church, Ambrose is the godfather.

We are interested, however, in Ambrose's confrontation with Roman civil authorities, which serves as a healthy guide for modern churchmen. In 390, according to the early church historian Sozomen, the people of Thessalonica, after a series of incidents, finally broke out in rioting against the Roman general Buthericus and killed him. The Christian emperor Theodosius immediately retaliated, killing seven thousand Thessalonians without trial, so that Sozomen wrote, "The city was filled with the blood of many unjustly slain; for strangers, who had but just arrived there on their journey to other lands, were sacrificed with the others."

News of the slaughter reached Milan. When Theodosius tried to enter the Milan cathedral, Ambrose blocked his way. Reminding the emperor of the enormity of his crime, Ambrose called him to account with these words:

> We must not because of the sheen of the purple fail to see the weakness of the body that it robes. You are a sovereign, Sir, of men of like nature with your own, and who are in truth your fellow slaves; for there is one Lord and Sovereign of mankind, Creator of the Universe. With what eyes then will you look on the temple of our common Lord—with what feet will you tread that holy threshold, how will you stretch forth your hands still dripping with the blood of unjust slaughter?

Finally, Ambrose ordered him out of the temple. "Begone. Attempt not to add another crime to that which you have committed."

Theodosius sought to change Ambrose's mind, but the strong-willed bishop refused to annul the sentence of excommunication. Finally, Theodosius relented, publicly confessed his sin, refrained from wearing his imperial robes during the period of penance, and decreed that imperial edicts would be executed only after a thirty-day waiting period, during which cool heads would presumably prevail. Ambrose, without for a moment overstepping the bounds of his office, had effectively challenged an unjust act, and, using the tools of the bishop— Word, sacrament, and discipline—forced the adoption of a more just imperial practice.

What would Ambrose do with our Christian politicians who permit and even defend the slaughter of innocent babies? No doubt he would have responded much as he did to Theodosius: "How in such hands will you receive the all holy Body of the Lord? How will you who in your rage unrighteously poured forth so much blood lift to your lips the precious Blood?"[3]

King of Kings

The place of political action in the growth of the kingdom of God—our second perspective on this question—is a hotly debated topic in evangelical circles these days. Although there are numerous disagreements about very significant issues, there seems to be a consensus that the kingdom cannot be established or advanced by political means. Typically the assumption is made that the kingdom is confined to the church or to the rule of Christ in the hearts of His people. Thus understood, the kingdom is established when men and women respond with living faith to the gospel, and the kingdom advances as more and more people become subjects of the Great King.

There is, obviously, a good deal of truth in this formulation. It is one of the fundamental perspectives of the preceding chapters of the present book. Christ does indeed rule savingly over men and women who respond to His call to repentance and faith, and the kingdom does advance as more and more people are saved.

In Scripture, however, the scope of the kingdom of Christ is not limited to the church. Again and again, Scripture emphasizes the cosmic dimensions of Christ's authority, His reign as *pantokrator,* ruler of all (Matt. 28:18–20; Eph. 1:19–23; Phil. 2:5–11). Thus, to *limit* the reign of the God-man to the church is a serious truncation of the biblical message. It is a dangerously one-sided reading of Scripture.

As the risen and ascended One, Christ demands that all kings and judges submit to His rule or face the punishing blows of the rod of His anger (Ps. 2). Though the church does have a unique place in the kingdom (Eph. 1:20), and though in certain senses, as I have argued, it can be said that the church *is* the kingdom, the Bible teaches that Christ also rules over men in their political activities. Christ is not only Head of the church; He is also King of Kings and Lord of Lords.

Evangelicals tend, moreover, to assume a dualism or dichotomy between faith and political action, between the kingdom of God and human culture. As should be obvious from the foregoing chapters, I believe that there is indeed a distinction to be made, a duality if you will, between the kingdom and culture. Faith is not the same as political action, and the kingdom of God is not the same as human culture. There will never be historical civilization that can be identified with the kingdom of God.

Yet, Scripture nowhere treats faith and politics in a dualistic fashion. Though faith is not the same as political action, faith can be *expressed* in political action. The kingdom of God is not the same as human culture, but one's seeking of the kingdom can be expressed in cultural pursuits, in painting and poetry as well as politics. By faith, the Old Testament saints conquered kingdoms, enforced righteousness, won military victories (Heb. 11:32–33).[4] It was by faith in the unseen things (Heb. 11:1) that the saints of old exercised godly political dominion. It was the Spirit of God who filled judges and kings with strength to defeat God's enemies. The same Spirit who gives wisdom unto salvation also gave wisdom to Solomon so that he could judge and lead the people (1 Kings 3:8–9).

There is therefore no inherent tension in Scripture between faith and political action, between spiritual and political things. It is by faith in and obedience to God's Word, and in the power of the Spirit, that Christians are to engage in political action (and in all other activities as well). The tension between human action and religious duty is ethical, the product of sin, not inherent and metaphysical.

It is important, of course, to avoid an *over*estimation of the role of political action. In that regard, the cautions of such leading evangelicals as Charles Colson are well taken. Paul's list of spiritual weapons in Ephesians 6 includes truth, right-eousness, the gospel, faith, prayer, and the Word. None of these refers in the first instance to political action, though it is surely possible for righteousness and truth to be manifested in, say, lobbying or leading a protest march. Elsewhere, Paul explicitly draws a contrast between the weapons of Christ's kingdom and those of the world of politics and war (2 Cor. 10:3–6). This does not mean, however, that war and politics are irrelevant to the kingdom of God; it means rather that the weapons of this world are neither our most important nor our most powerful weapons.

A Tool of the Kingdom

With these qualifications and cautions in mind, I believe that it can be shown that no matter how narrowly one defines the kingdom of God, political action is a tool that contributes to the growth of the kingdom.

First, Jesus Himself sovereignly rules nations so that the world will become an image of the heavenly kingdom. Political history is subordinate to redemptive history. Throughout the Old Testament, the Lord raised up and destroyed nations to chasten and deliver His people. In the New Testament, the book of Revelation, whether it is describing the destruction of Jerusalem or of Rome, shows that Christ orders political and military events so that they contribute to the extension of His rule. As part of God's sovereign and eternal plan for history, our political acts (and all our other acts as well) contribute to the realization of His historical purposes for mankind. In East-ern Europe since 1989, for example, we have witnessed po-litical events that have enormous spiritual consequences. Je-sus is ultimately responsible for the collapse of the Berlin Wall.

Political action is a tool of the kingdom also in the sense that it can be the key that opens doors for the gospel of the kingdom, or the foot that keeps a door from being closed. Sev-eral years ago, the Institute for Religion and Democracy re-ported that the Zimbabwean government was taking steps to force the churches of that nation to become agents of the continuing revolution. If this plan had been carried through, only those churches that "got on the side of history" would have been permitted to continue operations. Faithful churches would have been suppressed as a reactionary element in the society. The most significant thing American Christians could have done for Zimbabwe would have been to pray for the church, to appeal to the Supreme Court of heaven for justice. And, of course, the Lord uses persecution to purify and strengthen His church. Yet, a sustained political effort—letter-writing campaigns, newspaper editorials, public protests—to expose and head off this plan would have helped to prevent the kingdom's growth in Zimbabwe from being seriously impeded.

Similar examples could be multiplied from recent and more distant history. Historians speculate that the church historian Eusebius escaped martyrdom by using his political connections at the imperial court, and he eventually became Constantine's trusted advisor and biographer. Luther's reforming efforts would have come to nothing without the military and political protection of sympathetic noblemen. In the Bible, Paul's appeal to Rome enabled him to preach the gospel of the kingdom in Rome (Acts 25:11; 28:31), and in the Old Testament, Esther's courageous political act of appealing to the king saved the Jews from extinction (Est. 5–7). Political action is a tool to aid the spread of the gospel and to prevent persecution of the church.

Thus, even if we define the kingdom narrowly as Christ's rule over His church, political action is a tool that can contribute to the advancement of the kingdom of God in indirect ways. It is neither the most important nor the most powerful tool in the Christian arsenal, but it is one of the tools that the Lord in His grace has provided.

An Image of the Kingdom

I have argued that the task of Adam was to form the creation into an image of the heavenly city of God. The kingdom was established to restore humanity to the task of Adam—obedient and worshipful dominion. Political action can contribute to the realization of that task in several ways.

Political officials help in a positive way to make earth more like heaven by enforcing just laws. A young man living in the Massachusetts Bay Colony in 1638, when sodomy was punished as a crime, would have been far less likely to risk his life to satisfy his forbidden lust than is a young man living in San Francisco today. David C. Reardon's outstanding book, *Aborted Women*, provides another example. The vast majority of women who get abortions would not seek abortions if they were illegal. Laws do not make people good, but laws can prevent sinners from being as sinful as they want to be. And, however marginal the improvement, keeping sin in check makes the world more like the city of God.

Political action and political order also image and anticipate the kingdom. That is true first of all in the sense that political officials are images of Christ, and their exercise of political authority is an image of His rule. Political officials stand in the place of God. This is why the psalmist called them "gods" (Ps. 82), and this same conception lies in the background of Paul's discussion of the duties of magistrates in Romans 13.

Political officials are, to be sure, imperfect and often ironic images of Christ the King. But the Messiah, the "anointed One," is the original of which human rulers are but more or less imperfect copies. Objectively, political acts reflect and image the rule of Christ. Even Idi Amin revealed something of the rule of Christ in his exercise of power, though in the sense that a thing can be revealed by contrast with its opposite. In a more specific sense, righteous political acts and rulers alone reflect the perfect justice of Christ's reign. Whenever a political official acts in obedience to Christ, the king is a shadowy image of the King.

Since the fall of Adam, the transformation of the world into an image of heaven is in part a political task. The growth of the kingdom involves the healing of broken relationships and deep-seated animosities among nations, the political and legal embodiment of the Christian view of man and God—in short, the pursuit of justice, freedom, and peace.

True freedom, justice, and peace are found only in Christ, whose death, resurrection, and ascension liberate men from their bondage to sin, reveal the justice of God, and establish peace between men and the Holy God and among men. This is all-important, and implies that freedom, justice, and peace are realized primarily in the church. It is only where the Prince of Peace is acknowledged that there can be peace among men and nations.

But political action still has a role in our efforts to bring the heavenly pattern to earth. To illustrate, let us focus particularly on the punishment of civil offenders. Punishment is an act of just retribution against a criminal. It is in accord with justice insofar as it *reflects* the perfect justice of Christ's kingdom; in that sense, just punishment is an image of the eschatological judgment. But just civil punishment also *produces* a more just earthly situation.

For example, Vern S. Poythress of Westminster Seminary in Philadelphia has argued that the Mosaic Law's requirement of double restitution for theft is based on the principle that justice is achieved when the criminal receives the wrong he intended to do to the victim.[5] The thief intended to deprive the victim of, say, his bicycle. He must return the bicycle, but also give another (or its monetary equivalent) as punishment. The result is that the victim recovers his bicycle, while the thief is punished for his criminal intent. Double restitution produces justice by setting right a situation corrupted by a specific crime. The political act of enforcing restitution produces earthly conditions that dimly reflect the justice of Christ's final kingdom.

Moreover, by acting as a deterrent to violent crime and as judge of interpersonal disputes, political officials help to establish conditions of social peace. Peace is a mark of Christ's rule; while it falls short of the perfect peace of the final kingdom, and while political action is not our primary tool even for the achievement of earthly peace—still, the political acts of deterrence and mediation produce a peacefulness or settledness that reflects and anticipates the peaceableness of the kingdom of God. Similarly, the military protection of a nation from its enemies produces a security that again images the perfect security of life in the consummated new heavens and new earth.

All this is part of what we request when we pray that God's kingdom would come. We mean ultimately that Christ would return and achieve a final restoration of all things, but we are also asking that Christ would rule over the present world and cause the rulers of this world to produce conditions of justice and peace among persons and nations. Such conditions image the coming kingdom.

Conclusion

Political action is thus related to the kingdom of God in three ways. First, political acts are tools for the protection and advancement of the church; a political act can protect the church from her enemies or open doors for the gospel. Second, political acts may image or picture Christ's acts of government; whenever a political leader acts in a legislative, judicial, or executive capacity, He is imaging (directly or ironically) Christ's own acts of government. Third, political acts produce conditions that reflect and anticipate the perfect peace, justice, and freedom of the final kingdom; by restraining violence and ungodliness, political leaders make the world a bit more like the kingdom.

ELEVEN

Against the World for the World

I have argued that the kingdom of God, is the new world order inaugurated by Christ's death, resurrection, and ascension, and is a fulfillment of the original order of creation, and of the Old Testament order of Israel, in these specific respects:

- God, the King, created Adam and Eve to share in His rule over creation. David and Solomon represent preliminary fulfillments of this privilege. It is fulfilled supremely in Jesus Christ, the Last Adam and Son of David, who conquered Satan, ascended to a heavenly throne, and acquired a heavenly dominion that far exceeds the dominion of the First Adam (chaps. 2–3).
- Adam and Eve were to produce a race of rulers. The nation of Israel not only was a priestly nation, but by the power of God subdued their enemies under them. In Christ, the saints are now given authority beyond that of the First Adam and are seated on heavenly thrones to rule over Satan, sin, and death. Living with their minds set on heavenly things, they rule on earth (chap. 4).
- Priestly worship in the Garden was the alpha and omega of life for Adam and Eve. Under Solomon, the temple, a glorified garden, was built in Jerusalem. By His death,

Christ has opened the way into the heavenly sanctuary, where His people gather to commune with Him and to hear His Word around His throne (chap. 5).

- To empower them for their task, God blessed Adam and Eve with life by giving them access to His Garden and by letting them eat the fruit of the Tree of Life. Christ, the true Tree of Life, offers the life of the kingdom through the Spirit when He speaks to His people in the Word and when He gives His flesh and blood to them in the Eucharist (chap. 6).

- In obedience to God's covenant law and for His glory, Adam and Eve were to form the matter of creation into an earthly temple-city that reflects the heavenly city of God. Israel was to model to the nations the worship and obedience that God requires of all peoples. United to Christ in a new covenant, the church forms a new humanity that worships and obeys the Lord. Through Word, sacrament, discipline, prayer, and service, the church is to bring the nations of earth into conformity with the heavenly pattern (chaps. 8–9).

Popularly, what I have called the "millennial" and the "social activist" models seem to dominate contemporary evangelical discussions of the kingdom (see the Introduction). It is true that the kingdom of God will be perfectly consummated only at Christ's Final Advent (though I do not believe in a literal millennial period); and the church should, I have argued, seek to transform the world. Yet, the biblical teaching on the kingdom is not primarily intended to satisfy our curiosity about the future or to foretell political events in the Middle East. Nor is the biblical teaching primarily concerned with social and political questions. Without denying the insights provided by the two models mentioned above, the sacramental-ecclesiological model provides an important and almost forgotten perspective, a perspective without which the other models become distorted.

In the Bible, the kingdom of God is mainly concerned with the church, her sacraments and worship, her discipline and teaching, and her ministries of mercy. The kingdom has more to do with ecclesiology than with eschatology (narrowly defined) or with political theory. The really big kingdom activities do not take place in the halls of Congress or at the March for Life. Those activities of "normal war" are commendable and important, and they are related to the advancement of God's kingdom (see chap. 10). But the really big kingdom activity—the act that radically changes the world—is the gathering of the people of God on the Lord's day at the heavenly banquet table, when God's people hear His Word, offer humble petitions to the King, and feast on the flesh and blood of Jesus.

These are, in my judgment, not only the central emphases of the biblical theology of the kingdom, but also the dimensions of the kingdom that need most to be stressed in our day. To understand why that is the case, we need to take a brief look at the experience of the early church.

Triumph of the Meek

The transformation of the Roman Empire into the Christian empire within a few centuries is the most astounding of historical developments. The church began as a minuscule sect of Judaism, but by the first decades of the fourth century a Christian emperor was instructing his soldiers to paint crosses on their shields and requesting Christian baptism as he lay on his deathbed.

This turn of events seems all the more astonishing when we consider the cultural invisibility of Christians in the Roman world. As the writer of the famous *Letter to Diognetus* explained:

> Christians do not form a separate group marked off from other people by land, language or custom; they do not live in towns of their own nor speak a foreign tongue nor follow a special way of life. . . . In their dress and way of living and general outward behavior they conform to native usage. . . . They take in good

part all that comes their way for they are pilgrims.
. . . They live on earth but their city is in heaven.[1]

It would be wrong to conclude that the conversion of the
empire was wholly unanticipated. From the beginning, the
church claimed that Jesus was Lord of all, even of Caesar.
Christ claimed all things, and it was the duty of the church
to work out the implications of that claim. Roman Catholic
scholar Josef Jungmann has written that

> the task undertaken by the Catholic Church, to trans-
> form the ancient pagan world into a Christian one, was
> indeed a formidable one. . . . The world . . . had to
> be refashioned. Not destroyed, but reshaped; not de-
> molished, but converted, moulded into something
> Christian, transformed into the *Civitas Dei* [City of
> God]. The Church did not bow to the forces of pa-
> ganism; this was impossible. . . . The whole pagan
> world had to enter the kingdom of God in order to be
> sanctified. No sphere of life was exempted from Chris-
> tian "Baptism."[2]

More specifically, Alexander Schmemann wrote that for
the early Christians the state belonged

> to the dominion of the one Kyrios [Lord], Jesus Christ.
> In a deep sense [Christianity] rejects the "separation"
> of Church and state, if that separation is understood
> not in "institutional" or "legal" terms . . . but in those
> of a common perspective, a common reference to the
> same "end." Limited as it is by its belonging to "this
> world," the state is nevertheless capable of reflecting
> the ideal of the Kingdom, of living by it, of truly serv-
> ing the Kyrios of the universe.[3]

This was the view of Christians even before Constantine; already in the early third century, Origen was speculating on
the possibility of a Christian empire.[4]

What surprises us more than the fact of Christianity's triumph, perhaps, is the *way* that it triumphed. The early Christians, it is true, sometimes made use of their rights as Roman citizens to promote the gospel. The two apologies of Justin were addressed to the Roman Senate and represented attempts to convince the Roman government that the church posed no threat to the peace and stability of Rome. Justin demanded that Roman judges overcome their anti-Christian prejudices and condemn only those who had been convicted of crimes.

Many Christians, however, abandoned all legal claims and joyfully endured and even sought martyrdom, and there is no evidence of any large-scale "Christianization" agenda. For the most part, Christians simply went about their daily tasks, gathered each Lord's Day for worship, gave alms to the poor, and showed mercy to slaves. Out of their peacefulness, humility, joy, and mercy, a new world was born. Living with their eyes on heaven, they looked down one morning to find themselves sitting on earthly thrones. It is as clear as can be: the church did not grasp for dominion, but remained patiently faithful and humbly received dominion. Truly, the meek inherited the earth.

These events are of vastly more than historical interest. More than at any time since Constantine, the church in the West finds herself today in the same position as the early church. As in the first centuries, Christianity is under attack on the legal front; the legal effort to strip the public square of Christianity continues unabated. In view of these attacks, it is understandable that Christians have responded with legal and political counterattacks. Christian leaders have rallied Americans around an agenda emphasizing the use of the weapons of law, politics, and the media to protect the unborn, to secure equal treatment of Christians in public schools, to support the traditional family, to bring an end to anti-Christian bigotry in the media. But we may as well be blunt: Christianity is no longer in any sense "official," and, as T. S. Eliot noted several decades ago, there is little hope of its becoming official again for the foreseeable future.[5] It does no good to operate under the illusion that a Christian establishment or a Christian consensus can be legally reinstated.

It has not been my contention, however, that these legal and political strategies are wrong. These efforts are important and necessary in ways that I explained in chapter 10. Political action can indeed be an expression of faith (Heb. 11:32–34) and is a tool of the kingdom. It may well be that legal and political efforts will give the church the precious time it needs to rebuild. Yet, political and legal activities can never become the overriding priorities of the church. There are more important tasks to be undertaken, more pressing questions to answer, more powerful weapons for transforming the world into an image of the heavenly city.

A more biblical set of priorities has been suggested by Armenian Orthodox ethicist Vigen Guroian.

> Historically, the Church's ability to transform society has depended not upon a power of management over society or political brokerage of its own interests, but rather upon a willingness to exercise its freedom to redeem and re-create a fallen world. This the Church has done in its worship, with the strength of internal discipline and by building from within its unique polity more just and compassionate forms of human relations and services.[6]

As I have argued, this is not a historical fluke. It is the way God has ordained for His church to operate in the world. The church will not transform American society primarily by political or legal action. The church will have its most profound impact on the world by faithfully performing its distinctive tasks of sacramental worship, teaching the whole Word of God, evangelism, discipline, and mercy. The highest priorities of the church near the turn of the twenty-first century ought, then, to be to reform herself in these areas. These have always been the chief concerns of the church, and, regardless of the condition of the social world, they remain the chief concerns of the church today, the chief means by which the world will be transformed into an image of the coming kingdom. More than that, they are well pleasing to the Lord of the church.

Conclusion

To some extent, our perception of the church's present task depends largely on our perception of the current state of our civilization. Even from this perspective, however, I believe that the church will be most effective by being the church. If American Christians are victims of a vicious elite, working to regain the levers of power might seem a sensible strategy. If, however, American culture is a mess because the church is a mess, then the most sensible strategy would be to begin with the reform of the church. I hope to have at least made a plausible case for the latter interpretation.

If, furthermore, what used to be called Christendom faces not merely a temporary setback, but a large-scale collapse, the church's most prudent strategy is to prepare herself now to survive the dark age that is upon us. As Eliot warned, "The World is trying to experiment with attempting to form a civilized but non-Christian mentality. The experiment will fail; but we must be very patient in awaiting its collapse; meanwhile redeeming the time: so that the Faith may be preserved alive through the dark ages before us; to renew and rebuild civilization, and save the World from suicide."[7]

Endnotes

Introduction
1. On the use of "models" in theology, see Avery Dulles, *Models of the Church,* exp. ed. (New York: Image/Doubleday, [1974] 1987), 15–33; Howard A. Snyder, *Models of the Kingdom* (Nashville: Abingdon, 1991); and Vern S. Poythress, *Symphonic Theology* (Grand Rapids: Zondervan, 1987).
2. I am thinking, for example, of Herman Ridderbos, *The Coming of the Kingdom,* trans. H. de Jongste (Phillipsburg, N.J.: Presbyterian and Reformed, 1962); Geerhardus Vos, *The Kingdom of God and the Church* (Phillipsburg, N.J.: Presbyterian and Reformed, 1972); G. R. Beasley-Murray, *Jesus and the Kingdom of God* (Grand Rapids: Eerdmans, 1986).
3. I have explored this connection historically in an essay entitled, "The Great Awakening and American Nationalism," available from Biblical Horizons, P.O. Box 1096, Niceville, FL 32588-1096.
4. Journalism provides one barometer of the change. Robert Wuthnow notes the lack of substantive theological articles published in major Christian periodicals. "Pick up the latest issue of *Christian Century* or *Christianity Today;* observe the number of articles that deal with politics and note the paucity of material on theology or even personal spirituality. Or open the mail and count the letters from Moral Majority, Christian Voice, People for the American Way, the American Civil Liberties Union. The

219

issues are now national rather than local or regional," or, for that matter, ecclesiastical (*The Struggle for America's Soul: Evangelicals, Liberals, and Secularism* [Grand Rapids: Eerdmans, 1989], 25–26).

5. Quoted in A. James Reichley, *Religion in American Public Life* (Washington, D.C.: The Brookings Institution, 1985), 336, emphasis added.

6. John Calvin, *Institutes of the Christian Religion,* ed. John T. McNeill, 4.17.7.

Chapter 1: What Is the Kingdom of God?

1. Shakespeare, *The Life of King Henry the Fifth,* act 5, sc. 3:

> This story shall the good man teach his son;
> And Crispin's Crispian shall ne'er go by,
> From this day to the ending of the world,
> But we in it shall be remembered;
> We few, we happy few, we band of brothers;
> For he to-day that sheds his blood with me
> Shall be my brother; be he ne'er so vile,
> This day shall gentle his condition:
> And gentlemen in England now abed
> Shall think themselves accursed they were not here,
> And hold their manhoods cheap whiles any speaks
> That fought with us upon Saint Crispin's Day.

2. For a careful sociological study of this warfare, see James Davison Hunter, *Culture Wars: The Struggle to Define America* (New York: Basic Books, 1991), and Hunter's essay "American Protestantism: Sorting Out the Present, Looking Toward the Future," in Richard Neuhaus, ed., *The Believable Futures of American Protestantism* (Grand Rapids: Eerdmans, 1988), 18–48. See also Robert Wuthnow, *The Struggle for America's Soul: Evangelicals, Liberals, and Secularism* (Grand Rapids: Eerdmans, 1989).

3. Some writers, such as Alasdair MacIntyre and Thomas Molnar, go a step further, arguing that conflict is the only thing that binds us together as a society. Molnar cites Marcel Gauchet, "who insists that the main social code and requisite of modern society is that nobody is allowed to win, that nobody may be right. Conflict is then the essence of freedom, the red badge of

individuality, really a kind of common good in reverse. More than that, conflict has the vocation of being turned into a religion." In short, the "sacralization of continuity [in medieval European culture] has been replaced by the sacralization of conflict" (*Twin Powers: Politics and the Sacred* [Grand Rapids: Eerdmans, 1988], 100, 119).

4. My translation. Most translations mistranslate the word "discovered" as "burned up" or something similar. Textually and lexically, "discovered" is superior.

5. Alasdair MacIntyre, *After Virtue,* 2d ed. (Notre Dame, Ind.: University of Notre Dame Press, 1984); *Whose Justice? Which Rationality?* (Notre Dame, Ind.: University of Notre Dame Press, 1988).

6. Throughout this book I am using the definitions of "evangelical" and "fundamentalist" offered by A. James Reichley: "The distinction between evangelicalism and fundamentalism was, and has remained, somewhat hazy. Evangelicalism is best defined as a branch of Christianity, descended from the pietist movement of the Reformation by way of the Great Awakening, that emphasizes direct experience by the individual of the Holy Spirit (being 'born again') and that regards the Bible as an infallible source of religious and moral authority. Fundamentalism is an extreme form of evangelicalism. All fundamentalists are evangelicals, but not all evangelicals are fundamentalists" (*Religion in American Public Life* [Washington, D.C.: The Brookings Institution, 1985], 312).

7. Roger Kimball, *Tenured Radicals* (San Francisco: Harper and Row, 1990); Dinesh D'Souza, *Illiberal Education: The Politics of Race and Sex on Campus* (New York: Free Press, 1991); Allan Bloom, *The Closing of the American Mind* (New York: Simon and Schuster, 1987).

8. See George Gilder, *Men and Marriage* (Lafayette, La.: Pelican Press, 1986); Allan C. Carlson, *Family Questions: Reflections on the American Social Crisis* (New Brunswick, N.J.: Transaction, 1988); Bryce Christensen, ed., *The Family in America,* newsletter published by the Rockford Institute Center on the Family in America, Rockford, Illinois.

9. For a Christian view of environmental issues, see E. Calvin Beisner, *Prospects for Growth: A Biblical View of Population, Resources, and the Future* (Westchester, Ill.: Crossway Books, 1989).

10. Richard John Neuhaus, *The Naked Public Square: Religion and Democracy in America* (Grand Rapids: Eerdmans, 1984), 72.

11. Sidney E. Mead, *The Nation with the Soul of a Church* (San Francisco: Harper and Row, 1975), 73, quoting John E. Smylie's 1963 article, "National Ethos and the Church."

12. Understanding the conflict as one between "conservatives" and "liberals" is highly suspect even at a sociological level. The lines between "conservative" and "liberal" are blurry at best; there is such a myriad of subdivisions within each camp that the labels have become all but useless for thoughtful analysis. One bit of evidence in support of this conclusion is that some writers feel the need to define their positions with compound labels. Richard John Neuhaus identifies himself, among other things, as "culturally conservative," "politically liberal," "economically pragmatic." Moreover, alliances vary from issue to issue; some "liberals" are pro-life, while some conservatives call for a "conservative welfare state." Efforts to define the conflict in purely political terms fail to do justice to this complexity. Hunter's use of "orthodox" and "progressive" is more useful, but still fails to provide a sufficiently nuanced picture.

    I recognize, moreover, that there are Christians who reverse these equations, who see America as a uniquely evil nation, and who believe that Christian faith requires a radical restructuring of the American economy and political order. I have not addressed these sectors of American Christianity, primarily because my own experience has been in politically conservative circles, and so I am more confident critiquing that viewpoint than the liberal. I began my intellectual pilgrimage on the right, and there, to a large extent, for better or worse, I remain.

13. Vigen Guroian, *Incarnate Love: Essays in Orthodox Ethics* (Notre Dame, Ind.: University of Notre Dame Press, 1987), 151. I think the late Walker Percy got it exactly right when he sardonically commented in *The Moviegoer* that in the modern world 100 percent of the people are secular humanists, and 98 percent believe in God.

14. Quoted from a summary of a Washington, D.C. sermon by Randall Terry in *The National Rescuer* (December 1990/January 1991), 1. Terry is more on target when he calls, as he constantly does, for Christians to humble themselves in repentance. My contention is that his two emphases are incompatible with each

another. Either the "real Americans" are righteous victims of the elite, or the "real Americans" are themselves unrighteous.

15. Of course, the analogy of the early Christians and modern Western Christians is not perfect. We live in a culture that has thrown off Christianity, while they lived in a culture that had not yet heard the gospel. The contemporary West is not so much pagan as apostate. Yet, I think we will have a more accurate assessment of the church's present task if we make an effort to think like the early Christians than if we think like the temporarily vanquished Emir of Kuwait.

16. James B. Jordan, "The Holy War in America Today: Some Observations on Abortion Rescues," 3–4. Available from Biblical Horizons, P.O. Box 1096, Niceville, FL 32588-1096. Drawing on the Old Testament pattern of holy war, Jordan concludes that

> The Gospel is God's Holy War today. Like the Holy War of the Old Covenant, the Gospel:
>
> 1. Is initiated by God;
> 2. Involves sending God's warriors aggressively out into the world to change it;
> 3. Is made necessary because of man's Original Sin and actual sins;
> 4. Brings the judgment of Spiritual fire to man's life and cleanses him; and
> 5. Delivers men from the futureless fires of hell into the glorious inheritance of the saints in light.

17. I have discussed this point at somewhat greater length in "Marburg and Modernity," *First Things* (January 1992).

18. Quoted in Jonathan V. Smith, *To Take Place: Toward Theory in Ritual* (Chicago: University of Chicago Press, 1987).

19. Quoted in Archibald Robertson, *Regnum Dei: Eight Lectures on the Kingdom of God in the History of Christian Thought* (New York: Macmillan, 1901), 162.

20. "Clerical Illusion," *Crisis* (February 1990), 8.

21. I have explored the strengths and weaknesses of this definition in detail in an essay entitled, "What Is the Kingdom of God?" Available from Biblical Horizons, P.O. Box 1096, Niceville, FL 32588-1096.

22. The notion that the kingdom is "already" and "not yet" is so commonly accepted by New Testament scholars that I feel no need to defend it here. See Wendell Willis, ed., *The Kingdom of God in 20th-Century Interpretation* (Peabody, Mass.: Hendrickson, 1987); G. R. Beasley-Murray, *Jesus and the Kingdom of God* (Grand Rapids: Eerdmans, 1986), esp. chaps. 9–12. Rudolf Schnackenburg describes the various formulations of this "tension" in *God's Rule and Kingdom,* trans. John Murray (New York: Herder and Herder, 1963), 114–17.

The conclusion that the kingdom has present and future dimensions cuts across millennial lines. Among postmillennialist writers, see David Chilton, *Paradise Restored: An Eschatology of Dominion* (Fort Worth, Tex.: Reconstruction Press, 1985); Roderick Campbell, *Israel and the New Covenant* (Philadelphia: Presbyterian and Reformed, 1954; reprint, Tyler, Tex.: Geneva Divinity School Press, n.d.), esp. chaps. 12–18; Gary DeMar and Peter Leithart, *The Reduction of Christianity* (Fort Worth, Tex.: Dominion, 1987), 149–228. Among amillennial scholars, the reader can consult Herman Ridderbos, *The Coming of the Kingdom,* trans. H. de Jongste (Philadelphia: Presbyterian and Reformed, 1962), esp. chaps. 3–4; Geerhardus Vos, *The Kingdom of God and the Church,* chaps. 4–5; Vos, *Biblical Theology: Old and New Testaments* (1948; reprint, Grand Rapids: Eerdmans, 1983), 343–402. For detailed examinations of this same pattern in Paul's epistles, see Vos, *The Pauline Eschatology* (Princeton, N.J.: Princeton University Press, 1930; reprint, Phillipsburg, N.J.: Presbyterian and Reformed, 1986), and Ridderbos, *Paul: An Outline of His Theology,* trans. John Richard DeWitt (Grand Rapids: Eerdmans, 1975). Among premillennial writers, see George Eldon Ladd, *Jesus and the Kingdom: The Eschatology of Biblical Realism* (New York: Harper and Row, 1964).

Chapter 2: I Saw Satan Fall

1. For further details of the Matamoros incident, see the reports in the *Economist* (April 22, 1989), 27; *World* (April 22, 1989), 8.
2. For a helpful overview of this subject, see Greg L. Bahnsen, "The Person, Work, and Present Status of Satan," *The Journal of Christian Reconstruction* 1, no. 2 (Winter 1974), 11–43.
3. I used a number of sources in arriving at this formulation. See James B. Jordan, *Through New Eyes: Developing a Biblical View*

of the World (Brentwood, Tenn.: Wolgemuth & Hyatt, 1988); Vern S. Poythress, *The Shadow of Christ in the Law of Moses* (Brentwood, Tenn.: Wolgemuth & Hyatt, 1991); Alexander Schmemann, *For the Life of the World,* 2d ed. (Crestwood, N.Y.: St. Vladimir's Seminary Press, 1973); Calvin, *Commentary on the Book of Psalms,* 5 vols., trans. James Anderson (Grand Rapids: Eerdmans, 1949), especially at Psalm 36:8; William J. Dumbrell, *The End of the Beginning: Revelation 21–22 and the Old Testament* (Homebush West, Australia: Lancer, 1985); Meredith Kline, *Kingdom Prologue,* 3 vols. (by the author, 1983–86), 1:54–55.

4. I admit that there are some peoples who suppress the created "drive" to rule the earth. Various social scientists, for example, have documented that different cultures have widely varying attitudes toward their environments. Some accept whatever happens as the product of an inscrutable fate, while others seek, as Shakespeare's Henry V said, to "bend the world to their awe or dash it all to pieces." For more extensive thoughts on dominion, see my article, "Perspectives on Dominion," *The Biblical Worldview* 5, no. 1 (January 1989): 6–9.

5. On the priestly character of Adam's calling, see Kline, *Kingdom Prologue,* 1:64–69; Dumbrell, *The End of the Beginning,* 178–79; Schmemann, *For the Life of the World,* 14–16; Jordan, *Through New Eyes,* 136–38. For a brief exploration of the essential meaning of priesthood, see my article, "What Is a Priest?" *Biblical Horizons* (January 1992), 3–4.

6. Herbert Schlossberg developed this point brilliantly in his *Idols for Destruction: Christian Faith and Its Confrontation with American Society* (Nashville: Thomas Nelson, 1984). For a classic theological statement of this truth, see Calvin, *Institutes* 1.1.3–5.

7. C. van der Waal, *The Covenantal Gospel* (Neerlandia, Alberta: Inheritance Publications, 1990).

8. For detailed examinations of the sanctuary features of the Garden, see Jordan, *Through New Eyes,* 152–59; Kline, *Kingdom Prologue,* 1:37–38; Dumbrell, *The End of the Beginning,* 52; Gordon J. Wenham, *Genesis 1–15* (Waco, Tex.: Word, 1987), 61, 65. The idea that Eden, and later the city and temple of Jerusalem, were "world-centers" comes from Dumbrell.

9. This definition of blessing comes from Dumbrell, *The End of the Beginning,* 131.

10. Among the writers who find the pattern of the kingdom of God in the Garden of Eden are David Chilton, *Paradise Restored: An Eschatology of Dominion* (Fort Worth, Tex.: Reconstruction Press, 1985); Dumbrell, *The End of the Beginning*, 135, 194; Jordan, *Through New Eyes*.

11. See Kline, *Kingdom Prologue*, 1:82. Kline also rightly calls the tree the "probation tree," that is, the tree by which Adam and Eve were to be tested. On the connection of the tree with royal wisdom, see van der Waal, *Covenantal Gospel*, 49–51. Van der Waal well captures the sense of Genesis 2 when he writes that "the tree of the knowledge of good and evil was the Royal Standard Supreme of Yahweh Himself. This had to be honoured as a *Royal Standard*. Adam did not behave like a Royal *Keeper* of the Great Seal. He profaned the majesty, he committed *crimen laesae majestatis*" (51).

12. See James B. Jordan, "The Dominion Trap," *Biblical Horizons* 15 (July 1990): 1–4.

13. Kenneth A. Myers, *All God's Children and Blue Suede Shoes: Christians and Popular Culture* (Westchester, Ill.: Crossway, 1989), 46.

14. David Lamb, *The Africans*, 2d ed. (New York: Vintage Books, 1987), 109.

15. For introductory studies in typology, see Jordan, *Through New Eyes*, and Jordan's bibliography, 315–20. See also Edmund P. Clowney, *The Unfolding Mystery: Discovering Christ in the Old Testament* (Colorado Springs: NavPress, 1988; reprint, Phillipsburg, N.J.: Presbyterian and Reformed, 1991).

16. Dumbrell, *The End of the Beginning*, 139.

17. See my article, "He Shall Be Called a Nazarene," *Biblical Horizons* 13 (May 1990): 2–3.

18. I am relying on the careful exegesis of this difficult passage provided by G. R. Beasley-Murray, *Jesus and the Kingdom of God* (Grand Rapids: Eerdmans, 1986), 91–96.

19. I am not denying that Jesus is eternally and essentially God. Adam was not the Son of God in the same sense that Jesus is. But it makes sense in the context of the temptation to understand the phrase "Son of God" in a redemptive-historical rather than an ontological sense. See Geerhardus Vos, *Biblical Theology: Old and New Testaments* (1948; reprint, Grand Rapids: Eerdmans, 1983), 333–35.

20. On the "forensic" character of the resurrection, see Richard B. Gaffin, Jr., *Resurrection and Redemption: A Study in Paul's Soteriology*, 2d ed. (Phillipsburg, N.J.: Presbyterian and Reformed, 1987), 122–24.

Chapter 3: One Like the Son of Man

1. See my article, "Building the Church," *Biblical Horizons*, 14 (June 1990): 3–4, for a fuller discussion of Matthew 16:13–20.
2. Roderick Campbell, *Israel and the New Covenant* (Philadelphia: Presbyterian and Reformed, 1954; reprint, Tyler, Tex.: Geneva Divinity School Press, n.d.), 37.
3. Augustine, *City of God* 16.43.
4. G. R. Beasley-Murray, *Jesus and the Kingdom of God* (Grand Rapids: Eerdmans, 1986), 232–35, notes that the title "Son of Man" connotes authority.
5. See William J. Dumbrell, *The End of the Beginning: Revelation 21–22 and the Old Testament* (Homebush West, Australia: Lancer, 1985), 190–95.
6. This crucial point is missed in nearly every recent treatment of "dominion." While some authors who write about "dominion theology" admit that the Old Testament is to be interpreted typologically, they fail to work through the implications of this insight consistently. If Adam is a type of Christ, then Adam's dominion is also a type of Christ's, as the writer of Hebrews emphasizes. Christ's dominion thus includes something beyond the earthly or cultural dominion of Adam.

   Many treatments of the "dominion" theme in the Bible tend to isolate Genesis 1–3 from the rest of the Old Testament. Instead of being treated, as the Scriptures teach they should be, as types of Christ and His kingdom, these chapters are treated as raw materials for a Christian political, cultural, or social philosophy. I am not denying that these chapters have relevance to such issues, but to treat them exclusively or even primarily from the perspective of social theory seriously distorts their intended meaning.

   C. van der Waal makes a similar point: "The conclusion is often immediately drawn that creation concerns 'man' in general. If mention is made of the image of God, then the conclusion is: surely something of it remains in everybody. The 'first things' are easily separated from that which follows and from the 'last things.' The concept of 'creation' and the concept of 'man' are taken from Gen. 1 and 2, and become building blocks for a general philosophy or *theologia naturalis* or a humanistic train of thought" (*The Covenantal Gospel* [Neerlandia, Alberta: Inheritance Publications, 1990], 47).

7. See John M. Frame, *Perspectives on the Word of God: An Introduction to Christian Ethics* (Phillipsburg, N.J.: Presbyterian and Reformed, 1990), 12–13, for a brief and insightful discussion of the authority of God's Word.

8. For a thorough discussion of Christ's authority over the nations, see William Symington, *Messiah the Prince, or, The Mediatorial Dominion of Jesus Christ* (Edmonton, 1884; reprint, Canada: Still Waters Revival Books, 1990), chap. 8.

9. Leon Morris, *The Biblical Doctrine of Judgment* (Grand Rapids: Baker, 1960), 17.

10. See Frame, *Perspectives on the Word of God,* 10–12, for a discussion of the power of the Word of God.

11. Ibid., 13–16, for a discussion of the Word as the personal presence of God.

12. Compare the opposing view of Kenneth L. Myers, who has recently resurrected the old Presbyterian debate concerning the scope of Christ's "mediatorial reign" (*Public Eye* 1, no. 3 [September 1987]: 1, 3, published by Berea, Inc., 2809 Church Road, Mitchellville, MD, 20716). Myers, following Thomas E. Peck's 1863 article in *The Southern Presbyterian Review,* denies that Christ is mediatorial King over all things; His "saving rule" is over His church alone. For an extensive refutation of Peck's and Myers's position, see Symington, *Messiah the Prince.*

13. See the fascinating discussion of Jaroslav Pelikan, in his Rauschenbusch Lectures, *The Excellent Empire: The Fall of Rome and the Triumph of the Church* (San Francisco: Harper and Row, 1987), 53, which contrasts the views of Jerome and Gibbon on decline of Rome. Jerome emphasized that God was fulfilling His purposes in the midst of human history, while Gibbon believed that his purpose as an historian was to discover the mix of vice and virtue that made up the history of the church, and Gibbon was particularly interested in the vice. I am arguing that the biblical view combines Jerome's optimism with Gibbon's realism.

14. This imbalance seriously mars, for example, Abraham Kuyper's classic *Lectures on Calvinism,* and it is evident among those deeply influenced by Kuyperian thought.

15. See Archibald Richardson, *Regnum Dei: Eight Lectures on the Kingdom of God in the History of Christian Thought* (New York: Macmillan, 1901). The Reformers as well as the medieval Roman Catholic Church made this identification. Martin Bucer offered political advice to Edward VI in his *De Regno Christi,* but when he wrote about the "kingdom of God," he was referring to the church. The Westminster Confession of Faith similarly spoke of the church as "the kingdom of Christ" (25.1).

16. To put it differently, the particular and universal aspects of Christ's reign may be said to be "perspectivally related." Readers familiar with John M. Frame's work, *The Doctrine of the Knowledge of God* (Phillipsburg, N.J.: Presbyterian and Reformed, 1987), will recognize that I am using "perspective" in a rather technical sense. Two doctrines are "perspectivally related" when each includes or implies the other. The rule of Christ over His people is related in this way to His rule over all things. See Symington, *Messiah the Prince,* 62, 72, 193.

17. Edmund P. Clowney, *The Unfolding Mystery: Discovering Christ in the Old Testament* (Colorado Springs: NavPress, 1988; reprint, Phillipsburg, N.J.: Presbyterian and Reformed, 1991), 39.

18. Quoted in Jean Danielou, *The Angels and Their Mission, According to the Fathers of the Church,* trans. David Heimann (1957; reprint, Dublin, Ireland: Four Courts Press, 1988), 37.

Chapter 4: In the Heavenlies

1. C. S. Lewis, *The Weight of Glory and Other Addresses* (1949; reprint, New York: Macmillan, 1980), 93–105. In this entire chapter and the following, I am deeply indebted to James B. Jordan's continuing work on the "treasury of God."

2. C. E. B. Cranfield, *A Critical and Exegetical Commentary on the Epistle to the Romans,* The International Critical Commentary, 2 vols. (Edinburgh: T. & T. Clark, 1975), 1:288.

3. James B. Jordan, "The Church: An Overview," *The Reconstruction of the Church,* ed. James B. Jordan, Christianity and Civilization, no. 4 (Tyler, Tex.: Geneva Ministries, 1985), 19–21.

4. See Rousas John Rushdoony, *Salvation and Godly Rule* (Vallecito, Calif.: Ross House Books, 1983), 35–36.

5. Edmund P. Clowney, *The Unfolding Mystery: Discovering Christ in the Old Testament* (Colorado Springs: NavPress, 1988; reprint, Phillipsburg, N.J.: Presbyterian and Reformed, 1991), 39.

6. On Romans 6:14, Calvin comments: "The apostle is desirous of comforting us and preventing us from growing wearied in striving to do what is right, because we still feel the imperfections in ourselves. However much the stings of sin may torment us, they cannot subdue us, for we are enabled to conquer them by the Spirit of God." *The Epistles of Paul the Apostle to the Romans and to the Thessalonians,* trans. Ross Mackenzie, ed. David W. and Thomas F. Torrance (Grand Rapids: Eerdmans, 1980), 131. See the discussion of this passage in Philip Mauro, *The Church, the Churches and the Kingdom* (1936; reprint, Sterling, Va.: Grace Abounding Ministries, 1988), 125–32. Roderick Campbell summarizes the various ways in which believers reign with Christ in *Israel and the New Covenant* (Philadelphia: Presbyterian and Reformed, 1954; reprint, Tyler, Tex.: Geneva Divinity School Press, n.d.), 134–35.

7. Martin Luther, "The Freedom of the Christian Man," in *Martin Luther: Three Treatises,* rev. ed. (Philadelphia: Fortress, 1970), 289–90. This treatise was translated by W. A. Lambert.

8. Augustine, *City of God* 1.9–14.

9. Ibid., 1.8.

10. See Alexander Schmemann, *For the Life of the World,* 2d ed. (Crestwood, N.Y.: St. Vladimir's Seminary Press, 1973).

11. See, for example, my own argument in *The Reduction of Christianity* (Fort Worth Tex.: Dominion, 1987), 175–76. Though my discussion of *ek* in *Reduction* is accurate in itself, my exegesis was not sufficiently sensitive to the connection between origin and nature.

12. See Irenaeus, *Against All Heresies* 4.14.3: In the Old Testament, God "instructed the people, who were prone to turn to idols, instructing them by repeated appeals to persevere and to serve God, calling them to the things of primary importance by means of those which were secondary; that is, to things that are real, by means of those that are typical; and by things temporal, to eternal; and by the carnal to the spiritual; and by the earthly to the heavenly. . . ."

Also, Chrysostom, *Homilies on Matthew,* homily 1.12: In comparing the "commonwealth" of God with that of Plato, Chrysostom writes that the apostles "as a place for this their commonwealth have assigned Heaven, and God they have brought as the framer thereof." Chrysostom ends his first homily by stating that Matthew is a useful guide through the heavenly city of God (1.17). Similar statements about the heavenly character of the kingdom are found scattered throughout these homilies.

Calvin, *Institutes* 2.11.1: "Now this is the first difference [between old and new covenants]: the Lord of old willed that his people direct and elevate their minds to the heavenly heritage; yet, to nourish them better in this hope, he displayed it for them to see and, so to speak, taste, under earthly benefits. But now that the gospel has more plainly and clearly revealed the grace of the future life, the Lord leads our minds to meditate on it directly, laying aside the lower mode of training that he used with the Israelites."

Patrick Fairbairn, *Typology of Scripture* (New York: Funk and Wagnalls, 1900; reprint, 2 vols. in 1, Grand Rapids: Kregel, 1989), 1.158: Comparing the old and new covenants, Fairbairn writes, "*There,* the outward, the present, the worldly; *here,* the inward, the future, the heavenly." Fairbairn goes on to emphasize that the new covenant is not therefore to be understood as something unrelated to the world.

Testimonies of such theologians ought not be summarily dismissed as "neoplatonic."

13. I have defended this traditional translation, and attempted to explain the meaning of this verse, in "The Substance of Things Hoped For," *Biblical Horizons* 18 (October 1990): 2–3.

14. A dramatic example of this comes from F. Kefa Sempangi's *A Distant Grief,* an extraordinary account of Sempangi's ministry in Idi Amin's Uganda. When threatened after an evening worship service by several of Amin's henchmen, for example, Sempangi found himself replying calmly, "You can't hurt me. I'm already dead." His reply defused that situation, and one of the soldiers present at the encounter was later converted.

Chapter 5: The Torn Veil

1. See William J. Dumbrell, *The End of the Beginning: Revelation 21–22 and the Old Testament* (Homebush West, Australia: Lancer, 1985), chap. 2, "The New Temple."

2. The phrase is Peter Brown's. See his *The Cult of the Saints: Its Rise and Influence in Latin Christianity* (Chicago: University of Chicago Press, 1981), and *Society and the Holy in Late Antiquity* (London: Faber and Faber, 1982).

3. See James B. Jordan, "The Meaning of Clean and Unclean," *Studies in Food and Faith*, no. 10 (Tyler, Tex.: Biblical Horizons, 1990), available from Biblical Horizons, P.O. Box 1096, Niceville, FL 32588-1096.

4. See Meredith Kline, *Images of the Spirit* (Grand Rapids: Baker, 1980).

5. John M. Frame has written that God "prefers . . . not to speak to each person individually, though he is quite capable of doing that, but rather to speak publicly, to spread his speech out on the public record so that all alike can come and see. He prefers to place his words in a written constitution so that a *people* may be formed, a *body* of individuals, visibly and externally (as well as invisibly and internally) united and governed by their allegiance to a particular text." *Perspectives on the Word of God: An Introduction to Christian Ethics* (Phillipsburg, N.J.: Presbyterian and Reformed, 1990), 27–28. What Frame says about the Word applies to worship generally.

6. Dumbrell, *The End of the Beginning*, 40–42, for a discussion of the connections of Sabbath, creation, and sanctuary. See Irenaeus, *Against All Heresies* 4.16.1: "The Sabbath of God, that is, the kingdom, was, as it were, indicated by created things."

7. See Vern S. Poythress, *Symphonic Theology: The Validity of Multiple Perspectives in Theology* (Grand Rapids: Zondervan, 1987).

8. Herman Bavinck, *The Doctrine of God*, trans. William Hendriksen (Grand Rapids: Eerdmans, 1951; reprint, Grand Rapids: Baker, 1977), 120–24.

9. See Marc Bloch, *The Royal Touch*, trans. J. E. Anderson (New York: Dorset Press, 1989); Thomas Molnar, *Twin Powers: Politics and the Sacred* (Grand Rapids: Eerdmans, 1988).

10. The clearest evidence that the sanctuary and the kingdom are one is the fact that they are united eschatologically. When John saw the new heavens and new earth in a vision, he saw a city coming from heaven (see Rev. 21:2). But this city, like the Holy of Holies, was a cube: "Its length and width and height are equal" (21:16; cf. 2 Chron. 3:8). In other passages, this final state of things, this consummated new heavens and new earth, is called the kingdom of God that the saints will inherit (see Matt. 25:34). Others have suggested that the city coming from heaven is a pyramid, a holy mountain, but the connection of the kingdom and sanctuary would remain even in this interpretation.

For a more detailed defense of my conclusion that the kingdom and sanctuary are parallel, see my article, "What Is the Kingdom of God?" 15–18, available from Biblical Horizons, P.O. Box 1096, Niceville, FL 32588-1096. See the similar comments of Rudolf Schnackenburg, *God's Rule and Kingdom* (New York: Herder and Herder, 1963), 17, 21–30; G. R. Beasley-Murray, *Jesus and the Kingdom of God* (Grand Rapids: Eerdmans, 1986), 184.

11. The reader interested in examining the symbolism of tabernacle and temple at greater length is urged to consult James B. Jordan, *Through New Eyes: Developing a Biblical View of the World* (Brentwood, Tenn.: Wolgemuth & Hyatt, 1988), chaps. 15–16.

12. Augustine, *City of God* 17.3.

13. Some scholars have suggested that the Old Testament background to Jesus' "entrance" statements is not the sanctuary, but the land (see Schnackenburg, *God's Rule and Kingdom*, 161–62, 284–85). To enter the kingdom is to enter the true, heavenly land, for which Abraham searched. That is completely reasonable to me, and in fact is quite consistent with my argument here. The land, after all, was a *holy* land, a sanctuary land, where God was specially present in His tabernacle and temple. Thus, I am perfectly content to add another equation to an already complicated series of connections: to enter the kingdom is to enter the sanctuary is to enter the true Promised Land.

A further connection, which I have developed at some length in my article "What Is the Kingdom of God?" (16–17) is that between the kingdom and the glory of God. The two are clearly parallel in certain passages (see Matt. 16:27–28; Mark 10:37 with Matt. 19:28; 1 Thess. 2:12). Throughout the Old Testament, moreover, the glory of God is the visible revelation of God as *King* (see Isa. 6:1–5; Ezek. 1:26). This indirectly leads us back to the association of the sanctuary and the kingdom. The glory of God is His kingly presence, and the glory descends upon the tabernacle and temple, consecrating them as holy places (see Ex. 29:43). Thus, to enter the kingdom of God is to enter the glory of God in the sanctuary.

14. Dumbrell, *The End of the Beginning*, 42.

15. Ibid., 43.

16. This discussion is largely based on the work of James B. Jordan, *Sabbath Breaking and the Death Penalty: A Theological Investigation* (Tyler, Tex.: Geneva Ministries, 1986).

17. See Meredith Kline, *Images of the Spirit* (Grand Rapids: Baker, 1980), for an extended discussion of the interconnected symbolism of the tabernacle, the priestly garments, and the Holy Spirit.

18. The writer to the Hebrews also tells us that the veil was a symbol of Jesus' flesh. This is not an easy figure to interpret. It may mean that Jesus passed through the flesh to inaugurate a new way for us. That is, He passed through a fleshly existence to gain our access to the heavenly sanctuary, identifying Himself with us in our weakness and frailty so that He could bring many sons to glory. This figure also implies that it is only through Him that we gain access to the heavenly sanctuary. He is the door. Some have also seen here the implication that it was only by the rending of the veil of His flesh that we could gain entrance to God's presence.

19. Dumbrell, *The End of the Beginning*, 67. See also C. van der Waal, *The Covenantal Gospel* (Neerlandia, Alberta: Inheritance Publications, 1990), 83–85, where van der Waal describes the rending of the veil as an announcement of the impending judgment on Jerusalem.

20. On Luke 17:21, see Beasley-Murray, *Jesus and the Kingdom*, 102–3.

21. This conflation is not foreign, however, to the Old Testament itself. The tabernacle was symbolic of the people of God assembled around His throne. See Jordan, *Through New Eyes*, 213–16.

22. Geerhardus Vos, *The Kingdom of God and the Church* (Phillipsburg, N.J.: Presbyterian and Reformed, 1972), 81; see Beasley-Murray, *Jesus and the Kingdom*, 183–84.

Chapter 6: The King's Table

1. See my articles, "The Dew of Heaven," *Biblical Horizons* 4 (May 1989): 2–3, and "Additional Reflections on the Dew of Heaven," *Biblical Horizons* 16 (August 1990): 2–3.

2. See Richard B. Gaffin, Jr., *Perspectives on Pentecost* (Phillipsburg, N.J.: Presbyterian and Reformed, 1979), 14–20. Calvin said that the ascension of Christ and the sending of the Spirit are "antithetical," and explained Christ's presence in the Supper by saying that the Spirit is the "bond of union" (*Institutes* 4.17.12).

3. See Meredith Kline, *Images of the Spirit* (Grand Rapids: Baker, 1980).

4. This use of the phrase "kingdom of heaven" is found clearly in Matthew 21:33–46, the parable of the vineyard. In this parable, the vineyard is a symbol of the kingdom, which God gives to the nation that will produce its fruit. In verse 43, Jesus warns Israel that God will take the vineyard from them and given it to a new people (cf. v. 45). In this passage, the kingdom is not a rule or a people or a place, but something that can be given to and taken from a people. See also Luke 12:32 and 22:24–30.

5. Calvin said that because of the sin of Adam, Adamic men do not even have any right to the food they eat. Thus, they compound their unbelief by stealing what is not theirs. Only in Christ, and by prayer and thanksgiving, is our food sanctified for our use (*Commentaries on the Epistles to Timothy, Titus, and Philemon,* trans. John Pringle [Grand Rapids: Eerdmans, 1948], at 1 Timothy 4:4–5).

6. In systematic theological terms, we must be justified to enter into the life of the kingdom. This is repeatedly stressed in Romans: righteousness leads to life (see Rom. 5:18, 21). See John Murray, *Redemption Accomplished and Applied* (Grand Rapids: Eerdmans, 1961), 122–31.

7. Richard Baxter made these helpful comments about baptism: "As all true believers, so all their infants do receive initially by the promise, and by way of obsignation and sacramental investiture in baptism, a *jus relationis,* a right of peculiar relation to all three persons in the blessed Trinity. . . . The right and relation adhereth to them, and is given them in order to future actual operation and communion: as a marriage covenant giveth the relation and right to one another, in order to the subsequent communion and duties of a married life; and as he that sweareth allegiance to a king, or is listed into an army, or is entered into a school, receiveth the right and relation, and is so correlated, as obligeth to the mutual subsequent offices of each, and giveth right to many particular benefits" (*A Christian Directory* [Ligonier, Pa.: Soli Deo Gloria, 1990], 657). Of course, the rights that baptism confers are not irreversible. Just as a rebellious child can be disinherited by parents or an adulterous husband be divorced by his wife, so also a baptized person can, through faithlessness, forfeit the rights and relation to which baptism has entitled him.

8. On the significance of the number eight in the Bible, see Augustine, *City of God* 23.30; Alexander Schmemann, *Introduction*

to Liturgical Theology, trans. Ashleigh E. Moorhouse, 3d ed. (Crestwood, N.Y.: St. Vladimir's Seminary Press, 1986), 75–80; Jean Danielou, *The Bible and the Liturgy* (1956; reprint, Notre Dame, Ind.: University of Notre Dame Press, 1987), chap. 16.

The structure of the text itself leads me to conclude that these are eight dimensions or perspectives on the kingdom, or an eightfold blessing of the kingdom. The promises of verses 3 and 10 are the same: both the poor and the persecuted will inherit the kingdom of heaven. These promises provide "bookends" for the Beatitudes as a whole. Within these bookends, the reality of the kingdom is unfolded and explained in a variety of ways. Augustine took something like this approach to the Beatitudes in his homilies on the Sermon on the Mount. He argued that "the one reward, which is the kingdom of heaven, is variously named according to these stages." "Our Lord's Sermon on the Mount," chaps. 2–3, in *A Select Library of Nicene and Post-Nicene Fathers of the Christian Church,* ed. Philip Schaff (1887; reprint, Grand Rapids: Eerdmans, 1979), 4:4–10. See also Rudolf Schnackenburg, *God's Rule and Kingdom,* trans. John Murray (New York: Herder and Herder, 1963), 93.

9. Geerhadus Vos, *Biblical Theology: Old and New Testaments* (1948; reprint, Grand Rapids: Eerdmans, 1983), 392.

10. In this and the following paragraphs, I am indebted to Geoffrey Wainwright, *Eucharist and Eschatology* (New York: Oxford University Press, 1981), 18–42.

11. Ambrose quoted in ibid., 101.

12. Schnackenburg, *God's Rule and Kingdom,* 35–36, notes the connection between the re-creation of the world promised by the prophets (e.g., Isa. 9:6–9; 35:1–10), and the enjoyment of the fruits of the renewed earth in the feast. See also Alexander Schmemann, *For the Life of the World,* 2d ed. (Crestwood, N.Y.: St. Vladimir's Seminary Press, 1973).

13. See G. R. Beasley-Murray, *Jesus and the Kingdom of God* (Grand Rapids: Eerdmans, 1986), 342, for the assertion that the feast is Jesus' favorite image of the kingdom; similar comments may be found in Schnackenburg, *God's Rule and Kingdom,* 85, 93–94, 162, 249ff.

14. In this following discussion, I am relying on Wainwright, *Eucharist and Eschatology,* 147–51, and Schmemann, *For the Life of the World.*

15. Kenneth A. Myers, *All God's Children and Blue Suede Shoes: Christians and Popular Culture* (Westchester, Ill.: Crossway, 1989), 52.
16. Irenaeus, *Against All Heresies* 4.18.4–5; 5.2.2.
17. Schnackenburg, *God's Rule and Kingdom*, 36.
18. Calvin, *Institutes* 3.20.44: "Not even an abundance of bread would benefit us in the slightest unless it were divinely turned into nourishment"; 1.16.7: "There is nothing more ordinary in nature than for us to be nourished by bread. Yet the Spirit declares not only that the produce of the earth is God's special gift but that 'men do not live by bread alone' [Deut. 8:3; Matt. 4:4]; because it is not plenty itself that nourishes men, but God's secret blessing. . . ."
19. Wainwright, *Eucharist and Eschatology*, 150.

Chapter 7: After the Feast

1. For additional argumentation along these lines, see John M. Frame, *Perspectives on the Word of God: An Introduction to Christian Ethics* (Phillipsburg, N.J.: Presbyterian and Reformed, 1990), 39–56.

Chapter 8: The People of the Kingdom

1. See Geerhardus Vos, *The Kingdom of God and the Church* (Phillipsburg, N.J.: Presbyterian and Reformed, 1972), 82, interpreting the kingdom in the parables of the wheat and tares and of the dragnet as a community of men. On Luke 12:32, see G. R. Beasley-Murray, *Jesus and the Kingdom of God* (Grand Rapids: Eerdmans, 1986), 185–87.
2. See the extremely helpful article by Norman Shepherd, "The Covenantal Context of Evangelism," in *The New Testament Student and Theology*, ed. John H. Skilton (Phillipsburg, N.J.: Presbyterian and Reformed, 1976), where Shepherd distinguishes between "looking at the covenant from the viewpoint of election" and "looking at election from the viewpoint of the covenant," and argues that the latter is the biblical approach.
3. The question of judging a true church is too complex to treat fully here, but a few comments may be made. First, the Reformers generally argued that the true church was marked by the preaching of the Word, the proper administration of the sacraments, and the exercise of discipline. These criteria, of course, leave a great deal to interpretation: Do we judge the true

preaching of the Word by conformity to the Westminster Standards, or by conformity to the Apostles' Creed? Does neglect of infant baptism mean that a church fails to meet the test of proper administration of the sacraments? If a church celebrates the Supper once a year, and uses crackers and grape juice, is she administering the sacraments properly? If, finally, discipline is a mark of the true church, many evangelical churches will fail the test. In these matters, I think it best to formulate what Calvin called a "judgment of charity," using broader rather than narrower criteria to discern the true church.

The question of Roman Catholicism is particularly pressing for many evangelicals, especially since some prominent Protestant leaders have recently converted to Rome. I have fundamental and serious objections to Roman Catholic theology and practice, but I do not believe that Roman Catholic churches are uniformly false churches. To put it briefly, I would argue that by the criteria discussed above, many congregations of the Roman Catholic Church are, despite grievous errors, true churches of Jesus Christ. They adhere to many of the basic teachings of Scripture; though their interpretation of the sacraments is fallacious, they do administer the sacraments (sometimes more faithfully than Protestants); and they are frequently serious about discipline. Other Roman Catholic congregations differ little from the most radical sectors of mainline Protestantism, and have virtually nothing in common with orthodox Christianity.

For a provocative discussion of these issues, see James B. Jordan, *The Sociology of the Church: Essays in Reconstruction* (Tyler, Tex.: Geneva Ministries, 1986), 5-11, 51-82.

4. Westminster Confession of Faith 25.2.
5. Augustine stressed that God created the human race from one man precisely to emphasize the unity and concord that He intended the human race to have. "By this means the unity of society and the bond of concord might be more effectually commended to him, men being bound together not only by similarity of nature, but by family affection" (*City of God* 12.21).
6. See William J. Dumbrell, *The End of the Beginning: Revelation 21–22 and the Old Testament* (Homebush West, Australia: Lancer, 1985), 39, 122.
7. Ibid., 124. For a good discussion of the continuities and discontinuities between Israel and the nations, see the various ar-

ticles in William S. Barker and W. Robert Godfrey, eds., *Theonomy: A Reformed Critique* (Grand Rapids: Zondervan, 1990).

8. On Pharaoh, see James B. Jordan, "Primeval Saints: Studies in the Patriarchs," (Tyler, Tex.: Biblical Horizons, 1988), 77–68, available from Biblical Horizons, P.O. Box 1096, Niceville, FL 32588-1096.

9. Dumbrell, *End of the Beginning,* 147.

10. Israel's transfiguration was to take place through the branch from the root of Jesse. The calling of Israel was to be fulfilled by a single man, and through Him the nation as a whole was to be restored. Isaiah depicted this "narrowing down" of the promises to Abraham and Israel. Throughout the middle chapters of his prophecy, "Israel" is individualized and personified in the "servant of the Lord" (see Isa. 41:8; 42:1–4; 49:3; 52:13–53:12). Through the work of the true Israel, the nation would be reborn (see Isa. 54:1–17), and a new heavens and earth would issue forth (see Isa. 65:17–25). The macrocosm would be re-created from the microcosm, the whole creation transformed by a New Adam (Ibid., 5–20, 146–49). As Mark Strom explains, the new covenant is made with the true Israel, Jesus Christ (*Symphony of Scripture: Making Sense of the Bible's Many Themes* [Downers Grove, Ill.: InterVarsity Press, 1990], 136–37).

11. Paul's list corresponds to the discussion of the blessings of the kingdom in chapter 6. It is, however, a sixfold, not a seven- or eightfold blessing.

12. See my article, "Ephraim in Redemptive History," *Biblical Horizons* 14 (June 1990): 2–3, for some reflections on the Old Testament transfer of the kingdom from Ephraim to Judah.

13. Dumbrell, *The End of the Beginning,* 29.

14. See David Chilton, *Days of Vengeance: An Exposition of the Book of Revelation* (Fort Worth, Tex.: Dominion Press, 1987); Kenneth L. Gentry, Jr., *Before Jerusalem Fell: Dating the Book of Revelation* (Tyler, Tex.: Institute for Christian Economics, 1989).

15. There is an abundance of recent literature on the "preterist" interpretation of this and other New Testament prophecies. See David Chilton, *Paradise Restored: An Eschatology of Dominion* (Fort Worth, Tex.: Dominion Press, 1985); Chilton, *Days of Vengeance;* J. Marcellus Kik, *An Eschatology of Victory* (Phillipsburg, N.J.: Presbyterian and Reformed, 1971); Milton Terry,

Biblical Apocalyptics (New York: Eaton and Mains; Cincinnati: Curts and Jennings, 1898; reprint, Grand Rapids: Baker, 1988); Kenneth L. Gentry, Jr., *Before Jerusalem Fell;* Cornelius van der Waal, *The Covenantal Gospel* (Neerlandia, Alberta: Inheritance Publications, 1990). Gentry provides an extensive listing of commentators who have given the book of Revelation an early dating (pp. 30–38). Significantly, Rudolf Bultmann notes that messianic movements multiplied after A.D. 40 (*Jesus and the Word,* trans. Louise Pettibone Smith and Erminie Huntress Lantero, rev. ed. [New York: Charles Scribner's Sons, (1934) 1958], 21–22).

16. See James B. Jordan, *Sabbath Breaking and the Death Penalty: A Theological Investigation* (Tyler, Tex.: Geneva Ministries, 1986), 46–51; Dumbrell, *The End of the Beginning,* 48–50.

17. Jordan, *Sabbath Breaking,* 49.

18. See van der Waal, *The Covenantal Gospel,* 137–39. See also the exegesis of Romans 9–11 in Max King, *The Cross and the Parousia of Christ: The Two Dimensions of One Age-Changing Eschaton* (Warren, Ohio: Parkman Road Church of Christ, 1987), 271–316. I disagree completely with King's larger conclusions, but I think he is quite right to see these chapters fulfilled in A.D. 70.

19. This emphasis on the significance of the destruction of the temple is traditionally associated with a postmillennial interpretation of biblical prophecy. I believe, however, that the paradigm I am outlining here enables us to understand how Christians can come to such different interpretations of prophecy. Let me explain. Premillennialists say that Jesus will return in judgment before the Millennium begins; amillennialists say that the Millennium is the age between the First and Second Comings of Christ; postmillennialists stress that Jesus will return after the Millennium, and that the Millennium will be an age of glory for the church.

Each of these millennial positions fits into the scheme I am presenting. I believe that the Millennium is the age of new covenant, during which the saints are enthroned in heavenly places in Christ (Rev. 20:4–6; Eph. 2:6). This identifies me as an amillennialist. At the same time, in a sense the premillennialist is correct to say that Jesus returned in judgment at the beginning of the Millennium; He did return at the beginning of the Millennium to judge apostate Judaism and to destroy the remnants of the typological kingdom order. I also believe that postmillennialists are correct in saying that Christ will return *after* the Millennium, at the resurrection, when the entire creation will be transfigured, and I concur with the postmillennial emphasis on the growth of the kingdom.

20. The covenant is of course far too complex a subject to enter fully into here. For further reading, see van der Waal, *The Covenantal Gospel;* James B. Jordan, *Through New Eyes: Developing a Biblical View of the World* (Brentwood, Tenn.: Wolgemuth & Hyatt, 1988); Ray R. Sutton, *That You May Prosper* (Tyler, Tex.: Institute for Christian Economics, 1987); Thomas McComsky, *The Covenants of Promise: A Theology of the Old Testament Covenants* (Grand Rapids: Baker, 1985); O. Palmer Robertson, *The Christ of the Covenants* (Phillipsburg, N.J.: Presbyterian and Reformed, 1980); Meredith Kline, *The Structure of Biblical Authority* (Grand Rapids: Eerdmans, 1972).

21. Edmund P. Clowney, *The Biblical Doctrine of the Church* (Phillipsburg, N.J.: Presbyterian and Reformed, 1979), 109.

22. The doctrine of the motherhood of the church has roots in the New Testament and patristic teaching, and was clearly embraced by the Reformers. See John Calvin, *Institutes of the Christian Religion,* 4.1. For the patristic teaching, see Henri de Lubac, *The Motherhood of the Church,* trans. Sergia Englund (San Francisco: Ignatius, 1982), part 1.

23. Bornkamm comments: "In Eph. 3:4ff. the mystery is the share of the Gentiles in the inheritance, in the body of the Church, in the promise in Christ. This joining of the Jews and Gentiles in one body under the head Christ is a cosmic eschatological event" (*Theological Dictionary of the New Testament,* ed. Gerhard Kittel, trans. and ed. Geoffrey W. Bromiley, 10 vols. [Grand Rapids: Eerdmans, (1964–76) 1967], 4:820).

24. *Against All Heresies,* 4.24.1.

25. Christopher Dawson, *Christianity and the New Age* (New York: Sheed and Ward, 1931; reprint, Manchester, N.H.: Sophia Institute Press, 1985), 85. Beasley-Murray, *Jesus and the Kingdom of God,* 339, writes that God's "action of grace does not create a new existence in solitude; rather, it is intended to bring about a renewed *humanity,* wherein God's purpose for both the individual and the race reaches its fulfillment."

Chapter 9: On Earth as It Is in Heaven

1. G. R. Beasley-Murray, *Jesus and the Kingdom of God* (Grand Rapids: Eerdmans, 1986), 151: The Lord's Prayer is "a plea that God will act in such a way as to realize his 'good pleasure'—namely, the purpose he intended for the world when he created it." Similarly, p. 152: In the Lord's Prayer, "Jesus is seeking an act of God to produce a 'movement' that will be a part of the greater 'movement' God has already initiated in Jesus. Heaven has already invaded the earth in the mission of Jesus; here he is praying for a completion of what God has begun in him, for a securing of his purpose to unite heaven and earth." On the same page, Beasley-Murray approvingly quotes H. Traub's comments that through Christ a "new participation of heaven in earth . . . has replaced the division of heaven and earth."

2. William J. Dumbrell, *The End of the Beginning: Revelation 21–22 and the Old Testament* (Homebush West, Australia: Lancer, 1985), 194. See also Rudolf Schnackenburg, *God's Rule and Kingdom,* trans. John Murray (New York: Herder and Herder, 1963), 59: "It is in and through the Church that the cosmos is grasped by Christ—attracted or compelled." Through the church, Christ takes hold of the creation, and glorifies and renews it. See James B. Jordan, *Through New Eyes: Developing a Biblical View of the World* (Brentwood, Tenn.: Wolgemuth & Hyatt, 1988), 121–27.

3. The idea defended by many New Testament scholars, that the "parables of growth" do not in fact teach that the kingdom grows, is in my judgment absurd. Though the notion of growth might not be in the forefront of these parables, it certainly is part of the whole teaching of the parables. Small beginnings produce grand results only if between beginning and result some growth or progress has taken place. Indeed, Jesus Himself said that the mustard seed must be "full grown" so that the birds of the air can find rest in its branches (see Matt. 13:32).

4. On the power of the Word of God, see the discussion in John M. Frame, *Perspectives on the Word of God: An Introduction to Christian Ethics* (Phillipsburg, N.J.: Presbyterian and Reformed, 1990), 10–12.

5. Eusebius, *Life of Constantine,* 1.28. In Philip Schaff and Henry Wace, *Nicene and Post-Nicene Fathers,* Second Series (1890;

reprint, Grand Rapids: Eerdmans, 1982), 1:490. For full scholarly accounts of the incident, see Jacob Burkhardt, *The Age of Constantine the Great* (Berkeley and Los Angeles: University of California Press, [1949] 1983), and Ramsay MacMullen, *Constantine* (London: Croom Helm, [1969] 1987).

6. *On the Incarnation*, 30.4–5; 31. Josef Jungmann comments that in the early church the cross "was invariably depicted without the figure of the crucified. The reason that lay behind this was not so much an aversion to showing him in the state of humiliation as to bring out the richer significance hidden away in that symbol: The cross, the instrument of redemption, had become a sign of victory, a *tropaion*, (trophy)." *Christian Prayer Through the Centuries*, trans. John Coyne, S. J. (New York: Paulist Press, 1978), 18.

7. Irenaeus, *Against All Heresies* 3.23.7. See Schnackenburg, *God's Rule and Kingdom*, 313. On the seed of the woman, see Edmund P. Clowney, *The Unfolding Mystery: Discovering Christ in the Old Testament* (Colorado Springs: NavPress, 1988; reprint, Phillipsburg, N.J.: Presbyterian and Reformed, 1991), 35–42.

8. James B. Jordan, "The Holy War in America Today: Some Observations on Abortion Rescues," (Tyler, Tex.: Biblical Horizons, 1989), 1–4, available from Biblical Horizons, P.O. Box 1096, Niceville, FL, 32588-1096.

9. See the discussion of the keys in Schnackenburg, *God's Rule and Kingdom*, 228–29.

10. The Spirit also equips us with the peculiar gifts needed for the accomplishment of the church's mission. Each member of Christ's body has received from the Spirit of God a particular gift, and with it an obligation to use that gift in the service of others within the body (Rom. 12:3–8; 1 Cor. 12). As each member uses his gift, the church matures and grows up into Christ (Eph. 4:1–16), living in righteousness and holiness and fulfilling the mission that God has given His people in the world. There is a circular pattern involved in the work of the Spirit in the church. There is a movement from unity through diversity and back to unity. The "one Spirit" gives diverse gifts to the many members of the church, but these many members are gifted precisely to build up the church until it attains to the unity of the faith and of the knowledge of the Son of God (Eph. 4:1–16).

11. See James B. Jordan, *The Sociology of the Church: Essays in Reconstruction* (Tyler, Tex.: Geneva Ministries, 1986), 236–37.
12. See John M. Frame, *Evangelical Reunion: Denominations and the Body of Christ* (Grand Rapids: Baker, 1991).
13. See Jean Danielou, *The Bible and the Liturgy* (1956; reprint, Notre Dame, Ind.: University of Notre Dame Press, 1987), chap. 3.
14. On the peace of God, see Georges Duby, *France in the Middle Ages, 987–1460: From Hugh Capet to Joan of Arc,* trans. Juliet Vale (Oxford: Blackwell, 1991).
15. Frame, *Perspectives on the Word of God,* 4.
16. Schnackenburg, *God's Rule and Kingdom,* 313, 316.

Chapter 10: Into the Political Arena

1. Georges Florovsky, *Christianity and Culture,* vol. 2 of *Collected Works* (Belmont, Mass.: Nordland, 1974), 21.
2. It was remarked that one of the difficulties that President Bush faced in the 1992 campaign was his hesitance to call attention to himself.
3. According to the Scottish church historian W. H. C. Frend, it was through Ambrose that "a vital principle of Western society had . . . been established. A Christian moral order stood above the will of the ruler or any reason of state. No arbitrary destruction of human life could pass without challenge by the church. In the last resort a ruler's misgovernment could bring about his excommunication and deposition." Ambrose laid the groundwork of the road that led to Canossa (*The Rise of Christianity* [Philadelphia: Fortress, 1985]).

   It is heartening that some Roman Catholic bishops have disciplined members who actively promote abortion. The evangelical church would do well to follow their example.

   It is certainly possible to misuse church discipline for partisan purposes. Historians have noted that overuse led to the trivialization of excommunication during the Middle Ages. If the modern church is guilty of anything, however, she is surely guilty of underuse.
4. It must also be said, on the basis of Hebrews 11:35–38, that faith has other expressions as well.
5. Vern S. Poythress, *The Shadow of Christ in the Law of Moses* (Brentwood, Tenn.: Wolgemuth & Hyatt, 1991), 125–33.

Chapter 11: Against the World for the World

1. Quoted in Joseph A. Jungmann, *Christian Prayer Through the Centuries*, trans. John Coyne, S.J. (New York: Paulist Press, 1978), 7.
2. Josef Jungmann, *The Early Liturgy to the Time of Gregory the Great*, trans. Francis A. Brunner (Notre Dame, Ind.: University of Notre Dame Press, 1959).
3. Alexander Schmemann, *Church, World, Mission* (Crestwood, N.Y.: St. Vladimir's Seminary Press, 1979), 32.
4. Henri Crouzel, *Origen: The Life and Thought of the First Great Theologian*, trans. A. S. Worrall (San Francisco: Harper and Row, 1989), 48.
5. Quoted in Thomas Molnar, *The Church: Pilgrim of Centuries* (Grand Rapids: Eerdmans, 1990), 172.
6. Vigen Guroian, *Incarnate Love: Essays in Orthodox Ethics* (Notre Dame Ind.: University of Notre Dame Press, 1987), 131–32.
7. Quoted in Molnar, *The Church*, 172.

Scripture Index

General Index

259